Re-Choreographing Cortical & Cartographic Maps

Re-Choreographing Cortical & Cartographic Maps

Going West to Find East Going East to Find West

Henry Daniel

intellect
Bristol, UK / Chicago, USA

First published in the UK in 2022 by
Intellect, The Mill, Parnall Road, Fishponds, Bristol, BS16 3JG, UK

First published in the USA in 2022 by
Intellect, The University of Chicago Press, 1427 E. 60th Street,
Chicago, IL 60637, USA

A catalogue record for this book is available from the British Library.

Copy editor: MPS Limited
Cover designer: Aleksandra Szumlas
Cover image: from Project Barca by Bea Gamboa and modified by Henry Daniel.
Frontispiece image: Luciana D'Anunciação in Here Be Dragons/Non Plus Ultra.
Production manager: Laura Christopher
Typesetter: MPS Limited

Hardback ISBN 978-1-78938-671-4
Paperback ISBN 978-1-78938-769-8
ePDF ISBN 978-1-78938-672-1
ePUB ISBN 978-1-78938-673-8

This is a peer-reviewed publication.

Cette publication est financée par le fonds du Conseil de recherches en sciences humaines du Canada (CRSH) Nouvelles frontières en recherche (NFRFE: Référence N. 2021-0017).

This publication is funded by a substantial publication grant from Social Sciences and Humanities Research Council of Canada (SSHRC)'s New Frontiers in Research Fund (NFRFE: Reference No. 2021-0017.

Contents

Figures

Note: Unless specified, all images are taken from the author's personal research archives.

Acknowledgements

I would like to acknowledge my dear wife Diane and daughter Lauren, who put up with more than my absences and the many international moves we made to satisfy my research and teaching agendas. I would also like to thank all the performers and collaborators in the different countries (Germany, the UK, Canada, Spain and the USA) for their contributions to the numerous productions I staged, and the institutions that helped me do so over the years; this book would not have been possible without their assistance. These countries and institutions are all named in the chapters as well as in the Appendices at the end of the document. I would like to acknowledge my undergraduate and graduate students, especially as they were the first to experience some of these ideas in development, whether in course lectures or in the many studio classes and stage productions I organized. Thanks to all the professional dancers in the different countries who helped me to take that work to another level. A big mention to Dr Roaa Ali for her early feedback on the idea for the book, and acknowledgements to Research Assistants Anna Dueck, Rachel Silver, Tomoyo Yamada and Karla Desentis who worked hard on cataloguing the images and videos for the ongoing performance archive. Thanks to everyone at the Simon Fraser University (SFU) Digital Humanities Innovation Lab (DHIL), the SFU Library and SFU's Research Computing Group's Labs who advised and assisted in the early attempts to create an online archive, and finally, thanks to my publishers for their patience as I tried to meet their deadlines.

Prologue

To have a mind is to have the ability to reason, and to be sensitive to reasons in thought, feeling and action.

(Hacker 2014: 89)

[T]he Tibetan word for 'mind,' which is sem (Sanskrit citta), covers not just the realm of thought but also that of emotion.

(His Holiness, The Dalai Lama, Tenzin Gyatso 2005: 122)

In our direct and immediate awareness of the body, we know it primarily through the various tactile sensations involved in any activity of touching something.

(Welton 1998: 47)

Beginning with a prologue and ending with an epilogue – between which are seven chapters with multiple scenes that function as intermissions, interruptions and resumptions in a dramatic play – I am suggesting that this book functions as a kind of performance. The links to my online website archive, where much of the dance material being discussed here can be witnessed by the reader, helps to support that idea. However, the book is also a scholarly document where the three Acts with their seven Chapters knit together a set of arguments concerning relationships between dance, choreography and performance and the search for and generation of new knowledge. The idea here is to combine my extensive background as a professional dancer and choreographer with my academic scholarship and an enduring interest in transdisciplinarity as a coming together of what may seem as disparate ideas but which, to me at least, permits a better understanding of dance and choreography as practices that allow us to claim embodied knowledge.

My research methodology is transdisciplinary and transcultural in nature, meaning it draws on approaches from different disciplinary and culturally specific constructs to explain how the movement of bodies in space/time is analogous to the unfolding and/or initiating of a thought process. Why transdisciplinarity?

Because it suggests that there is a larger knowledge field that, for valid reasons, was divided up into different disciplines, which unfortunately resulted in a loss of important connections between them. It also suggests that the Cartesian strategy of separating things of the body from those of the mind contributed immensely to the opening and subsequent widening of these gaps. In Roberto Poli's words, 'the task of transdisciplinarity is to bring to light, to make visible, the usually hidden links among the various disciplines' (2009: 137). Transculturality, on the other hand, suggests a hybridity that is often the norm for those born into colonial and post-colonial societies. Hence, an eye towards disciplinary reconnection, holistic thinking and cultural complexity is necessary in order to understand how practices that emerge from such communities, and the bodies that perform them, can and have contributed to the development of contemporary dance and performance discourses worldwide. The writing style of the book, therefore, is at times autobiographic and at other times critical in a scholarly sense. This is deliberate.

Part of this strategy has to do with my attempts to undermine the accepted epistemological and ontological paradigms that the Western European scholastic tradition has passed on to those of us who were forced to give up our own ancestral ways of being and thinking in the world in favour of systems of power that the colonizers imposed on us. But just as my own ancestors were asked to adopt the institutional structures and educational mandates that colonialism provided – which these same ancestors 'messed' with, and in so doing created new hybrid structures that contained elements from their own epistemological and ontological 'past' – so too I am 'messing' with the accepted notions of what the arguments and disciplinary norms for proper critical debate in a document should look, read and feel like.

I begin with a hypothesis, which claims that human beings are cognitively embodied through their own lived experiences of movement through space and time; the spaces we inhabit and the practices we engage in are documented through cortical and cartographic maps. In short, as we inhabit and move through spaces our brains organize our experiences into unique cortical and spatial maps, which eventually determine how we see and deal with, i.e. 'become' subjects in a world that we also help create. This 'hypothesis' is also foundational to studies in embodied cognition, the 4Es so to speak; embodied, embedded, extended and enacted cognition (Menary 2010). Although my approach here is quite different to those who make a career out of exploring the nature of these 4Es through scientific methods, I make what I argue is an equally rigorous attempt to explore the nature of embodiment through my own disciplinary frameworks, i.e. dance, choreography and performance as modes of exploring, re-articulating and hence claiming information that is in the body and in the environment as personal knowledge. Building on some of de Bruin's, Newen's and Gallagher's more recent insights (2018), I also agree with Menary that 'the once homogenous framework of cognitivism is being replaced by a multi-dimensional analysis of cognition as incorporating our brains, bodies and environments' (2010: 462). As such, I argue that it is extremely critical for our development as human beings that we are not deprived of opportunities to exercise these creative instincts. And by 'we' I mean everyone, not just Black people like myself.

Cartography is the discipline that deals with the conception, production, dissemination, representation and study of maps of geographical territory, while cortical mapping is the method by which the brain – through the spine and the peripheral nervous system – dynamically represents relationships between the body and its movement experiences in space/time (Shadmehr and Mussa-Ivaldi 2012). Since this 'representation' is an internal process of the brain that organizes and 'interprets' space/time relationships, we can say that the human body moving through space and time presents an opportunity to claim the information in those spaces as personal knowledge. Thus, if dance is the intentional movement of bodies that leads to an experience in space/time, then choreography becomes the deliberate organization of those movements into coherent and meaningful structures towards some specific goal. In other words, movement is analogous to the unfolding and/or initiating of a thought process, and through dance and choreography that simultaneous unfolding and initiating becomes an opportunity to understand and therefore claim the knowledge that is in the body as well as in the spaces through which it travels. It unfolds in the sense that it receives a signal from somewhere and it initiates something in the sense that it has a degree of agency in how that signal is interpreted and acted upon. Therefore, if we wish to fully know and understand ourselves and our relationship to the rest of organic life, unique investigative procedures based on sound theories of performance need to be developed. This book is an attempt to ground a theory of practice that pursues such a path.

With this hypothesis, I can begin to pose questions such as: How are mental, emotional and physical maps generated and stored within the body as short and long-term memories? And how are they articulated through our actions as the capacity for embodied knowing? How does the re-articulation and/or re-organization of these movement maps create a dynamic such that new knowledge can emerge? And most importantly, what happens in and through the body as people become displaced from their lived environments? How can the dancer, choreographer or performing artist facilitate a shift in the audience's perceptual landscape for them to share the deeply lived experiences that are foundational to that knowledge? These are some of the fundamental questions that inform my decades-long choreographic practice, in which I utilize new technologies as part of an extended experimental toolkit. It is important, therefore, that the reader understands that, as an artist and scholar coming from a specific background but working in an international context, I find it useful to define the term performance in a very specific way, as follows:

1. Performance is a multi-levelled activity that human beings engage in to make sense of themselves and to establish a meaningful relationship with the world around them.
2. Performance allows us to explore different roles and personalities that comprise what we often think of as a single stable identity.
3. Because there are levels of consciousness that exist in 'domains' or 'dimensions' that have different behaviours or operational characteristics, these behaviours can appear to be contradictory. Hence, a strategy is needed to understand how and why this complexity works the way it does *before* we attempt to change anything about it.
4. History, as it individually or collectively unfolds, is a dynamic process that accounts for people's actions in space/time. Thus, understanding history and the architecture of its processes is an important aspect of performance – in other words, understanding how cortical and cartographic maps are created and how they have evolved historically.
5. Exploring these maps through choreography and performance is a method for cultivating embodied knowing, and hence understanding what 'being' in the world entails.
6. Bringing artistic practices into a transdisciplinary discourse with science and technology, cultural, colonial and post-colonial studies and philosophy, is a useful strategy for understanding the complex dimensions that the term performance evokes.
7. A theory of practice that benefits from this type of exploration has the potential to transform our understanding of and relationship to the world we live in.

To fully appreciate where some of the key ideas in this publication originate and why they are being presented here in this format, the reader should know that I come from a colonial upbringing; my ancestors were forcibly removed from their homes on the African continent and brought to the New World as slaves. This fact inevitably influences the way that concepts such as 'identity', 'self', 'performance', 'embodied knowledge' and 'becoming' are framed throughout this document. Initially, I was educated in an all-boys school (Naparima College) founded on the Caribbean island of Trinidad by Canadian Presbyterian missionaries for the sons of Indian indentured labourers brought in to replace the 'emancipated' African slaves. My theatre training began in this environment. I subsequently received additional professional artistic and intellectual training in the USA, the UK and Germany; widely practicing my craft in each of these countries while touring internationally. Extensive travel and learning some of the languages in countries where I lived widened my perspectives but also left me feeling somewhat nomadic (Hall 1990; Braidotti 2011; Meerzon 2012). I begin this book, therefore, recognizing that I come from a place where power has always been exercised through external sources, a condition that I argue applies to those bodies that have had to perform their way through a range of geo-political, socio-economic and psychological frameworks that colonizing processes have imposed on them.

The subtitle *Going West to Find East/Going East to Find West* thus begins as a performative conjecture, with the fifteenth-century Columbian initiative playing a prominent role in how transnational movements of bodies have created – and continue to create – new movement maps across extended physical, psychological and geographic spaces. A key aspect of that performance is based on survival; how to survive the institutions and systems of power these colonialists created but at the same time use some of those structures against it as one tries to create alternate forms. A key premise of the book's argument is that the framing and overt compartmentalization of knowledge that a Western European Enlightenment agenda, informed by a Cartesian dictate, imposed on the knowledge acquisition process served to marginalize large groups of 'others' (Dussel 1995, 1996), and that current institutional processes continue to present serious challenges to the efforts by these 'others' to redefine their role in contemporary neo-liberal societies (Nolan and Knowles 2016). I, therefore, suggest that bringing a new approach to the table – a trans-disciplinary and trans-cultural one that engages more equitably with contrasting views, frameworks and philosophies – can address some of these inherited imbalances. To this end, I organized and led four multi-year choreographic research projects that collectively demonstrate how these transdisciplinary and transcultural links can be made and why it is important to strengthen them[1]:

(1) Transnet (2003–05)[2] investigated the potential for a transdisciplinary dialogue between artists and scientists on notions of performance that ranged from human expressive behaviour to computation, efficiency and optimization in digital systems (Daniel 2009); (2) The Touched Project (2007–10)[3] looked at how human beings and new technologies together create a dynamic systems ecology that challenges the notion of agency in both humans and technological systems (Daniel 2010a, 2010b) and (3) Project Barca (2011–14),[4] looked at the implications of a colonialist/expansionist agenda that began with attempts by Europeans to reach a fabled 'East' by going 'West', and in so doing the positioned race as the basis for determining who has power and who does not, along with who deserves to be treated as human and who not. Inverting the phrase to 'going east to find west' and playing on the inherent paradox of going in either direction to find the other, the project explored how the concept of circumnavigation opened opportunities for cultural encounters that would fundamentally impact

the fates of many (Daniel and Ezpeleta 2014). (4) The fourth and final project, Contemporary Nomads (2017–21),[5] sought to extend the scope of what cultural theorist Stuart Hall once described as 'the prototype of the modern or postmodern New World nomad, continually moving between centre and periphery' (Hall in Rutherford 1990: 234) in an attempt to establish a presence in the world. This 'New World presence', according to Hall, is 'not so much power, as ground, place, territory [...] the juncture-point where the many cultural tributaries meet, the "empty" land (the European colonizers emptied it) where strangers from every part of the globe collided' (Hall in Rutherford 1990: 234). It is in this final project that the concept of movement as a process of a thought unfolding and/or being initiated finds its transdisciplinary anchor.

The trajectory of these four multi-year projects address a set of questions that are all related to an exploration of dance and choreography – and performance in general – as (1) key practices for expanding awareness of the multiple dimensions of self; (2) for exploring how different systems and institutions of power exploit the notion of the human and the non-human; (3) as a means of experimentally drawing out and testing knowledge about bodies and their relationship to space, time and identity; and (4) as valid vehicles for both artistic and academic research. Also, as the three short quotes at the beginning of this prologue suggest, I am interested in the epistemological bases that different disciplines and cultures use to speak about the experience of knowing, as well as the methods they use to explore those knowledges.

Re-Choreographing Cortical & Cartographic Maps: Going West to Find East Going East to Find West comprises a three-part book structure with eight subsections. It begins with this Prologue and continues with an auto-ethnography in Act 1, Chapter 1 that explains why I adopt the approach I do for this book. In Chapter 2, I conduct an in-depth examination of the hypothesis introduced in the prologue, explaining its ontological, epistemological, methodological and ethical foundations. The ideas and unique events mentioned here open the way for a wider framing in Chapter 3, which draws on my own artistic works as well as the work of other theorists, scientists and artists, many of whom were collaborators. Act 2, Chapters 4, 5 and 6, looks at three multi-year research projects; Transnet (2003–05), The Touched Project (2007–10) and Project Barca (2011–14), where the reader can see how the 'Theory of Practice' develops and plays out over time through technological interventions, live performances, documentary videos, short films, audio-visual installations, essays, conference presentations and refereed academic publications, many of which can be found on the author's website-as-archive.

In Act 3, Chapter 7, the fourth multi-year research project (Contemporary Nomads 2017–21), makes an argument for the seemingly chaotic large-scale movement of bodies across international spaces in the first decades of the twenty-first century as a continuing transnational event that reflects the deep fragmentation that exists between communities within as well as outside national borders, between nationalized and personalized bodies, and between disciplines that seek to carve out their own spaces within social and political institutions that often alienate the very people they were meant to serve. The works in this project provoke thinking about the underlying reasons for and causes of these dynamic cortical and cartographic shifts, which result in radical socio-economic and political changes (Ross et al. 2018). Finally, An Epilogue 'Fitting [Out-fitting] In' transforms the thematic of dislocation and/or displacement into a process of what I call 'worlding' – portrayed here as an engagement with the world as an extended performance event.

Two appendices plus links to the web-based performance archive mentioned above and a comprehensive bibliography complete the document. Appendix A gives a detailed breakdown of the productions in each of the four multi-year projects and a few of the single stand-alone projects mentioned in this publication, while Appendix B comprise three maps that trace my movements to and from the countries where I lived and worked and the places to which I travelled while exploring the ideas outlined in this book. The links to my web-based performance archive give the reader access to an electronic tool that allows him/her/them to witness some of the choreographic material cited in this volume and to form their own opinion about its efficacy.

NOTES

1. Video excerpts from the works choreographed within the four projects can be found on my website at www.henrydaniel.ca. The handle henrydaniel.ca is a permanent performance archive and is therefore always accessible. All other URLs in the notes throughout this book were accessed 3 Aug. 2022.
2. www.henrydaniel.ca/transnet.
3. www.henrydaniel.ca/the-touched-project.
4. www.henrydaniel.ca/project-barca.
5. www.henrydaniel.ca/contemporary-nomads.

ACT 1

1

Autoethnography as a Methodological and Ideological Starting Point

A beginning of sorts

> *Only when 'seeing things as they really are' means something essentially different from our usual 'seeing' does one become aware of the problematically different 'levels' or degrees of being. Otherwise, the term 'being' can only appear as the most general and vaguest of concepts.*
>
> (Morris 1981: 66–67)

I begin the first act of this academic treatise with a rough autobiographic outline. Autoethnography is a research approach that enables systematic analysis of personal experience in order to understand the cultural experience,[1] while posing relevant questions about the researcher's assumptions and prejudices. In this chapter, I position autoethnography as a methodological and ideological starting point and frame of reference for my research, which focuses on lived personal experience as the basis for an investigation into dance, choreography and performance as ways of knowing and strategies for becoming. As a choreographer with an extensive background in the professional world of dance, theatre and performance, and as a scholar with a good grasp of the intellectual field and investigative procedures that surround dance and theatrical performance research, I am fully aware of the difficulties involved in evaluating performance research that employs this kind of approach. However, I think it crucial that the reader understands more about who I am and how, as an author, I choose to navigate the dynamics of subject/object relations.

Within the professional dance community, there is a deep scepticism about the scholarship that assesses artistic work, arising from dance artists' experience of scholarly critiques based on little or no knowledge of the processes that artists go through in making these artworks nor of the sustained and embodied experience these forms involve. Much of the work of dance artists occurs in their studios and rehearsal rooms and never makes it to the performance stage. Hence, one can argue that it is an invisible aspect of performance work that is extremely difficult to assess. References in scholarly writings on dance often come from a body of work that was not designed with the discipline in mind. Although the introduction of Practice-as-Research (PaR) into the academy has shifted this dynamic somewhat, the privileging of verbal language and the history of those traditional aesthetic discourses as an integral part of the education of minds and bodies still dominate how we apprehend non-verbal art forms such as dance. What therefore concerns me is the ignorance or misapprehension of significant layers of information within the somatic spectrum that leads to an inability to fully understand what claiming knowledge of one's own embodiment means. In other words, the embodied practice in dance research is too often absent from the critics' analysis.

Nevertheless, scholars have increasingly adopted a view of performance material as work-in-progress as a way to evaluate the knowledge produced. Given that some of these scholars are increasingly being allowed privileged access to the studio processes of individual artists, some of that information is becoming increasingly accessible to the wider reading public. Yet the matter of who authors those evaluations – who claims this knowledge and how – is still subject to the power structures within the academy. However, since more and more artists are writing about their own practices within an academic context, the traditional academic position is no longer the sole source of written critical opinions exploring the body's expressive potential in rigorous performance contexts.

What is therefore increasingly under scrutiny is the validity of the philosophies that have intellectually framed (Gilroy 1994; Farred 2003) interpretations of current and past performance works on theatrical stages as well as the codified movement vocabularies and the legitimizing processes that allow those in power to negate, invalidate, appropriate and even simulate 'other' bodies as it suits their agendas. If nothing else, the power relations surrounding the creation, dissemination and assessment of work need to be re-examined and decolonized if you will. Since I write from the position of both performer (choreographer/dance artist) and scholar, it makes my situation simultaneously easier as well as more difficult.

As an Afro-Caribbean male occupying these multiple positions, I recognize the importance of acknowledging the work of past diasporic scholars on the issue of decolonization, especially work on repositioning the minds and bodies of those of us who were brought up in colonial and post-colonial spaces. New World theorists who have contributed to this discourse and who have since left us include Franz Fanon (1925–61), Eric Williams (1911–81), C. L. R. James (1901–89), Édouard Glissant (1928–2011) and Stuart Hall (1932–2014), for example. Like them, I choose to start my conceptualizing by looking into the not-quite-forgotten past;

specifically, to the fifteenth century and the year 1492 when Columbus first set sail across the Atlantic. Also like them, I am not afraid to remain in contact with what Paul Gilroy called the 'insinuating rhythms of everyday life' as I attempt to 'read the signs in the street in defiance of contemporary pressures to retreat into a contemplative state' (Gilroy 1993: 47).

The fifteenth century is historically important in the colonizing process insofar as it set into motion a series of processes that account for my being where I am now in the twenty-first century. According to some New World scholars, it marks the beginning of the European concept of modernity (Reid-Pharr 2016; Gordon 2008; Wynter 1994; Dussel 1995), by which a radical shift in thinking about the past and the future of humanity took place. According to Jamaican scholar Sylvia Wynter, this shift saw an interpretation of humanity that not only justified the mass enslavement of African peoples but it also created the terms for the social, economic and political support for that idea (Wynter 2003). This idea was that Africans were less than humans; they were no more than animals that needed to be trained to behave as humans did. Harsh and sustained violent treatments were therefore justified.

Successive crossings landed my ancestors in a 'New World', entangling them in a deadly web that systematically tried to reprogram their bodies and minds to erase the memory of their previous existence in another part of the world. This colonization of bodies and minds which accompanied the annexation of physical territory (wa Thiong'o 1986) still plays a significant role in how people like myself understand our place in the larger world, how we fit into contemporary institutions and how we continue to, or are allowed to act both within and outside them. The task here, then, is to produce a document that is consistent with my position as an artist and scholar, creating performance works and experimental frames of knowledge for a wider international audience while trying to follow Gilroy's missive to use the 'languages' of the streets if needed. I argue that such a strategy has the potential to produce completely new choreographic landscapes that foreground the movements of diverse bodies, encompassing their restrictions and freedoms, personal as well as extra-personal, and that can be performed anywhere.

However, a serious problem presents itself for those of us who work in institutions where bodies like ours are absent from the rehearsal studios, lecture rooms and performance stages, making the possibility for a wider cultural understanding unlikely. The question then becomes: how can we do work that is truly different when the bodies we need to do such work are absent or choose not to be in these educational institutions in the first place?[2] And how can we generate new choreographic frames and cortical mappings at the very site where opposing forces have the potential to be at their strongest when that site is in some ways designed to keep out or refuse to accommodate bodies that attempt to cross its borders.

Also, how can we manipulate existing conditions in order to generate a 'hidden' potential that proves new solutions are indeed possible? To begin answering such difficult questions I need to take a significant step backward.

Will the artist please stand up?

> *[N]either trained introspection nor creative insights would lead to the systematic accretion of knowledge needed for the foundation of a science of mind. That sort of foundation requires more than insight, it requires experimentation.*
>
> (Kandel 2006: 40)

I appropriate Kandel's use of the term 'experimentation' in relation to the 'systematic accretion of knowledge' about 'minds' here to introduce my methodological approach to Performance-as-Research, Artistic Research, Research/Creation and PaR. Kandel is an acclaimed scientist who did extraordinary work on the foundations of both long and short-term memory, work that has been instrumental in guiding current knowledge on how the mind/brain/body operates. Since the term 'mind' and its association with the brain and spinal cord (the central nervous system) is inseparable from the peripheral nervous system that runs throughout the entire body, one can say that the mind is embodied, and its knowledge is always operationally available to us. But, to avoid the classical mind/body dichotomy, and to decouple it from the historically programmed Western understanding of how the body is 'controlled' by the brain, I prefer to think that there are three different 'brains' with degrees of an agency located throughout the body: brain, spinal cord and peripheral nervous system. In this way, the idea of control is distributed between different systems, and embodied knowledge involves knowing how this extended nervous system operates and how the information it holds can be claimed.

Hence, to understand the intention behind the aphorism 'know thyself' attributed to ancient Greek, Egyptian and Arabic/Islamic sources via scholars such as Pythagoras,[3] Hermes Trismegistus[4] and the Ikhwan al-Safa',[5] one needs to first look within. But what exactly does this looking inward entail and how does it work? More importantly, how can one escape the obvious subjective biases, assumptions and prejudices that accompany such attempts? I believe this process should begin with the researcher's examination of the experiences that have been foundational to his, her or their beliefs. For example, what were my thoughts, where did they come from, what kinds of actions did those thoughts motivate in me and how did I feel about them? As a larger picture begins to emerge, one can appreciate the importance of the self-observation process where the body appears to *think*, the mind to *feel*, the emotions to *move*, and vice versa. In this way, we are able to communicate with different aspects of ourselves to understand the complex organisms that we are.

Among the many events and experiences that have influenced my own intellectual and artistic development – which include the works I created over time – three are seminal, and I examine them in some detail here. The first involves a broken radio, which prompted my independent learning about the principles of physics and that of human behaviour. I grew up on a small island in the southern Caribbean in a culturally diverse, post-colonial but essentially colonial-minded environment, which out of necessity fostered a deep sense of embeddedness in community, land and territory. The corporeal expression came easily to me: I played soccer and cricket with people much older than myself, sang at church, recited poetry and debated in elocution and oration contests (the content of which was determined by faraway authorities in the United Kingdom). I developed a fascination for algebra and geometry, loved my chemistry and English teachers, was good at literature, was terrified by my Latin teacher but found my Spanish and French instructors quite agreeable; I loved geography and art and had a penchant for drawing in charcoal. By most standards, I had a good education.

However, for some strange reason, I never formally studied physics. Nonetheless, my curiosity once drove me to dissect the family radio, and when I was unable to put it back together, I knew I was in a good deal of trouble. I was so deeply fearful of being punished that I dared not tell my grandmother – with whom we were living with at the time – that it was I who broke her radio. At that point, I knew as much about electronic technology as I did human behaviour – which was not much at all. I had therefore conducted my experiment without any learned method. While intrigued by the apparent magic of that enigmatic black box on the outside, I was completely ignorant of the physical/mechanical mode of its operation on the inside. In a broader sense, I was also ignorant about what my African ancestors did before their fateful encounter with European slave traders and their subsequent brutal transport to the Americas. The same was true about the Indigenous people they encountered, except that most of these latter had already perished by the time 'we' arrived. Very little of that history was on the imported British syllabus. Not only was the English language in an 'unassailable position' in our lives and in our literature (Achebe 1975: xii), *they* made sure that all our institutions of learning were structured according to British logic, which included assumptions about our learning capacities and their limits. Many of us were therefore streamed at an early age in the directions they thought we could manage. Those who were 'lucky' or 'smart' enough to get a secondary education were destined to think and behave as the colonizers did, in the fields that they assumed we could handle, but without the hope of ever becoming as competent or learned as them.

But let us return to the broken radio incident. By some means unknown to me, the device started to work again, and my grandmother did not punish me – at least not that time. Determined to understand how the radio and other electronic devices functioned, I started educating myself on the basic principles of physics with various textbooks – some of which belonged to my younger brother. To solve the mystery of why my normally discipline-minded grandmother never 'took me to task' I began desperately trying to decipher books by Sigmund Freud and Carl Jung borrowed from the library. Reading physics soon led me to understand that the most common component on any electronic circuit board was the resistor and that the principle of modulated resistance drove most of the other components. Even the amplifier, which does precisely what its name suggests, I learned, consists primarily of two substances of different resistances joined in such a manner that a current passing through the more resistant side accelerates when it encounters the more conductive material on the other side. Much later, I would learn that the transistor, a semi-conductive device that facilitates complex processing through sophisticated 'switching gates', also makes use of the principle of modulated resistance and levels of energy, but in a far more complex manner, where subtle changes in temperature, illumination, magnetic fields and minute amounts of impurity in atoms could cause enormous increases in electrical conductivity.[6] This, in turn, would lead me to understand the idea behind quantization, where electrons, as energy, never manifest as a continuous stream of values, but literally jump from one value – or level – to another.

Even in those early years, my undeveloped mind drew comparisons between the principles of physics that governed the behaviour of electronic currents, and the chemistry and behaviour of human beings, which included what I perceived as the unpredictable logic of grandmothers. I learnt that if one stayed with a problem long enough, the answer often came when one left it alone, or when one was doing something completely different and not actively thinking about it. Hence, I came to understand that persistence was not such a bad thing, and that one could conserve energy by leaving a problem and returning to it later with new insight. Perhaps the only thing I learnt from my youthful readings of Freud and Jung was that even though there was information in the unconscious that influenced my conscious behaviour, the two might as well be separate domains. What took place in the depths of one domain rarely made it to the other, and whenever such information did cross from one domain to the other, it was so confusing that one needed time and quite a different logic to decipher it. As for how I was to make my way in the world, my dear grandmother made sure that I did well at school by learning everything that was fed to me from those who 'came down to teach us' or those who 'returned with knowledge gained from studies abroad'.

The second incident that shaped my early mode of thinking came during an introductory lesson in my secondary school chemistry lab. The lesson consisted of practical demonstrations of chemical transformations that we had previously learnt about in theory. Studying abstract formulas of different chemical reactions was one thing but seeing those material transformations take place in glass beakers in the lab was quite another; colours changed, beakers foamed and strange-smelling fumes emerged. We were even encouraged to taste some of the substances. I distinctly remember being deeply moved by knowing that these same substances were also present in my body – in different amounts of course – and were being processed there during every moment of my waking and sleeping life, transforming my feeling, sensing and mental states. It was clear to me even then that my experiences of these two principles – of modulated resistance and its curious effects on the behaviour of energy, and the transformation of matter through different chemical processes, which affected my physical, mental, emotional and psychological states – would influence my desire to know more about how and why things, and people, behaved the way that they did. Interestingly, I never did equate the term 'behaviour' with that of artistic performance at the time, even though I was deeply engaged in both.

The third of my earliest experiences was more dramatic, and although it occurred prior to the aforementioned two, I never understood the importance of the event until much later. This experience would fundamentally change my understanding of the relationship between space, time, body and notions of reality, which would be the basic elements I would try to manipulate in my career as a dancer and choreographer. As I mentioned earlier, I was generally good at sport, especially football, or soccer as it is called in North America. I was about eleven years old when I was chosen to play against another team coming from a different district. During the match, I leapt up to head a ball and collided in mid-air with an opponent much bigger than me. I have no memory of the collision, but I do remember waking up on the bicycle seat of one of my teammates, holding onto his shoulders as he pedalled the several miles back to my house. Apparently, I was knocked unconscious, the match was cancelled, and my friend had offered to take me home. This gap in my perception of being embodied in space and time had consequences that would resurface years later, revealing extremely strange and bizarre memories that I would find difficult to understand and almost impossible to reconcile without changing my view of the world and the constitution of the reality I knew. For reasons that I didn't realise until much later, my interest in the phenomenon of consciousness was stimulated.

The key insight that would assist me in understanding some of that experience occurred many years later when, as an adult, I was living in the southwest of Germany in the city of Freiburg-im-Breisgau. I had 'woken up' in the early hours of the morning but, to my utter confusion, woke up a second time to the everyday reality I thought I recognised. But, as far as I was concerned, I could have remained in that first waking state and not realised that I was still asleep if I had not woken up that second time. It was after this second 'waking up' that I felt my body slipping back into a state I had little control over. Standing terrified under a cold shower did not help much, but standing on the balcony of that apartment, stark naked and in the dead of winter, very slowly brought me back to the body I was more or less accustomed to.

Now, we all dream, and some of us do not remember much of those dreams after waking. Others do remember and place great importance on them. Up to that point I cannot say how much value I myself placed on them. But there was a very distinct feeling in my body from this particular dream that felt like a sort of decompression. In fact, I would later call the event my first 'decompression dream', where I instantly knew on that second waking up that it was very different from any experience I had ever had. There was a specific pressure in the body, as if I were surfacing from a great depth and normal consciousness was returning to my body. It also seemed as if the blood was hesitant in returning to my body, which resulted in a very strange alienating feeling that eventually turned into a 'tingling' throughout. Later I would reason that, if dreaming was a manifestation of the brain's ability to organize things into discrete memory categories at different levels of consciousness, then the deeper the dream, the closer one gets to understanding how and why one's memories were structured the way they are. This, in turn, meant that one might be closer to the earliest moments of consciousness and hence the origins of certain ideas. In other words, I had accidentally accessed part of an immense unfolding that had a seemingly endless series of sophisticated but discontinuous 'switching gates'.

With respect to other experiences that I will explain later, I remember thinking that if consciousness existed outside the body, one could also inherit well-formed thoughts, or that these well-formed thoughts could enter bodies at a very early age and remain as memories that could be accessed in different body states. Therefore, when the body is asleep, it is possible that it connects to one's deepest memories, but when it returns to being fully awake, it enters a state of forgetfulness as a protective strategy. Such a hypothesis could explain early traumatic experiences, where the brain 'forgets' events that actually took place. I would have more of these decompression dreams, not at the depth of that first one where I woke up twice, but certainly ones with information that would completely confound me. I would experience the sense of resurfacing that my body remembered from that first instance of returning to 'everyday consciousness'. My struggle to remember and to recognize the value of these dreams would play a significant part in my artistic work.

Another 'decompression dream' occurred in that same city and apartment in Germany, which again I sensed as returning or emerging from a 'space/time hole' that connected experiences that had occurred decades apart. The scene of the dream was the location of my football accident in Trinidad, before I 'woke up' on my friend's bicycle. But I was looking at a room in a house with a lake in the background close to the site of the accident. I do not remember such a lake near that location. Nevertheless, there was a bed in a room of that house with a body on it, and I had the distinct feeling that that body was mine. After much trepidation and hesitation, I tried to enter the room but immediately woke up. That familiar feeling of resurfacing, decompressing and tingling recurred and I immediately felt that the two scenarios were related beyond the fact that they shared the same physical location. This linking of a dreamscape with the experience of a traumatic event occurring in a specific location in my childhood disturbed me. And it would happen again.

Other 'holes' linked to different incidents in my life would surface during that eventful decade living in Germany, generating an elementary working theory of my own consciousness that would influence my artistic work and my academic thinking. This kind of 'speculative philosophy' (Whitehead 1978) constituted my elementary attempts at forming a 'cosmology' in which many things were connected at the same level, but where other things seemed to be connected at different levels. Much later it would also help me understand how my own ancestors may have negotiated the traumas they underwent during slavery and how the implications of those experiences would continue to resonate in the bodies of their descendants and in their communities across time. The radical changes to their lifestyles, their sense of identity and the new realities they were introduced to must have been truly terrifying. I would argue that the practices they devised to maintain some degree of sanity continue to play a foundational role in how their descendants negotiate the intersection of the conscious and the unconscious while being awake to the known and the unknown in their everyday lives. It would also explain how cultural practices from a previous land underwent transformations because of the new environment these ancestors found themselves in and the treatment they were subjected to. Those practices would become methods for dealing with a reality that would have otherwise consumed them, and in many cases certainly did.

The personal experiences mentioned above, and the awareness of historical parallels, led me to question what seeing things as they really are entails, and what it means to become aware of the problematically different levels or degrees of being that the Islamic philosopher Mullā Sadrā speaks about through Morris (1981) in the quote at the beginning of this chapter. I would also seek explanations for these experiences from other sources, very much in the spirit I did many years ago in my grandmother's household, but from those who were experts in these fields.

Introducing the map

> *Philosophy emerges where problems that stimulate critical reflection come to the fore. By critical reflection I mean subjecting each assumption to conditions of evidence, rational assessment, or reason. But simply thinking about one's assumptions and prejudices, while a necessary aspect of philosophical work, is insufficient to make such thought itself philosophical. Thought transcends mere critical reflection when it begins to raise certain questions. These include, but are not limited to, 'What is there? How should we conduct our lives? What can we know? How is knowledge possible? How do we know what we know? What matters most? Why is there something instead of nothing? What must be the case?' or 'What is reality?'*
>
> (Gordon 2008: 8)

> *That knowledge has been colonised raises the question of whether it was ever free. The formulation of knowledge in the singular already situates the question in a framework that is alien to times before the emergence of European modernity and its age of global domination, for the disparate modes of producing knowledge and notions of knowledge were so many that knowledges would be a more appropriate designation.*
>
> (Gordon 2014: 81)[7]

Lewis Gordon is an American philosopher who works in Africana philosophy, postcolonial thought, theories of race and racism and philosophies of liberation. He makes some key points in the quotations above that I believe are equally relevant to performance artists. I would argue that such questions can and have been addressed by constructs outside of mainstream Western epistemic frames. As a practicing artist and a scholar working in academia and in the professional performing arts world, I choose to begin my questioning by drawing on ideas from the field of philosophy. However, I do not see my position here as a philosopher per se. Rather, I see it as a choreographer working with the body in performance – my own and that of others – whilst observing how these bodies provoke, invoke and generate questions that have also long troubled philosophers.

As the subtitle of this book suggests, I am deliberately bringing seemingly divergent philosophical and scientific ideas and practices into dialogue with a specific set of historical and cultural events that, collectively speaking, have had enormous repercussions for entire peoples on both sides of the Atlantic, in particular those from Indigenous populations across the Americas and throughout the African diaspora. I refer here to the voyages of discovery that Christopher Columbus and others began in the late fifteenth century as a search for wealth and influence in a fabled 'East', but which eventually opened the way for genocide, slavery and mass migration in the newly rediscovered lands of the 'West'. This volume thus represents my own grappling with some of the complex questions regarding movement in space/time as processes of thought unfolding and/or being initiated and how those processes are interpreted through dance as a unique research enterprise, as a discipline that helps cultivate a state of embodied knowing, of choreography as an investigative practice that generates as well as frames that knowing in unique ways, and of performance as an activity that reveals much about how that knowing operates in the world.

As I mentioned earlier, my research methodology is transdisciplinary and transcultural in nature because it draws on approaches from different disciplinary and culturally specific constructs to generate new perspectives. Such new perspectives position the body in a central position and its movement in space/time as relationships of thought and feeling. For example, the history of the Black body in its forcible removal from an African continental space to a Western New World space can be seen as a process of separating it from a known land with a specific culture, system of knowing and familial ties within a coherent ontological and epistemological schema, and forcibly indoctrinating it into a system in which the mental was separated from the physical and the emotional, i.e. a Cartesian landscape. I argue that these modes of separation between the African body and a coherent ontological and epistemological schema deeply disoriented it as well as gave justification to the White hierarchy to treat the newly arrived as inhuman and thus incapable of valuing human treatment. Examining these movements from novel perspectives can therefore reveal new knowledge of the bodies themselves, the experiences they went through, are currently going through, as well as what potential they have for creating future scenarios.

If, as I suggested earlier in my introduction, cortical and spatial cartography is an internal process of the brain organizing and interpreting space/time relationships, and that the human body moving through space and time presents an opportunity to claim the information in those spaces as personal knowledge, this forced movement and incarceration of bodies through slavery not only hijacked the entire mental and spatial landscapes of the enslaved but it also compressed them into cells that knew only forced labour and dream of escape. Hence, the new practices that would emerge from such bodies became ways of dealing with such an intense physical, mental and emotional conundrum. I argue that these same practices can be seen as charting individual and collective processes of becoming. And although this process of becoming has an initial stage where there exists a kind of 'double-consciousness' in the sense that Du Bois meant it (1989), this double-consciousness sets the foundation for a triadic unity that creates new possibilities for being. To be clear, such processes are true not just for those who experienced the trauma of an Atlantic crossing and subsequent slavery, they are true for every single body that experiences traumatic situations in life. A key point in this book is that, eventually, different groups come to learn the 'movements' of others and hence gain the possibility of understanding as well as displaying empathy, compassion and mindfulness towards them.

A key premise of my research into choreography and dance is that movement in space and time is foundational to the experience of knowing, and as such, the body achieves a certain conceptual status. It must be clear here that when I say movement, I am not simply referring to the physical or macro movements of bodies, but also the movements of ideas and emotional states that those bodies experience moving through space. The idea of a human 'being', or of a 'being' in a process of 'becoming', is understood here as movement that is capable of redefining who we currently are as well as what we can become. This, then, is the conceptual foundation for the idea of choreography as a re-mapping of cortical and cartographic coordinates, i.e. the process of first knowing those complex structures and then creating the capacity for reorganizing the maps that constitute our being in space/time, with performance as a method through which this can be articulated.

Microcosm vs. macrocosm

Philosophical literature from at least as far back as Plato's *Timaeus* (Moor and Sattler 2010) has described the human body as a microcosmic part of a macrocosmic whole that we call the Universe.[8] But what does this really mean, and how does such an idea fare in the context of modern science? What also would it mean to say that the human body, moving through space/time, accepting, resisting, defying and mediating its way through and/or around every obstacle, is the performance of that microcosmic part attempting to establish an individual presence within a macrocosmic whole? I argue that a transdisciplinary linking of thought, movement and lived experience with the idea of dance and choreography as practices for knowing is very much like the dance of creation, maintenance and destruction that is embodied in the image of the *Nataraj*, the tenth-century Hindu bronze statue depicting Shiva as the Master of Dance. By donating a copy of this statue to the CERN Laboratory in Geneva, Switzerland,[9] where some of the latest experiments in nuclear science are carried out, the Indian government and the CERN Laboratory were both aware that a powerful metaphor was being drawn between the dancing body and the creative potential that exists in the physical world at cosmic and subatomic levels.[10]

But it is no small fact that Shiva's body is portrayed split down the middle – half male and half female – as a symbol of creative balance. However, this balance is certainly not a dualistic one. In fact, it masks a third element in a triad of principles insofar as there is a hidden or partially concealed principle that is the creative potential that brings worlds into existence, maintains and then destroys them in extended cycles. Shiva is standing on a living creature, the 'demon' of ignorance called Apasmara. The image, therefore, represents how ignorance is transformed into knowledge through a process that involves the body grappling with and eventually overcoming that ignorance. I would like to think that as a choreographer, my practices follow these same processes of 'worlding', in the sense that I enact (Varela et al. 1993; Thompson 2007), in conjunction with performers and audiences, temporary worlds that exist for a moment but continue virtually in the minds and bodies of those same performers and audiences. And although some of these choreographic experiments may not result in a traditional performance onstage with an invited audience, the process is always performative, in the sense that it is designed to facilitate a shift in the awareness spectrum of dance artists and observer/participants alike.

The term performance, therefore, is framed here as a 'doing' and an 'experiencing' of different kinds of movements as they unfold in space/time; one experiences oneself as an inalienable part of a dynamic and extremely complex world with the possibility of influencing some small aspect of how that world functions. As someone constantly aspiring to a greater awareness[11] of self, identity and 'becoming', I attempt here to frame dance, choreography and performance within a theory of practice, or theory of 'artistry',[12] which deeply engages with all of the above-mentioned issues. Such a theory recognizes that the notion of 'being' is itself complex, or as Mullā Sadrā once described it: a 'modulated and graded existence [that] only admits of degrees by perfection and deficiency' (Sadrā in Corbin 1964: 68–69). Sadrā's description characterises a world that is full of movement and continuously in flux, where the individual is always in a state of becoming; his core argument being that this modulation goes from 'God', the most real and most intense, to matter, the least real and least intense.

The issue of 'being', therefore, exists as a matter of scale, and since human beings are composed of the same material 'stuff' that constitutes the physical universe, one can argue that we have the capacity to make a movement toward change within that 'God/Human' scale, however small. The concept of 'being' and the notion of 'self' thus depends on our ability as human beings to be consciously aware of who, what and where we are within that scale. *Going West to Find East/Going East to Find West* suggests that there is an interactive multi-directional movement flow between ideas and concepts across disciplines, cultures and geographic locations, all having the potential to oppose and to regenerate one another, and through which an individual's sense of becoming emerges and evolves.

Mediating difference

To fully exploit the idea of a mediating principle that assists in the generation of creative outcomes, this research proposes that the human body be seen as a physical territory within and upon which maps of all our actions are constantly being inscribed and re-inscribed. In short, the body becomes the field where three fundamental principles, or forces – two opposing and one mediating – are constantly being played out. And since these same forces act on and interact with human as well as non-human systems across personal and wider environmental spaces (Ingold 2000), we literally become entangled within an extensive set of multidimensional maps (Salter 2010; Rothberg 2009; Shadmehr and Mussa-Ivaldi 2012).

Performance is thus further defined here as the art of negotiating the physical, geographical, psychological, real and imagined borders that exist between different kinds of territory; it is an act of doing that assists in the generation and regeneration of maps. In this theory of practice, bodies become agents of performance, and dance and choreography become expert practices through which the capacity for embodied knowing is cultivated. And I say cultivated since embodied knowing is not a given simply because one possesses a body – rather, it is an awareness achieved through ongoing practice. An essential dynamic of this transdisciplinary and transcultural methodology is that an active engagement with difference creates new possibilities for action. In other words, new possibilities emerge through the principle of mediation between opposing forces, different perspectives and/or ways of knowing. This logic of the included middle, as it is called in the literature on transdisciplinarity (Nicolescu 2002; Brenner 2005, 2011), operates in complete contradistinction to the law of excluded middle, one of the three classic laws of thought.[13] The law of excluded middle states that either a proposition or its negation can be true, essentially implying that there can be nothing between the two parts of a contradiction. The idea of mediating difference through the law of an included middle, on the other hand, suggests that something else exists, hidden or not obviously apparent, that holds the possibility for movement to a higher level or plane. The 'lower level' here is Apasmara or ignorance, and one achieves real power at the possibility of moving to higher levels first through knowledge of self. Thus, the principle of transdisciplinarity supports the idea that there are different scales or layers of information that exist in complex phenomena such as human bodies, and its concerns are 'the dynamics engendered by the action of several levels of reality at once' (Nicolescu 2002: 45).

One finds support for such a principle amongst writers from quite different disciplinary fields and cultural backgrounds. Philosopher/psychologist Felix Guattari, for example, argues that an excluded middle creates an 'ontological binarism' that leads to a closing out of possibilities for all kinds of action (Guattari

1995: 50). Alfred North Whitehead's 'speculative philosophy' claims that the idea of 'becoming', or movement within a larger cosmological scheme, essentially requires a mediatory principle (Whitehead 1978). Theoretical physicist Basarab Nicolescu argues that the logic of the included middle, together with 'complexity'[14] and 'levels of reality' (Nicolescu 2002; Poli 2001, 2009) are three key axioms that form the basis of a transdisciplinary theory where any reality is always already multi-layered. Crucially, Nicolescu argues that the logic of the included middle is grounded in the work of quantum mechanics pioneers Max Planck (1885–1947), Wolfgang Pauli (1900–58) and Werner Heisenberg (1901–76)[15] and hence displays the unique characteristics of phenomena at that level of 'being'. Further, transdisciplinary theorist Joseph Brenner (in Magnani et al. 2010) argues that, based on the work of these three physicists, the characteristics of energy can be formalized 'as a structural logical principle of dynamic opposition, an antagonist duality inherent in the nature of energy (or its effective quantum field equivalent) and accordingly of all real physical and non-physical phenomena – processes, events, theories, etc.' (Brenner 2010: 338).[16]

Brenner himself argues that this new logical system follows the original work of the French/Romanian philosopher Stéphane Lupasco (1900–88), who claimed that for every phenomenon there is an anti-phenomenon such that the actualization of one is the potentialization of the other, without either ever disappearing entirely. Thus, the point at which equilibrium occurs is also the point of maximum antagonism or contradiction and the place where the included third term, as the only possibility for growth, emerges (Brenner 2011). It is this third term, force or mediating principle that, with the other two, enables the shift to a different level or energetic plane. In other words, it facilitates our understanding of the complex behaviour of phenomena, whether that be the movement of elementary particles through the famous double slit experiment,[17] the ability to remember events that took place in altered states of reality, or the ability of an audience to fully experience, understand or truly 'witness' (Goldman 2017) the complexity of what is taking place between different kinds of bodies on both public and private performance stages (McFee 1992; Coates and Demers 2019).

My understanding and use of the concept of levels of reality borrows from Poli's articulation that these levels are material as well as psychological and social. Poli claims that the material acts as a bearer of the psychological which then supports the social. In other words, the one is the environmental prerequisite for the other. They are what he calls 'referents of a coordinated group of ontological categories' (2009: 14) where psychological phenomena, for example, 'form a specific level of reality, and perception should be considered a specific sub-level within the psychological level' (2009: 143). These psychological phenomena and their perceptual coordinates are at the base of key decisions that alter the course of history. For example, given that Europe was the known 'West', and India, China and Japan the unknown 'East', the discovery of new territories farther west across the Atlantic gave Europe the chance to reposition itself as the influential 'Centre' of the modern world, thus surpassing the ancient and somewhat mythical centre that was thought to be India (Dussel 1995). In this way, those belonging to this new Centre gave themselves the right to develop the newly discovered territories as they saw fit.

The events that transpired on the Iberian Peninsula specifically and in Europe generally, and which led to Columbus's departure on 3 August 1492, established a potent dialectical base for the idea of going West to find East and going East to find West;[18] essentially grounding the seemingly paradoxical idea that anyone travelling in a straight line will eventually find themselves going in the opposite direction to which they began, even though that person would literally still be travelling in the same direction. Extrapolating further, one could say that if any point of view is held long enough without modulation, it transforms into its opposite, even as we would like to believe that nothing fundamental has changed. Transdisciplinary scholars Nicolescu (2002), Brenner (2011) and Bernstein (2015) all agree that the place where opposing forces meet generates a third possibility *without* the destruction of either of the two initial forces. Only then, when all three are working together, can a new phenomenon be created. Here, an arbitrary 'West' meets an equally arbitrary 'East' to generate a dynamically moving 'Centre' that negotiates or mediates between the two. These three, together, reveal new possibilities or 'dimensions', of existence. This idea of modulating difference in service of one's own personal knowing becomes an extremely powerful practice in support of the collective issues this book addresses.

It is imperative, however, that one understands that these positions are never static; 'East', 'West' and 'Centre' are relative positions in that one easily changes into the other depending on one's position at any moment. I argue that the geographic spaces that were previously opened up, explored and claimed, and those who did the opening up, exploitation and claiming, misunderstood this dynamic and, as such, created institutions that were not willing or able to accommodate the different knowledges of the many 'others' they encountered. I also argue that support for these ideas and for the debates they generate can be found in the work of scholars writing from different disciplinary and culturally diverse positions.

Gordon (2008: 28),[19] for example, claims that Africana philosophy recognizes the significance of the conquest of the Americas and the Atlantic slave trade in how we as a society think of the notion of modernity and hence the conception and institutionalization of knowledge within contemporary societies. Homi Bhaba conceptualizes a 'third space' (Bhaba 2004) where the real and the imagined, the concrete and the virtual generate boundaries that are continually being renegotiated and identities that are always in flux. Geographer and self-styled urbanist William Soja's conceptualization of a 'third space' (1989, 1996), which has the potential to 'change the spatiality of human life' with an 'awareness that is appropriate to the new scope and significance being brought about in the rebalanced trialectics of spatiality–historicality–sociality' (Soja 1996: 57) provides a third reference point. All three, I argue, embrace the potential within hybrid cultures to generate 'something new and unrecognizable, a new area of negotiation of meaning and representation' amongst different peoples (Bhabha in Rutherford 1998: 211).

In *Going West to Find East/Going East to Find West: Re-choreographing Cortical and Cartographic Maps*, my objective is to set up an engagement with history that pits a geographic and conceptual 'East' against an oppositional 'West' mediated by an uncertain centre, but where these three forces/principles together create a set of moving physical, metaphorical and conceptual co-ordinates that force us to reconsider what 'doing' and 'being' in the world entails. I am introducing the idea here that performance is a conscious act of negotiating this complexity, and choreography a strategic mode for organizing and re-organizing the actions of 'bodies' and the cartographic and cortical maps they create in space as well as in their own materialities (Lewin 1999). The performer thus has the possibility of becoming a significant contributor to his or her own embodied knowing and hence to a more dynamic topography of their presence in space/time. This, to me, is what decolonization means.

Choreographic organization

The book's title gestures towards choreographic practice as an organization and re-organization of physical, emotional and mental maps and the multilayered territories they inhabit. In this way, choreography and performance become disciplined practices that facilitate bodies being aware of their own 'becoming' in space and time. A key premise, therefore, is that we have the potential to remember and to recognize information that may be 'hidden' in the recesses of our own bodies and in the spaces through which it travels. The dancing body presents us with a unique opportunity to study what is already there as well as learn how that relates to what is beyond its immediate physical borders. More importantly perhaps, dance, choreography and performance constitute an approach to the idea of PaR, Research/Creation and Arts-based Research that expands the epistemological, ontological and ethical bases through which different knowledges meet and interact.

This strategy of bringing together ideas from different disciplinary contexts to create a more comprehensive and holistic understanding of notions of 'self' and 'becoming' is much like the brain's capacity, through the spine and the peripheral nervous system, to create connections between cells and neurons in very different locations throughout the entire body,[20] hence contributing to a more integrated knowledge of the body and its capacities. This aptitude for logical organization, for connectivity, and hence for different levels of understanding, is demonstrated in the artistic works presented in this book as well as the links between each of its four multi-year artistic projects.

In formulating a theory where dance, choreography and performance can be thought of as practices of 'becoming', I have taken great care to follow Michael Shermer's advice about the power that theory has to shape the researcher's observations. In *Why People Believe Weird Things: Pseudoscience, Superstition, and Other Confusions of Our Time* (1997), Shermer warned against the popular use of scientific theories – quantum theory in particular to explain how the perceptions of an observing consciousness helps shape the reality being observed simply through the act of measurement. And arguing that doing so has been dangerous in the past. In this book, I take a mediated route, using the knowledge gained from my own rigorous dance, choreographic and performance practices over time and viewing them through the combined lens of lived experiences as well as disciplinary fields outside my own, drawing valuable analogies as I do so, and paying careful attention to the resonances that occur across these different knowledge fields. In other words, there is no one knower and no one form of knowledge, the situation is far more complex and entangled than that.

NOTES

1. Ellis, Carolyn; Adams, Tony E. and Arthur Bochner. 'Autoethnography: An Overview.' *Forum Qualitative Sozialforschung/Forum: Qualitative Social Research*, vol. 12, no. 1, Art. 10, p. 1. http://nbn-resolving.de/urn:nbn:de:0114-fqs1101108.
2. I write from a West Coast Canadian context.
3. The sixth-century Greek mathematician/scientist/philosopher who reportedly travelled widely throughout Egypt accumulating knowledge that would influence many, including his student Plato and thus all of the Western philosophical discourse (Kahn 2001; Ferrari et al. 2000).
4. Four volumes by Hermes and Walter Scott titled *Hermetica: The Ancient Greek and Latin Writings Which Contain Religious or Philosophic Teachings Ascribed to Hermes Trismegistus*, 1985.

5. *Epistles of the Brethren of Purity: On the natural sciences: An Arabic critical edition and English translation of epistles 15–21*, edited and translated by Carmela Baffioni; foreword by Nader El-Bizri.
6. Britannica, The Editors of Encyclopaedia. 'Semiconductor.' *Encyclopedia Britannica*, 5 March 2021, www.britannica.com/science/semiconductor.
7. Gordon, Lewis R., 'Disciplinary Decadence and the Decolonization of Knowledge.' *Africa Development*, vol. 39, no. 1, 2014, pp. 81–92, www.jstor.org/stable/24484677.
8. Richard McDonough discusses this in some detail in his contribution to the Encyclopaedia of Philosophy, www.iep.utm.edu/platoorg/#SH2b.
9. www.cds.cern.ch/record/745737?ln=en.
10. www.home.cern/resources/faqs/cern-answers-queries-social-media.
11. The term awareness is used here in the sense of being conscious of one's own consciousness (Brenner 2011: 10; Depraz et al. 2003).
12. This phrase 'theory of artistry' borrows from the work of Japanese philosopher Yasuo Yuasa in his *The Body: Toward an Eastern Mind-Body Theory* (1987). In this book, Yuasa attempts to bring the phenomenological writings of European thinkers into a dynamic discourse with Buddhist philosophy and practice.
13. The three classical laws of thought or the three fundamental laws of logic are (1) the law of contradiction, (2) the law of excluded middle (or third) and (3) the principle of identity. Encyclopaedia Britannica www.Britannica.com/topic/laws-of-thought.
14. Barrett describes complexity as 'a metric to describe any structure that efficiently creates and transmits information. A system with high complexity can create many new patterns by combining bits and pieces of old patterns' (Barrett 2017: 282).
15. Niels Bohr's Principle of Complementarity and its opposition to Heisenberg's Uncertainty Principle must briefly be flagged here as it enters into my later arguments dealing with language, discursive logic and the performer/audience relationship.
16. Magnani, Lorenzo, Walter Carnielli and Claudio Pizzi, editors. *Model-based Reasoning in Science and Technology*, Springer-Verlag, 2010.
17. I refer here to Thomas Young's initial experiment in 1801 to measure the wavelength of light, and subsequent versions of this experiment by renowned scientists such as Niels Bohr, Werner Heisenberg and Albert Einstein in their attempts to resolve the wave/particle duality of both light and matter. The experiment proves that several realities can exist simultaneously until observation forces them to be limited to just one possibility (Tucker 2005: 189).
18. Centuries of Islamic occupation of the Iberian Peninsula and numerous Crusades conducted by European powers against Islamic powers pre-empted Christopher Columbus' 1492 voyage of discovery.
19. See https://plato.stanford.edu/entries/africana/ for a general definition of Africana Philosophy. Lewis Gordon defines it as 'a species of Africana thought; which involves theoretical questions raised by critical engagements with ideas in African cultures and their hybrid, mixed, or creolized forms worldwide' (Gordon 2008: 1).

20. The Enteric Nervous System (ENS), in the gut or digestive tract, for example, has neurons that connect directly to the brain. (1) Sonnenburg, Justin, and Erica. *The Good Gut: Taking Control of Your Weight, Your Mood, and Your Long-term Health*. Kindle Edition. Penguin Books, 2016. (2) David, Marc. *The Brain in your Belly*, Institute for the Psychology of Eating, 2015, https://home.web.cern.ch/news/press-release/cern/cern-director-general-outlines-seven-point-strategy-european-laboratory.

2

The Hypothesis Explained

Theory, perception, process and practice

> *That theory shapes perceptions of reality is true not only for quantum physics but also for all observations of the world. When Columbus arrived in the New World, he had a theory that he was in Asia and proceeded to perceive the New World as such. Cinnamon was a valuable Asian spice, and the first New World shrub that smelled like cinnamon was declared to be it. When he encountered the aromatic gumbo-limbo tree of the West Indies, Columbus concluded it was an Asian species similar to the mastic tree of the Mediterranean. A New World nut was matched with Marco Polo's description of a coconut. Columbus's surgeon even declared, based on some Caribbean roots his men uncovered, that he had found Chinese rhubarb. A theory of Asia produced observations of Asia, even though Columbus was half a world away.*
>
> (Shermer 1997: 46)

It is a scientific fact that our bodies take in and regulate enormous amounts of information every minute of our lives without us being consciously aware of it (Dennett 1991; Damasio 1994; Rolls 2014). We also act on and react to this information, often without knowing or fully understanding precisely how or why (Tononi et al. 2009; Tononi 2013; Graziano 2013). Being aware that the body holds memories of these experiences as maps become crucial if we are to creatively utilize them (Barrett 2017). It is also important to know that different strategies are necessary to gain access because of how this information is configured within the body, and how the organization and re-organization of these maps play out as human behaviour in the real world (Kandel 2006). Knowing this is an important step towards directing one's choreographic investigations and hence what kind of knowledge might be available through these processes.

The first thing to keep in mind is that embodied information exists at different levels within the human body and appears in different behavioural modes. There is also a significant discontinuity in our apprehension, perception and understanding of these different levels and modes that are reflected as different 'personalities' in us. The manner in which different disciplines investigate these behaviours speaks to how they are categorized as well as what we expect to learn from them. For example, physics, biology, chemistry and psychology have their own investigative procedures, and look at human behaviour in different ways. Their procedures and methodological approaches are also quite different from the performing arts, making communication between these fields difficult and sometimes even impossible. The term behaviour, for example, can be seen through the arts as performance actions, and we tend to think of these actions as roles being performed on different stages. However, we also tend to frame these roles as being performed by a single stable identity. I argue that the roles we perform are all aspects of a complex 'I', with preferred positions consolidated through practice and 'performed' to the world. My 'theory of practice' therefore argues for the notion of identity in human beings as something that is multiple or fractured.

To state my position more clearly here: we are fragmented beings with layered consciousnesses in need of expert holistic practices to claim true embodied knowing. Only by understanding the spectrum of awareness between our conscious and unconscious states, and deliberately integrating this knowledge into our everyday practices, can we hope to better understand what it means to be human and hence capable of ethical and responsible actions. Playing on the terms 'actions' and 'behaviours', performance artists attempt to influence their audiences through a tacit re-staging of these same actions and behaviours that audiences have become accustomed to in their daily lives. And since these performances emerge from, as well as are received by bodies that have had extensive 'rehearsals' from an evolutionary perspective, it is impossible to predict how they will be received. Any performance can therefore be seen as an experiment for performers as well as audiences to discover or verify something about themselves. Given that the information that feeds this knowledge is stored in maps that exist at different levels within the body itself, one can say that we exist in different states of being; some of which can be classified as awake though without full consciousness of what is happening around us, or 'asleep' but not fully unconscious of our immediate surroundings.

Research by Tononi et al. (2013) has confirmed that we can even achieve states of hyperawareness, though this is rare. It is normally the case that we forget what happens in one state when we return to normal, as in the case of sleep and wakefulness. In other words, what takes place in one state is often lost to the other. And although our bodies can act on what one might call 'unconscious reminders', it is difficult to claim the information that the body has access to in those states without developing specific re-membering and re-cognising practices. My hypothesis is that the strategic distribution of key biological functions throughout the body and the nature of their operations significantly affect our *capacity* for action. This means that when the body is resting in sleep, normal communication with others stops; although the control mechanisms in the brain, the organs in the chest, abdominal and pelvic cavities for breathing and life regulation continue to operate, we lack the ability to control those actions.

And whilst we do have a certain level of control when awake, we do not normally have that control over information that flows in other 'nonconscious' networks or structures in the brain (Varela et al. 1993; Tononi 2013; Damasio 2010; Graziano 2013). Our potentials are therefore hindered by this discontinuity; we are a collection of functions and roles that are automatically coordinated at a level that keeps us alive. However, since there are other levels of 'being' beyond just staying alive, which we have some access to, we must consider what these are, what procedures exist or can be developed to access them, and how we can consciously use them in our creative work and life. In the following chapters of this book, I make a rigorous argument for the idea that consciousness is indeed relative; it exists in different degrees or layers with their own unique 'performative signatures' (Assmann 2008; Eckstein 2006), and we can explore these 'signatures' by putting them in dynamic opposition to one another. It is therefore possible to re-cognize and re-member these different layers through performative approaches to our everyday behaviour as well as through staged performance practices. In this way, the artist sees and treats the world as the dynamic performance of emergent choreographic scripts; what emerges is the knowledge of how these maps are made, how and why they behave the way they do, and to what extent we can use this information in our creative work and in our everyday lives.

Neuroscientist Lisa Feldman Barrett discusses some of these dynamics in her book *How Emotions Are Made: The Secret Life of the Brain* (2017). She claims that the way we see and deal with the world is the result of interactions between a triad of 'ingredients' that she describes as (1) affective realism, (2) concepts and (3) social reality (Barrett 2017: 283). Barrett argues that 'affective realism' is the capacity and tendency to experience what we believe to be true because of the way our brains are wired; 'concepts' result from the brain being wired to construct a conceptual system that regulates the body, keeps it alive and makes predictions about how it should act in the world; and 'social reality' is a process where the brain wires itself to an environment that contains others who also have brains and hence behaviours that they learn in order to survive in a shared social space. Since all these constructs operate uniquely in each person, i.e. no two brains are alike, Barrett claims that we constantly mistake what are 'perceiver-dependent concepts' for 'perceiver-independent reality' (Barrett 2017: 286). This enables conclusions, often based on superficial stereotypes, that create and maintain our everyday realities. Barrett suggests that 'by virtue of our values and practices, we restrict options and narrow possibilities for some people while widening them for others, and then we say that stereotypes are accurate' (Barrett 2017: 289).

Barrett further argues that emotions result from acts of perception that make sense of information coming in from the world around the individual, how that individual body feels at that moment in time, and everything that person has ever been taught to understand as emotion (Lende 2013). In short, emotions are constructed very differently for each person and there is no such thing as a universal emotional response. This 'theory of constructed emotion' (Barrett 2017: 291) takes issue with work that has been done by facial expression and emotion specialist Paul Ekman and his co-writers, who propose that emotions are displayed and recognized in universal ways (Ekman 1972, 2003; Ekman et al. 1987, 2010, 2011). Barrett's theory integrates the latest scientific evidence about relations between emotion, the mind and the brain, thereby challenging commonly held views about how our brains work, how our minds are structured and why 'discontinuities' or differences of opinion arise between individuals, communities and institutions. Seen within the larger context of history as a cyclic process of behavioural scripts unfolding, it is no surprise that many of these biases continue to shape our contemporary societies and institutions.

Barrett's theory of constructed emotion provides a useful foundation for some of my choreographic strategies. Since audiences come to performances with their own preconceptions, the challenge is to unsettle those preconceptions through new choreographic constructs. To get an audience involved in and committed to understanding what any theatrical production is about, one needs to appeal to multiple aspects of their being, be that through physical, emotional, mental or psychological stimulation of one kind or another. Drawing on stereotypes for roles can achieve a certain amount of mileage in a theatrical sense, but the more important challenge for choreographers or theatre artists is how to create a more expanded repertoire that enables the awareness of one's audience to grow and/or change.

Returning to my transdisciplinary hypothesis, the idea of a discontinuity between levels of awareness, degrees of understanding and information that is mapped in complex ways throughout the body, i.e. theory, perception, process and eventually practice, finds an interesting analogy in the field of quantum physics. Keeping in mind that transdisciplinarity as a methodological and theoretical construct has much of its conceptual basis in quantum dynamics, I see a benefit in using the analogy of movements that occur within the smallest particles of matter, i.e. the negatively charged electron, the positively charged proton and the neutral or uncharged neutron within the internal spaces of the atom. The analogy begins with the idea that the fundamental basis of our emotional life is grounded in our biology and our chemistry, which are in turn determined by physical processes, Newtonian and quantum; the former explaining what we experience as the everyday and the latter what happens in extremely large cosmic and extremely small sub-atomic processes. One could argue that the quantum in our lives operates more in the realm of the subconscious and hence the creative imagination, while the Newtonian is visible in the physical processes that define what we do in our day-to-day interaction with nature. This begs the question of how a phenomenon in one dimensionality manifests its presence in another, which is the purpose of drawing this analogy.

The single electron in an uncharged hydrogen atom has a specific orbit that can only change from its ground state under certain conditions, i.e. it will instantly drop to a lower orbit if light energy is emitted, or it immediately moves to a higher orbit if it absorbs light energy. In other words, electrons remain in a stable orbit only so long as their very specific energy levels are maintained. I argue that the analogy of the so-called quantum leap, where the change from one energy level to another is discontinuous, i.e. quantised, is apparent, for example, when we move from a waking state to sleep, or when we wake up and within a few moments forget crucial aspects of the dream state we were in. It can also become apparent in our everyday activities, again depending on the level of energy that affects our awareness of what is happening in the world around us. Since these behaviours all have mental correlates in our synaptic architecture, the solution to our 'forgetting' lies in our efforts to remember, as in being aware of the body's actions as it obeys the intelligence of its internal systems interacting with that of the external world. The intelligence of a thing is therefore determined by its materiality as well as its place, and consequently its energy level within a complex system. In the physics analogy, a 'down-shift' or 'up-shift' in energy is an unfolding where something new is revealed.

Since the body is both a receiving and a transmitting system, the choreographer, or any performing artist for that matter, finds ways to explore these competences in their creative work. The body responds to what takes place in the environment and it utilises this information for its own homeostatic balance (Damasio and Parvizi 2001). Therefore, when we perform, we are responding to as well as transmitting information about the environment and about ourselves to others. On a practical level, re-cognizing and re-membering is the ability to use one aspect of the body to be aware of another aspect in a dynamic way – and by dynamic, I mean that these positions are not static, they shift. This is to say, by 'observing' or 'being aware' of one's 'selves' in action from different positions, one can develop a more integrated practice, and consequently, real embodied knowing. Self-observation couples the physical, the emotional and the mental and psychological aspects of a body in such a way that the individual has a better sense of how he or she is entangled in nature. However, just as the terms 'East', 'West' and 'Centre' are conceptually never static positions, so too is the notion of an integrating self, which I argue is always dynamic, in the sense that it is an ongoing project that goes through different stages or levels of reality. Eric Kandel, Nobel Prize winner in Physiology or Medicine (2000), once described the learning process as 'a set of signals from the environment, with different forms of learning resulting from different types or patterns of sensory signals' (Kandel 2006: 257). I argue that the capacity of the body to reference itself is a powerful tool that performers, because they are in the business of role-playing, have many opportunities to observe in themselves and to utilize in their practices.

My hypothesis further states that because of the mediating process, any one of these three aspects of a self-undergoing processes of integration can take on some of the qualities of the other. For example, the physical body can appear to 'think', the brain to 'feel' and the emotions to 'move', all because of a set of integrated 'feedback loops'. And this 'integrating self' is a far cry from the fragmented or discontinuous state mentioned earlier in my introduction. Such a body has better access to the larger knowledge field that it is embedded in, a knowledge field that I argue is replete with consciousness, as is the larger universe of planets and solar systems (Chopra et al. 2017). I will return to this idea of consciousness as a field that some scientists argue exists throughout the universe later on, but for the moment, I will only say that through consciously being aware of these 'mapping' processes throughout the body (not simply in the brain) as it interacts with everything outside it, the creative individual develops a more acute awareness of their physical, emotional and mental states and hence the capacity for embodied knowing. I argue that through this expanded definition of choreography, one can illuminate and dynamically integrate the group of personalities or positions that are typically subsumed under the false cloak of a stable identity. The benefits of a more integrated self are enormous, not least of all the ability to see the world in a much clearer manner, to act more responsibly within it and to understand one's position within the larger scheme of things.

Implications

The ideas embedded in the subtitle of this book, with their seeming dichotomy, suggest a methodological approach which defines a socio-historical, cultural and performative landscape wherein key events have determined the future of entire peoples. The scope of the choreographic plane that I am investigating here is the larger environmental landscape on which the behaviour of different peoples with their own identities, cultures and ideas are played out. Whenever these identities, cultures and ideas are disturbed, large-scale changes in their 'performative landscapes' take place. For example, if we look at the European colonizing enterprise, we can see how the imposition of the colonizers' languages – beyond and including the verbal – literally unhinged the perspectives of entire peoples.

The Kenyan writer wa Thiong'o once commented that the real aim of colonialism was 'to control the entire realm of the language of real life [...] the destruction or the deliberate undervaluing of a people's culture, their art, dances, religions, history, geography, education, orature and literature, and the conscious elimination of the language by the languages of the coloniser' (1986: 16). He also argued that there were specific 'technologies' that served to enforce those colonizing practices. What comes to mind here are the ships, guns, germs and steel (Diamond 2005) that Columbus and those who came after him wielded in the New World, as well as the commercial, corporate and religious institutions that thereafter supported their enterprise. These technologies conspired to destroy entire peoples and undervalue the 'languages' they could not completely eliminate.

'The Admiral' rightly concluded that he needed to travel constantly in one direction to get to his desired destination on the opposite side of the known world. The problem was that he never calculated for the possibility of finding an entirely different continent – and people with very different perspectives, well-developed institutions and deeply engrained cultural practices – lying directly in his path. Furthermore, introducing Africans as human chattel into these New World spaces and destroying many of the cultural foundations for their appreciation of their own human 'being' set the stage for a struggle to redefine selves that has persisted over centuries and is still ongoing. Nevertheless, one could say that these spaces also contained the potential for developing new creative practices, and hence cortical structures that gestured towards a different kind of becoming.

As mentioned previously, this mediatory agency emerges at the point where opposing forces are at their strongest potential; that is, within or at borders or zones of conflict. This New World, the Americas, was the zone of conflict that changed the way entire nations saw and defined themselves for the centuries that followed. It would also become a space where new hybrid cultural forms emerged to help diasporic Africans redefine themselves. As a descendent of those who were forcibly taken and traded from Africa to the new spaces across the Atlantic, I am interested in introducing other epistemological, ontological and ethical understandings of 'bodies' and their 'being' that engage and otherwise challenge those imposed on us through one idea of modernity.

However, if this 'conceptual decolonization' is to be achieved (Wiredu 2006), we must be clear about who did the aforementioned imposing, what value it brought them and how the structures of colonization need to be changed to accommodate other perspectives. This last point is key since the Black or Indigenous 'other' in a predominantly White environment understands the effects of colonialism and its attendant structural racism more than most and hence must be allowed their own agency in the implementation of changes. They also know that, in order to undo some of the damage to their own psyche, they must work towards what

Bragato and Gordon (2018) call a 'diversification of the epistemological locus of enunciation, replacing it with an interdiscursive, intercultural and complex epistemic field' (Bragato and Gordon 2018: 5).

I hope it is clearer to readers at this point why I see the performing body as a unique source of knowing and the construction of new 'choreographic maps' or 'organized space/time structures' as a key strategy in the unfolding of this knowledge. These new maps, with their attendant cortical and cartographic coordinates, i.e. coordinates that determine who can articulate or 'perform' what and in which spaces, can then engage those discourses that have always sought to 'other' Black and Indigenous bodies. And since so many of these 'others' are marginalized within mainstream training and performance institutions, I make deliberate efforts to change this. I am speaking here of generating a larger movement in service of the 'new dance' through which change can be performed. At stake here is the potential for human becoming (Wynter 1994, 2003), for attaining a state that is fully aware of and capable of accessing the information that adjoins or lies beyond our normal waking consciousness and claiming it as embodied knowledge.

Practically speaking, if thoughts are agents that set bodies in motion, and bodies reveal their relationship to other bodies through these movements in space and time, then it is possible to open up new avenues for understanding how and why these bodies operate the way they do. For example, by examining colonial history, we can see how a particular mode of thinking resulted in the removal of millions of people from one continent and how their enslavement in another served the insidious purposes of a Western European enterprise. It also allows one to see how that the same mode of thinking is still being perpetuated against some of these same peoples.

Embodiment and disembodiment

The term embodied knowledge assumes that bodies possess information about their origin and subsequent development and that this information can be known by their owners. It also assumes that these bodies have a biological substrate, and, crucially, have undergone an extensive evolutionary process (Jones 2000). While bodies are, ontologically speaking, the place where the concept of embodiment is more or less 'at home', scholars and performance artists must also be prepared to explore the implied 'opposing' idea of disembodiment. I am proposing that a movement between one and the other defines the possible scope or spectrum within which human awareness operates. While embodiment can be defined as the coming into being of a body with memories and experiences within particular space/time contexts, disembodiment suggests the potential for all of this to disappear in a moment, i.e. death. Therefore, this research sees embodiment and disembodiment as performative acts, where 'to perform' means to consciously actualize an event or phenomenon in space/time (Austen 1962, 1970; Butler 1997, 1999), and where 'to embody' implies giving that phenomenon a physical presence or incarnation in the world of matter.

Disembodiment would then be the process of moving consciousness outside the body to engage with whatever is beyond it; in which case the experience of 'waking up' outside one's own body and viewing it from that position could constitute such an experience. In fact, many West African and Diasporic African ritual practices engage with this idea of performing disembodiment, some of which I will examine in a later chapter. For the moment, I will preface this by citing a Buddhist concept that 'the various instances of consciousness we experience come into being because of the presence of preceding instances of consciousness' (The Dalai Lama 2005: 132). This, in turn, points to the idea that within Buddhist ontology, the property of consciousness exists outside human bodies and can therefore enter those bodies at birth as well as leave them at death. Thus, if the primary act of performance is the body becoming consciously aware of itself as an indissociable part of its surrounding environment for a limited time in a human form, disembodiment suggests a movement of 'consciousness' out of the body to engage with whatever exists 'out there', but which is in some way intimately connected to it. And this is precisely where some of the aforementioned West African ritual practices come into play within Diasporic communities in places such as Brazil, the Caribbean islands and southern Louisiana in the USA.

This 'dance' of embodiment – or disembodiment as the case may be – has always been of great interest to me. It is also intimately related to Shiva's symbolic dance of creation, maintenance and destruction in the *Nataraj*.[1] We can find a version of the embodiment/disembodiment dynamic in African cultural ontology (Soyinka 1998), where it exists in many of the dances and other cultural forms across the diaspora. It is also an idea that researchers in Buddhist philosophy and practice, in the neurosciences, quantum physics, the biological sciences and the science of mind have been debating in one form or another for quite some time. Varela et al. (1991, 2016), Crary and Quinter (1992), Damasio (2010) and Tononi (2012a, 2012b, 2015) all allude to the fact that we help create as well as maintain the phenomenal world through the complex operations of our entire perceptive apparatus. Coates and Demers (2019) argue that, although the spatial scales are quite different, grappling with the differences between physics and dance can lead us to understand the deep connections between the two. Crabtree (1993) argues that there exists a reflexive loop between sensation, perception, action and reaction that is highly creative, and our senses play a large part in *enacting* an environment that is teeming with the pervasive force of electromagnetic energy.

The dynamics of difference that are inferred in the subtitle of this book initiate a methodology that points to the spaces where these processes have played out in the past and continue to do so today. 'East' defines 'West' through a dynamic intra-action that creates a third field of action in the so-called New World. I argue that these oppositional processes and their spatiotemporal and material coordinates together reveal a hidden tertiary principle, hidden in the sense that one only detects it through results that are often unanticipated, unpredictable and sometimes 'miraculous'. Columbus and many others of his time were quite ignorant of what lay to the West beyond Europe, even though those lands existed and countless peoples with well-developed cultures and transformational practices lived there. And although the traumas that marked the establishment of contact between these different peoples remain, they also mask the metaphorical doorways that Trinidadian/Canadian writer and poet Dionne Brand (2001)[2] suggests can lead to a different potential. Brand's *A Map to the Door of No Return* (2001) is an exploration of identities that have been arrested, lost or misplaced after passing through a metaphorical door. And though this passage has resulted in the inability of many in the African diaspora to completely reorient themselves within a space defined by a condition of imposed powerlessness, she suggests that this very inability holds possibilities for designing entirely new futures, free from many of those constraints.

The chapters in this volume and the creative works that have emerged from this mode of research are designed to remind us that there are ways of knowing that we do not yet know and perhaps may never know, but which we constantly need to seek out if we are to understand the potential they contain (Hunter et al. 2016). In setting out an agenda, I am cognisant of the fact that the very idea of embodied knowledge suggests a location in a particular body that inherits a certain set of experiences, develops its potential and makes claims to knowledge. How that body moves through the world, interfacing and/or interacting with others and with the environment, suggests that history and memory, conscious awareness and unconsciousness, are different aspects of a complex spectrum. Negotiating this spectrum through our own 'nomadic' cortical and cartographic wanderings (Hall 1990; Braidotti 2011; Meerzon 2012) is the driving force behind my choreographic explorations.

Science, art, culture and the transdisciplinary mandate

> *Modern science was born through a violent break with the ancient vision of the world. It was founded on the idea – surprising and revolutionary for that era – of a total separation between the knowing subject and Reality, which was assumed to be completely independent from the subject who observed it. This break allowed science to develop independently of theology, philosophy and culture.*
>
> (Nicolescu 2006: 142)[3]

Now, one might ask, what has this quote and any of the incidents I described so far to do with dance, choreography, performance, a theory of practice or any of the issues I promised to address? A preliminary answer would be that I have always sensed there were connections between many things at the same level, but other things that seemed to be connected at different levels and across different disciplines. Therefore, I would need to investigate what those connections were and where they occurred. Some of those connections, according to Nicolescu, were also embedded in historical events. For example, though most historians identify the industrial revolutions in the eighteenth and nineteenth centuries as the onset of European modernity, there are New World writers (Reid-Pharr 2016; Gordon 2008; Wynter 1994; Dussel 1995) who claim that it began with a radical break in ways of thinking during the fifteenth century. This new state of mind led ultimately to the emergence of mechanisation, ideas of mass production, principles of telecommunication and a scientific logic that denied humanity to certain 'others'.

However, one could also see this transformation as the result of an encounter between cultures that had developed separately, perhaps because of even earlier breaks or transitions. In *Greco-Egyptian Interactions: Literature, Translation and Culture 500 BCE–300 CE* (Rutherford 2016), Ian Rutherford writes about the links between ancient Greek and Egyptian knowledge systems as early as the 2nd millennium BC and the potential loss in the 'translations' that occurred when Egyptian knowledge entered the Greek sphere. According to Alexandra von Lieven in Rutherford (2016), when Greeks referred to Egyptian deities, they commonly avoided the Egyptian names and preferred to translate them into an equivalent form within their own religious system, a process known as 'interpretatio graeca' (von Lieven in Rutherford 2016).

Von Lieven cites the 'Book of Thoth' as a potential model for the *Hermetica*, the works associated with the god Hermes, as an example. Thoth was the Egyptian god of writing and knowledge and Hermes the messenger for the entire pantheon of gods in Olympus. We can only speculate on what kind of misinterpretations took place in these 'knowledge translations' but what we do know is that the focus and scope of knowledge in these two systems were very different. Because of my own personal experiences and an early curiosity, I became interested in what may have been lost in this so-called exchange.

In the small world of my youth, the discovery of the three key principles mentioned earlier would influence my work for decades to come. First, modulated resistance revealed how energetic states could be manipulated in non-biological material. It also suggested how those same modulations in the human organism could translate into states of consciousness. Second, the transformation of matter through different chemical processes suggested that bodies could physically change and so too could the range of emotional states accompanying those physical changes. Third, my heightened perception of space, time and hence reality revealed a world that is multi-dimensional and indicated that our experiences could also be so. Simply taking apart a 'black box' (the radio), even without fully understanding how and why it functioned the way that it did, would eventually lead me to make connections between different disciplinary fields and to develop an experimental strategy (as recommended by Kandel) for the 'systematic accretion of knowledge'. This would also lead me to look at art works, architectural constructions and writings attributed to pre-Greco-Roman periods.

These experiences made me think deeply about the nature of consciousness and how its study involved a range of disciplines from physics, chemistry and biology to psychology and different kinds of spiritual practices. Curiosity became a dynamic mode for investigating and experimenting with overlaps between different knowledge modalities in order to understand how an immensely complex system behaved. In addition to recognizing the importance of those three principles in the formulation of a theory of practice, I also saw the possibilities in the concept of relationality, in that I could draw valid inferences between disparate events and experiences that could reveal crucial interconnections between them. It became clear to me that this kind of 'night science'[4] or 'workshop of the possible' (Yanai and Lercher 2019) was a good starting point for my methodological investigations. The idea that, at some time in the past, human beings had important knowledge about the relationship between the knowing subject and reality, and that this was lost when we changed our vision of how reality itself was constituted, is quite a tantalising one. And the fact that this knowledge, to some extent, still exists as information in some bodies is even more so.

The key point that Nicolescu makes in the quotation above is that particular knowledges can be completely inaccessible through certain frameworks while being transparent through others. And he is not the only respected scientist to express doubts about how much certain scientific frameworks can explain. Cognitive scientist David Chalmers (2014) once commented, 'We've got this wonderful, great chain of explanation, we're used to it, where physics explains chemistry, chemistry explains biology, biology explains parts of psychology. But consciousness doesn't seem to fit into this picture.'[5] He called this the 'hard problem' of consciousness or 'the subjective state of being in the human body – a specific individual body – and experiencing the world from there' (Chalmers 2010: 4). In fact, Chalmers even suggested that if we think of consciousness as a fundamental building block of nature, we might get somewhere beyond the hard problem.

The observations above allude to the fact that too often we forget that our individual disciplines are all trying to explain aspects of a much larger picture and that we need to find ways of connecting those disciplinary perspectives if we are truly interested in understanding their relationship to the whole. Chalmers suggests that there are increasingly fundamental explanatory levels that we need to be more aware of. While psychology on its own may not be able to explain the nature of consciousness, how we construct our daily realities and how those constructions can be seriously disturbed through trauma of one kind or another is certainly worth looking at. This book attempts to get closer to that larger integrated picture through a different route. It attempts to understand how the human being/body as a complex unit performs within an equally complex world and how we can understand both through our own performative actions. It also looks at how relationships between different states of the body influence its overall behaviour, and, in so doing, tries to make an argument for dance, choreography and performance as practices that can make us more aware of the conscious and unconscious processes that form the ordinary and extraordinary in our lives. Self-observation, self-remembering and recognition thus become important tools in the quest to acquire knowledge about ourselves and the different 'worlds' we are embedded in.

Neuroscientist Antonio Damasio's notion of 'self comes to mind' is useful here in terms of how we approach the issue of self-remembering and recognising (Damasio 2010). Damasio argues that 'mind' is created by the flow of sensory images through the brain, and 'self' is the ability to insert oneself into the process as the owner of that brain. A conscious mind is therefore a mind with a self in it, and hence we are only fully conscious when self comes to mind. Crucially, however, I argue that these images of self are distributed throughout the entire nervous system, and extends to the entire body, not just the head. The two most important questions for Damasio in this process are: (1) how minds are put together and (2) how selves are constructed. In my own attempts to identify notions of self in a mental, emotional and physical landscape, I was drawn to Chalmers's description of the 'hard problem' of consciousness and its potential solution long before I knew anything about molecular biology, psychology, neuroscience or the history of consciousness studies. Even in my early youth I felt the need to formulate an individual perspective, an elementary theory of practice, so to speak, which took into consideration the memory of my personal experiences and the way they shaped my mentation and subsequent actions over time.

While the trauma I experienced growing up was accidental, I had not given any thought to the idea of a larger 'cultural trauma' (Alexander et al. 2001; Eyerman 2001) that surrounded me and of which I was also a part. Even though the effects of that trauma were always present, I would only recognise the extent of its power and influence after I moved out of its immediate sphere. Living and working in the European and North American spaces where many of the ideas that were responsible for that trauma originated would give me a new perspective on the matter. Only then was I able to fully grasp what Reid-Pharr (2016)[6] described as a Western-European dictated humanism widely disseminated through specific forms of education. It became clear that the history of my people's transport to the West had already condemned me to a place as an 'other' who had to be educated to see the world through Western European eyes. Colonization revealed itself to me as a grossly unequal transaction that involved a tacit 'surrendering' of important parts of oneself to a system that was created by a historically White male hierarchy that claimed a 'God-given' autonomy and power over all 'others'.

Self-knowing

> *Since culture is a product of the history of a people which it in turn reflects, the child was now being exposed exclusively to a culture that was a product of a world external to himself. He was being made to stand outside himself to look at himself.*
> (wa Thiong'o 1986: 17)

As I mentioned earlier, the aphorism to 'know thyself' advises determined knowledge seekers to first look within. The idea behind knowing oneself suggests that the body contains information that the owner is unaware of, knowledge that connects to the conscious and the unconscious in us, and which we need to find ways of claiming. It assumes that strategies for re-membering and re-cognizing must involve deliberately putting one or more systems or structural configurations of the body up against one an other. I have cited these 'structural configurations' as belonging to three broad categories: (1) bodily sensations that generate spontaneous acts of physical agency, (2) mental and intellectual decision-making processes that produce more considered results and (3) an emotive/affective apparatus that tends to align with one or the other of the former two in key decision-making situations, and, in so doing, favour the outcome in a particular direction. I then briefly touched on how some of my earliest experiences of this process influenced how I understood the world and asked questions about being in it. Since my questions went unanswered or could perhaps only be answered by a more mature mind with more sophisticated knowledge, it occurred to me that I had no other choice but to look to the world and my own phenomenological experiences as I sought to be creative within it. Given my circumstances at the time, I felt all I could reliably do was look, observe, engage myself in rigorous physical practices and take note of what was happening around me in the hope that the relevant answers would present themselves and become coherent over time. This creative work became an investigative tool, a process for, an object of and eventually an outcome of that search for knowledge. In other words, the work encompassed PAR, Artistic Research and Performance-as-Research.

However, trusting my undeveloped mind to understand its own complexity, particularly given my inherent attraction for a range of seemingly disparate interests, made this strategy somewhat problematic. The quote at the beginning of this section offers a tacit warning about the problems one can encounter with such a methodology. In *Decolonising the Mind: The Politics of Language in African Literature* (1986), wa Thiong'o argued that the process of standing outside oneself in a colonial context worked to alienate many Africans from their own Indigenous cultures. Thiong'o claimed that colonialism's two distinctly interlinked forms – (1) 'distancing oneself from the reality around' and (2) 'identification with that which is most external to one's environment' – were equivalent to separating the mind from the body so that the two occupied 'unrelated linguistic spheres in the same person' (wa Thiong'o 1986: 28) which, as I will explain later, could eventually be used to one's benefit.

It was therefore fortuitous that I had early opportunities in my career to explore the power of those verbal and non-verbal 'languages' and to consider the nature of the relationships between them. I acted in original plays that were specifically written or re-imagined for a Caribbean context by directors and writers such as the future Nobel-Prize-winning poet Derek Walcott,[7] while at the same time, training and performing original works in Afro-Caribbean and Contemporary Dance styles in one of the most important dance companies in the Caribbean at the time.[8] I did all of this before deciding to go abroad to continue training to become a professional dancer, knowing that such a career was impossible to achieve at the time in my own country. As wa Thiong'o warned, my growing fascination and identification with things external to my environment would have consequences. Like so many of my generation who experienced a colonial secondary school curriculum, I wanted to see and experience first-hand those geographical and cultural spaces that I had read so much about and with which, to a great extent, I identified. This became somewhat of an adventure as I pursued the career of a professional dancer and choreographer. I was always going to or leaving new places, seeking or perhaps running away from one location or another, the only constant being the desire to see and experience the wider world and to develop a set of survival strategies and practices for creating a unique artistic voice.

This type of performativity, of exploring different facets of myself in different locations and circumstances, was extremely beneficial for building my confidence. And it was within this framework – the body in performance – that my artistic and later academic investigations to 'know myself' would grow and flourish. In the long run I would come to appreciate wa Thiong'o's cautions about standing outside oneself to gain self-knowledge, as I adopted a deeply experiential approach to gaining such knowledge. But this revelation would come only after numerous struggles to fit into others' frameworks, whether by learning a new language or by performing someone else's view of who I was. The lesson I learned was that only after a lengthy and difficult process of self-exploration and self-questioning is any kind of decolonization possible. But this process must, of necessity, involve standing outside the different selves one constructs in order to understand where one's authenticity lies.

As I mentioned earlier, one of the first issues this book tries to address is the ontological dilemma posed by the individual's attempt to know a self that is always already multiple and/or fractured, as well as the epistemological and methodological problems posed by any attempt to map those selves in a process of 'becoming' one. And there is the additional difficulty for those whose ancestors were violently uprooted from one continent, transplanted into another and subjected to prolonged enslavement and indoctrination in unfamiliar and hostile environments. The embodied effects of this immense psychic trauma and forced diasporic existence in the past cannot be underestimated in those who inherited them in the present. However, even in these hostile conditions, the ancestors were able to grasp the potential to create survival strategies and develop expressive languages that charted their navigations of assimilation and innovation. These forms offered ways to mitigate the many discontinuities and fractures that were ever-present in their daily lives. Contemporary artists can adopt similar strategies of 'double consciousness' of standing outside the self to discover the authentic triad of mind, body and emotions.

To the point, writers such as W.E.B. Du Bois spoke of a 'double consciousness' in *The Souls of Black Folk* (1989); Paul Gilroy saw the duality as neither a consistent privilege nor a consistent disability (McNeil 2010), but as an opportunity to develop a creative hybridity (see Gilroy 1993, *The Black Atlantic: Modernity and Double Consciousness*); and in *Performing Exile, Performing Self: Drama, Theatre, Film* (2012), Meerzon spoke of fracturedness and double consciousness as a condition of the exiled – the individual who belongs neither here nor there but who uses that form of punishment as a privilege. Although many recognize this condition as central to an understanding of modernity, and to the development of civilisation and humanity, somehow the contributions of Black people to this cause have always been understated or often completely ignored.

Africana philosopher Lewis Gordon claims that since Whites considered Black and Indigenous peoples less than human, they felt the latter did not deserve any such recognition. Gordon argues that a fundamental tenet of Africana philosophy has been to understand those who 'lived the dubious status of a questioned humanity' and 'to see the liberating aspects of thought among those who live the question of "being" or "becoming" from "the underside of the modern world"' (Gordon 2008: 32–35). In using the phrase 'underside of the modern world', he was, of course, drawing on the work of the Argentinian-born philosopher Enrique

Dussel, who consistently argued that the Global North, beginning with the conquest of Al-Andalus in Spain, hijacked the minds of those in the Global South with its White male European-based philosophical foundations. Such a philosophy 'consistently confused its economic, political and cultural domination, and the resulting crises in other philosophical traditions, with a Eurocentric universality claim, which must be questioned' (Dussel 2008: 1).

If we take the time to abstract the idea behind Du Bois's double-consciousness from its original meaning, imagining consciousness itself as a spectrum, and link it with Gilroy's idea of a creative hybridity, an interesting perspective emerges. The challenge here becomes how to establish lines of communication between different states of being, frames of reference, disciplinary constructs and categories of being, while keeping track of the different aspects of the complex self or 'personalities' that are linked to these states. Whether the frame of reference is a language, a discipline, a culture, a race or simply a point of view, I argue that a shift to a wider perspective is required to understand the complex nature of identity. And just as moving from waking to sleep or from sleep to wakefulness results in forgetting information that was available in one state of consciousness, shifting perspectives requires a tacit remembering of one state so that one is not completely lost on entering another.

What I'm concerned about here is rejecting the dualistic characterization of our thought processes for something more dynamic. This, in turn, could allow us to imagine space and time in a more expansive and multi-dimensional way. Although the so-called Age of Exploration opened up immense geographical spaces for Europeans, it did not open up their minds to the possibilities that there were others with very different but equally important cultures, belief systems and ways of being in the world. Nicolescu's claim of a radical break between different forms of knowledge and its implications for 'humanity' means that different groups of people lost contact with one another during not just one, but several violent breaks at different times throughout our evolutionary history. The fifteenth century, so important for the creation of new nation states, the expansion of social, economic and political ideas, and the opening up of new territories, was also an opportunity to reconnect with distant parts of the world (namely China, Japan and India) that at one point was known. In its attempt to reconnect with a distant 'East', Western Europe located some undiscovered 'others' in the Americas, and after decimating populations in search of wealth and power, forcefully dragged another group from the African continent to serve its colonizing agendas. Not content with colonization, they also appropriated for their artistic, cultural and economic profit, resources that these Indigenous and African peoples held sacred.

In classifying those whom they dragged to this New World as inferior, Europeans erased the contributions that many on the African continent made to human knowledge prior to the Age of Discovery. I argue that the genocidal actions perpetrated on

Indigenous peoples across the Americas, as well as attempts in different centuries to ethnically cleanse Europe of Jews and Muslims, represented the initial coming together of opposing forces *without* a mediating third principle, inevitably causing mass destruction. What was destroyed was the potential of moving to a 'higher' level of understanding, which is what transdisciplinary theory claims the hidden third principle can generate. What Europeans missed was an opportunity to recognize the humanity in those 'others' they encountered. There were many losers in this game of power, but arguably none so much as Indigenous populations across the Americas and the imported African slaves who were brought in to replace them in the human labour market. The European search for the 'other' in the 'East' revealed not only how cruel human beings could become in their treatment of one another but also how Europe's ideas of humanism did not extend to others different from themselves.

In his *Archives of Flesh*, Robert Reid-Pharr accused the Spanish of being the 'primary architects' of a globalizing process that fuelled the 'engine' of slavery and eventually led to the occupation of much of the Americas (Reid-Pharr 2016: 24). He clearly identifies the imperialist agendas that shaped not only the way race would determine how bodies were to be used but also how race would create different categories of labour and hence social status. To try to understand the extent to which this new order disenfranchized so many, Dussel himself called for an 'inter-philosophical global dialogue' with quite different epistemological and ontological foundations than those forced upon the disenfranchized (Dussel 2005: 3).

My own position is that this colonialist, historically White, male-dominated hierarchy will continue to prevail if the institutions that profess to teach, research and disseminate knowledge continue to operate the way that they currently do. I also argue for the recognition of non-verbal and non-discursive thinking as key processes one needs in the search for knowledge and the construction of new vocabularies to support it. Restating my map-making strategy of bringing dance and other movement practices into the discourses of science and technology, cultural studies, philosophy and post-colonial studies, my intention here is to understand history itself as a construct written by those who have for centuries held the reins of power and who will certainly not release them voluntarily. And, as wa Thiong'o so poignantly reminds us, an enormous amount of that power lies in language.

Movement, language and non-discursive thinking

> *To approach the body as capable of generating ideas, as a bodily writing, is to approach it as a choreographer might. Dance, perhaps more than any other body-centered endeavor, cultivates a body that initiates as well as responds.*
>
> (Foster 1995: 15)

> *Language carries culture, and culture carries, particularly through orature and literature, the entire body of values by which we come to perceive our place in the world.*
>
> (wa Thiong'o 1986: 16)

discursive *adj.*

1. passing from one topic to another, usually in an unmethodical way; digressive.
2. *(philosophy).* of or relating to knowledge obtained by reason and argument rather than by intuition.

(Collins English Dictionary 1995: 50)

Although I fully support Susan Foster's claim that the human body is capable of generating ideas, I have always been cautious of using her term 'bodily writing', if only because of what is implied by the term 'writing' and the power and status that this activity carries in the academic world (Derrida 1978). One could argue that Foster did not necessarily presuppose writing in the traditional sense of the term or that for dance to be a valid research enterprise it must adopt writing as its primary mode of inscription. However, she does draw attention to a certain activity that conflates two very different forms of inscription, i.e. dance as language-like use of movement, versus academic written and spoken word. Dance is certainly 'language-like' in the sense that choreography uses human bodies to inscribe a set of temporal relationships in space/time. But the terms 'reading' and 'writing' the body not only blur the relationship between movement and verbal or written language but also deeply prioritize the latter, perpetuating not only its institutionalisation in the academy but also a certain marginalization of movement and the non-discursive.

I am therefore much happier examining thought, movement and sound as processes that define a 'coming into body'. However, in this context, writing, or at least academic writing, frequently tries to 'fix' the inherent indeterminacy of dance/performance in space/time, drawing on very specific and pre-determined intellectual frameworks. Movement and its organization into choreography and hence dance does not need anything else to 'be', it already 'is', and the nature of that 'being' is what makes it unique. If, as I mentioned before, movement is analogous to thought unfolding, talking and writing about it is an attempt to make clear to others what one understands about it. But there are many other forms that can be used for sharing knowledge, especially when verbal languages have such deep psychological levels of meaning specific to the groups that develop them.

Discourse, which Julia Kristeva once argued 'implies first the participation of the subject in his language through his [*sic*] *speech, as an individual*', and where 'the subject forms and transforms himself in the discourse he communicates to the other' (Kristeva 1989: 11, original emphasis), is part of a process of differentiation, i.e. that of becoming a thing, or something. While I would like to think of my choreographic work as generating forms of discourse, I am always hesitant to use the terms 'writing' and 'reading' to describe its modes of inscription and apprehension. I prefer terms such as 'dancing', 'performing temporary spatiotemporal inscriptions' and 'spatial mapping' to better account for the succession of bodily images and movement attitudes that I utilise to challenge the viewer's psyche.[9] Performing this material in space/time is fundamentally different from intellectual discourse. It is movement that (1) allows thought to enter a prescribed space or (2) allows thought to define a space for itself. These two are different: the first functions as an invitation to the audience to think about what they are witnessing, and the second is an expression of the thoughts of those who contributed to the making of the work. Both take place during the live performance event. In this way, the relationship between thought, inscription, language and writing becomes more interactive, with movement at the beginning of a two-way process that may or may not produce an emergent *langue*.[10]

Kristeva herself has argued that instead of asking what language is, one should ask 'How was it possible to conceive of language?' (1989: 5). The question I pose here is: how can we think of choreography as a reconfiguration of space/time, hence allowing us to extend an experience that is prior to the establishment of any written language? In other words, how can we think of movement as the unfolding of a thought that, in turn, seeks to attach itself to another body. The two definitions of discourse cited in the quotation at the start of this section point to different methodologies: the words 'passing from one thought to another', 'unmethodical' and 'digressive' a striking contrast to 'reason' and 'argument', suggesting different states of a phenomenon, before and after its naming. The first set of words points to a general definition of discourse while the second refers specifically to its role in Western philosophy.

Gilles Deleuze and Félix Guattari argued that philosophy is a search for knowledge of phenomena through 'the art of forming, inventing, and fabricating concepts' (Deleuze and Guattari 1994: 2). And, after Spinoza (1994, 2012), they define two types of discourse: one as the logical activity characterized by the exposition of claims, premises and proofs in verbal and/or written arguments, i.e. linguistically, and another as affect, which contains some of what is traditionally attributed to the emotions. In fact, neuroscientist Antonio Damasio (2017) chose to define affect as a collection of processes that includes drives, motivations, emotions and feelings, and especially this latter as a motivator, monitor and negotiator of the cultural process.

Here, then, lies the foundation for a great deal of what we come to understand as embodied knowledge. In what I consider a commendation of the power of the non-discursive, Damasio argues that feelings – an important component of affect – seems to be systematically neglected in how we understand the nature of our intellectualizing, socializing and culturalizing processes. He claims that the power behind affect is homeostatic regulation, or the ability of an organism to remain within certain operating parameters such that it maintains its own healthy existence. What this essentially means is that the human organism has a built-in automatic ability to regulate itself, and it is this regulation that enables us to be what we are, which means to think, to feel, to move and to make decisions without recourse to words or writing. Affect and homeostatic regulation are thus doorways to embodied knowing, and eventually to claiming the knowledge that is inherent in our organism.

Mirroring

My objective in trying to understand how embodied information and its relationship to other bodies in space and time could be revealed through movement as a creative non-discursive practice received some unanticipated support through the work of the Italian neurophysiologist Giacomo Rizzolatti and his research team,[11] who were looking at the relationship between language, gesture and the body at the level of neurons in the brain.[12] Experimenting initially with macaque monkeys, Rizzolatti and his team noticed that when the animals saw an action performed by someone – say for example a researcher in the lab – this triggered responses in their brains even when they did not actually perform the same action. Moreover, they found that these 'mirroring' cells fired when the animals made associative actions, or actions related to a particular task, with their hands or mouths. For example, if the animal made a picking action with its fingers, neurons associated with that picking action would fire, regardless of what was being 'picked'. The cells also fired when a target object was in the visual field of the animals as well as when the animal touched parts of its own body associated with the potential touching of the target object. Rizzolatti's team concluded that these patterns of neural activity contradicted the previously held idea that 'action and perception were completely independent processes confined to their separate boxes' in the brain (Iacoboni 2008: 14).

Working on the assumption that there is an evolutionarily more complex 'firing' system of these 'mirror' neurons in the developed human brain, neurologist and neuroscientist Marco Iacoboni argued that this research indicates that 'the visual receptive field (that part of the surrounding space in which visual stimuli trigger the firing of the cell) and the tactile receptive field (that part of the body that, when touched, triggers the firing of the cell) are related in these neurons' (Iacoboni 2008: 15). The fact that these mirror neurons are 'premotor neurons' i.e. 'implicit, automatic, and pre-reflective' (Iacoboni 2008: 270) means that they are not really concerned with reflective behaviour. However, as Iacoboni and his own team proved, the neuroscientific discovery of mirror neurons 'disclosed the pre-reflective neurobiological mechanisms of mirroring to our reflective level of understanding other people' (Iacoboni 2008: 270). In other words, our ability to grasp and thus empathize with the actions of others is fundamentally instinctive. To return to my earlier support for the idea of consciousness being a fundamental building block of nature, does this then mean that it manifests as instinct at a base level? Further, does this mean that instinct in animals, and human beings, is really the manifestation of a lower degree of conscious awareness that exists within a far more comprehensive or profound spectrum of consciousness?

Iacoboni also claimed that something like physical contact occurs when people 'orchestrate' movements in their minds when watching someone else move. The conclusion I make here is that this relational mapping of intentional actions to people, objects in one's environment and the environment itself, creates a kind of reciprocal 'dance' that lays the foundation for a more formal language of reflective understanding. Again, it is the ability to tap into and re-organize this complex information that determines the degree of conscious awareness someone has. Here then are grounds for my argument that dancing is a way of performing spatio-temporal inscriptions or spatial mapping that challenge the viewer's psyche at a place before and beyond speech and written language. Thought defines a space for action through intention, or inversely, movement articulates the thought that enters a prescribed space, all of which takes place prior to speech or the formulation of a written language. This space is where a 'proto-language' is developed. Michael Arbib would build on the work of Rizzolatti and his team by setting out to prove that mirror neurons were the precursors of neural systems for language (Arbib 2005).[13] Arbib argued that proto-language is:

> an open system of communication used by a particular hominid grouping that was a precursor of 'true' language – where language is an open-ended system in which words and then phrases can be assembled according to some grammar that makes it possible to infer plausible meanings for novel utterances created 'on the fly'.
>
> (Arbib 2012: 252)

Arbib also claimed that the development of language from proto-language occurred not from adding syntax or syntactic categories, but from what he calls 'a process of *bricolage* (tinkering), which yielded many novelties to handle special problems of communication' (Arbib 2012: 253). It is from this 'tinkering' that the tools for constructing the rules of grammar eventually emerged. His Mirror System Hypothesis claims that the human being's capacity to use complex imitation in the development of communication protocols is a praxis deeply embedded in people's cultures and hence their systems of expression. And as I argue here, this occurs even in the way that one culture absorbs the language of another culture's colonizing enterprise. Any attempt to speak about embodied cognition or embodied knowledge must therefore consider how particular neurons in the brain negotiate relationships between perception, action and cognition, and hence the development of spoken and written language through gesture. This, I argue, is the same mechanism that lies behind every movement learned in the dance studio, every gesture observed and utilized in a choreographic setting, every emotion that provokes a movement and every thought that generates an action.

It becomes interesting to reflect on Deleuze and Guattari's definition of philosophy as a search for knowledge of phenomena through the art of forming, inventing and fabricating concepts, which of course assumes that philosophy cannot exist without language. But if languages are particular to the thinking of those groups of people who form, invent and fabricate the concepts surrounding them, is it not clear that there can be different philosophies based on the thought processes of different groups of people? I would respond to this question with a resounding yes. Perhaps the reader can now understand my scepticism about positioning dance as 'writing' and 'reading', and the consequent usurpation and limitation of an inherently dynamic process by an academic and often colonizing enterprise intent on institutionalising, i.e. imposing its own structures and ideological frameworks on others who not only have firmly established languages, thought processes, ideas and philosophies about existence of their own but who also have creative processes that work within these parameters.

Félix Guattari (1995: 5) once claimed that 'it was a grave error on the part of the structuralist school to try to put everything connected with the psyche under the control of the linguistic signifier!' He made this claim within the context of a larger argument on the complexities involved in the production of subjectivity beyond its classical definition, which, he argued, necessitates a revision of models of the unconscious (Guattari 1995). In the words of Black scholar, dance artist and activist Halifu Osumare, one finds that the 'insidious nature of cultural hegemony: [that] is embedded in the deep structure of the language, representing the unconscious thought patterns [...] can often be more oppressive than overt racism' (Osumare 2018: 32). What she means is that language, as it emerges from sound and a particular mode of thinking, is local and particular to the group that devises it. Its structure reflects the unique thought processes of that group or culture and hence, to forcibly impose it on another group is itself an attempt to colonise their minds.

To be clear, my argument goes beyond the obvious attack against the agency of the academy or of academics to a concern for identifying the different levels of the dynamic process we call performance and the techniques needed to train the body/mind to be aware of its complexities. The point here is that some of these stages have for so long been hijacked by other frameworks that they have become sufficiently institutionalized in miseducating rather than opening minds and bodies to more extensive possibilities. In their examination of the formation of methods in the pursuit of knowledge and hence the establishment of knowledge institutions themselves, Deleuze and Guattari claim that philosophy, art and science each engage in the activity of thought as an act of creation, and hence the sphere of creation will differ in each discipline.

Their position is that 'art is concerned with the creation of percepts and affects' (Deleuze and Guattari 1994: 164), i.e. sensations, while science is an activity of thought that creates 'functions' which are 'propositional', thus forming fragments from which it pieces together a makeshift language (Deleuze and Guattari 1994: 117). Art, science and philosophy, therefore, all have relationships to language that are discipline specific. In other words, individual disciplines define the terms of their relationship to the process of language-making differently. And since, according to them, science and philosophy use 'concepts' and 'functions', and art 'percepts' and 'affects' as tools in their pursuit of knowledge, these terms arguably serve to define the nature and scope of their disciplinary discourses.

Now this might be the case for Western philosophy and its attempts to rid itself of a historical emergence from a mind/body dichotomy, but regardless, I see possibilities for Performance-as-Research and Artistic Research that go beyond Deleuze and Guattari's classifications. This option utilizes functions, propositions, affects, concepts and percepts in a transdisciplinary manner, meaning that it operates with a different logic. I speak here of trying to make sense of my own rather confusing and somewhat irrational experiences cited earlier. In these experiences, percepts and affects work in conjunction with concepts and functions. In fact, they generate new meanings through what I would call a 'coming-up-against to work out new directions'. Knowing this, my starting position as a choreographer and scholar is that learning begins with trying to understand the information that is already contained within the materiality of one's own body, its thoughts, actions, desires, experiences and its own self-reflexivity. However, it also considers the irrational order of unusual, traumatic and even bizarre experiences of those bodies and the opportunity to understand what they mean. Thus, all experiences are relevant, and the performance becomes a mode through which we can experiment with new ways of thinking and being.

Bodies can therefore be seen as complex systems with units that monitor and regulate other units within themselves in a highly interactive manner; in the sense that one part (the nervous system, e.g.), makes maps of every action another part of the body takes as it senses and 'feels'. Additional maps are thus created within different levels of our organism in an increasingly abstract manner. Since the cerebral cortex contains almost 90 per cent of the neurons in the brain, it becomes the recipient of and host to an archive of extremely complex sets of information via attention, perception, awareness, thought, memory, language and consciousness (Damasio 2010; Kandel 2006). And as my main argument here is that dance and choreography can be seen as tools for the deliberate investigation and creative exploration of movement as a basic function of our human existence in space/time, it is important to remember that whether one is a trained dancer or not, the body can become so accustomed to moving in particular ways that we no longer think about it. 'Catching oneself' in the midst of a formally learned movement or action that the body instinctively makes must therefore become part of one's re-cognizing and re-membering strategies.

Movement, then, is far more than the physical expression of the body's inner state of being, or the manifestation of a 'lived experience' that is communicated to others; it is a window on how everything in the world is fundamentally entangled and how that entanglement functions. Complex expert movements are therefore ways of investigating how one kind of thought operates in bodies. Instinctive movement is another and stillness while the world outside the body continues to move is still another. Bodies generate a special type of 'discursivity' for which movement is foundational. Unlike words, movements are more open to interpretation and their symbolic or semiotic references vary widely from culture to culture. Metaphorically and scientifically speaking, they are indeterminate and complementary. They also become whatever the viewer sees and feels through his or her own culturally determined measuring instrument. Wordlessly, movement reveals a great deal about an individual's internal state, can engender uncertainty, instability and conflict. The key point to remember is that thought, movement and verbal language are different processes that span a multi-layered spectrum of becoming.

My argument is that since movement is a more primary response and thus closer to the deeper layers of our unconscious states, it plays a fundamental role in how we position ourselves within the world prior to verbally expressing ourselves as part of it. In other words, I am claiming that the body communicates things that verbal language later attempts to interpret and then writes into existence. Speech then has the additional function of articulating a thought that emerges from places of consciousness and unconsciousness. This is itself part of understanding and claiming knowledge, while writing allows one to settle on specific terms in different languages that locate, explain and eventually fix a perception within a specific language or cultural domain. Movement, on the other hand, reveals what the body tacitly knows and is therefore a window to a state that is prior to verbal expression.[14] Movement, speaking and writing are therefore different states of the knowledge process, the last being how one presents that knowledge to others.

The French phenomenological philosopher Maurice Merleau-Ponty (1962) recognized this when he argued that academic discourse must always return to the 'lived experiences' of bodies to rediscover their unique epistemological foundations. Movement operates at a level that often evades verbal explanations, especially when the language has no adequate terms for what one sees or senses and therefore is forced to make up a new term. In making up these terms, the writer's or speaker's verbal arguments function to convince listeners or readers to accept certain premises as valid, conclusions as strong and reasoning as interesting.[15] The act of convincing thus switches to the efficacy of the academician's language skills rather than any original affective experience. Clearly then, there are significant benefits to exploring the spaces between the conscious and what is still un-conscious through movement as non-discursivity, which could, in turn, give us a better understanding of the world and our role in its unfolding.

Preliminary conclusions

From what we have been looking at so far, the lived experience of the body as it moves through and interacts with others in space/time is fundamental to knowing. Through our perceptive functions we cultivate awareness of what is in the body as well as what it interacts with in the environment. Without these experiences, there is no basis for the establishment of a self or for knowing its parameters. The more complex our experiences, the more interesting the performances that emerge from bodies. But, to communicate what one knows to others requires quite a different set of skills. These include a kinaesthetic awareness that is initially generated through the pre-reflective neurobiological mechanisms of mirroring. However, the real power of dance as a performance discipline lies in the spaces where thought, movement and sound overlap before the verbalizing intent takes over.

In his early research on psychopathology, Carl Jung observed a set of relationships between images and sounds in his patients' dreams and fantasies. According to Kugler (1982), the experiments that Jung and his associates carried out at the Burghölzli Klinik in Zürich resulted in two major contributions to psycholinguistic theory. The first is that a person's speech is dominated by 'autonomous groups of associations' (Kugler 1982: 16–18), whose core is a psychic image, and the second is that the unconscious processes of association follow phonetic considerations. The emergence of sounds, and later speech, from a psychic image is a movement from a potential in the unconscious to physical expression, and hence an engagement of the kinaesthetic sense. This 'mirroring' facilitates the interaction between three signifying systems, images, movement or 'body language' and speech, thus revealing much about the underlying architecture of our desires and intentions.

Kugler's comments about how our psychic complexes structure our dreams as well as our speech are important; not only because they point to how these processes influence artistic creativity but also how linguistic structures are almost immediately imposed via the socio-political, cultural and educational institutions we have constructed, inherited from others or had forced upon us.

Kristeva's interpretation of the semiotic, and by extension the non-discursive, as a 'bodily drive' that manifests itself in 'signification' (Kristeva 1984; 1995) is useful for assessing the relationship between verbal language and movement in terms of the spaces they both strive to bridge. She argues that the rhythms, tones and movements of speech give rise to the grammar and structure of signifying practices. For her, meaning arises through the interaction between words and movements (Kristeva in Welton 1999). Thus, when choreographers use verbal language in their performance productions to draw attention to bodies, they deliberately problematize the social institutions around which these languages are constructed. This is quite evident, for example, in the *Tanztheater* work of choreographers such as the late Pina Bausch in Germany, and Lloyd's Newson Physical Theatre work with DV8 in the UK. The work that these choreographers staged[16] – many of which I was personally able to witness during my sojourn in Europe – uses movement and speech in performance to critically comment on issues particular to the social context of these two societies. Their works demonstrate how putting verbal language up against movement – and vice versa – generates a powerful expressive force that bridge dance and theatre as disciplinary forms, helping to establish Physical Theatre and *Tanztheater* as performance genres in their own right.

Both Bausch and Newson exploited movement and text as devices to stage interdisciplinary choreographic works that were extremely powerful in their presentation of social situations. They also used it to ambiguate meaning, by which I mean using the structures of verbal expression to question its very use, especially when one's audience may not understand some of the languages that are spoken in a production. In his early choreographies for DV8, Newson claimed that he wanted to take risks 'aesthetically and physically', to be 'radical' yet to 'break down barriers between dance, theatre and personal politics', and to reinvest dance with meaning 'particularly where this has been lost through formalised techniques'.[17] According to him, the goal was to construct a forum for the communication of 'ideas and feelings clearly and unpretentiously'.[18] Bausch, on the other hand, bore out Kristeva's argument for the body's return to modes of contemporary discourse through a combination of the semiotic and the psychoanalytic. In her work, she deliberately and creatively utilized the different languages of the members of her ensemble. And, like Newson, she developed a radical direction in relation to her own established traditions and institutions, the aim being social commentary through a personal investigation of the means that permitted or inhibited change.

Both choreographers demonstrated that such ideas require us to continually revisit the movement and verbal vocabularies we use, so that we can challenge ourselves and re-invest our work with a more contemporary relevance. The power in those works therefore came from a combination of individual gendered, nationalized and culturally embodied narratives of the members of her company, the society that supported those works, the means through which they could be shared and the attempt to re-organize the established cortical and cartographic maps that provoked its audiences to feel, think and move beyond their accustomed ranges. In doing so, those works ask us to revisit the ontological and epistemological bases of our knowledge systems as we continue to make an argument for dance as a unique research enterprise; how it assists in cultivating a state of 'embodied knowing', how choreography as a practice frames that knowing in creative ways and how the activity of performance reveals the way that bodies, especially ones 'othered' by the very discourses that claim to speak for them, continue to renegotiate their positions in the world.

NOTES

1. The Hindu god Shiva's dance of creation, maintenance and destruction in the *Nataraj* was partly the subject of my choreography *Touched* (2008), in the research project with that same name.
2. *A Map to the Door of No Return*. Doubleday Canada, 2001.
3. In Haverkort and Reijntjes (2006).
4. '*Night science*' is a term invented by the French scientist François Jacob (1998). It is the place where the unstructured realm of possible hypotheses and ideas not yet fully fleshed out are explored, whereas in *day science,* scientists falsify hypotheses and observe which ones are left standing. Itai Yanai and Martin Lercher. *Genome Biology*, vol. 20, 2019, p. 179.
5. Chalmers, D. [Filmed March 2014 at TED 2014], www.ted.com/talks/david_chalmers how_do_you_explain_consciousness?language=en. Also archived in text at www.ted.com/talks/davidchalmershowdoyouexplainconsciousness/transcript?language=en.
6. Reid-Pharr, Robert F., *Archives of Flesh: African America, Spain, and Post-humanist Critique*, New York University Press.
7. Derek Walcott (1930–2017) founded the Trinidad Theatre Workshop in 1959 and arguably wrote his most successful plays for this group. These works included *Ti-Jean and His Brothers* (1958), *Dream in Monkey Mountain* (1967), *The Joker of Seville* (1974), and *Oh Babylon* (1976). Walcott won the Nobel Prize in literature in 1992.
8. The Trinidad Repertory Dance Company was founded in 1972 by Astor Johnson (1930–85), who was its original director/choreographer.

9. I use the term psyche here to mean a complex where physical, mental and emotional experiences are stored, sometimes synthesised and mostly forgotten to the conscious mind, but which continue to influence our actions.
10. This term is used in the Saussurean sense as the abstract, systematic rules and conventions that define any signifying system (1983, 2013).
11. Vittorio Gallese, Luciano Fadiga and Leo Fogassi.
12. Gallese, V., L. Fadiga, L. Fogassi and G. Rizzolatti, 'Action Recognition in the Premotor Cortex.' *Brain* vol. 119, Pt. 2, 1996, pp. 593–609; Rizzolatti, G., and L. Craighero, 'The Mirror Neuron System.' *Annual Review of Neuroscience* vol. 27, 2004, pp. 169–192.
13. Arbib, M. A., 'From Monkeylike Action Recognition to Human Language: An Evolutionary Framework for Neurolinguistics.' *Behavioural and Brain Science*, vol. 28, 2005, pp. 105–124; discussion pp. 125–167.
14. Eugenio Barba and Nicola Savarese's *A Dictionary of Theatre Anthropology: The Secret Art of the Performer* deals with the issue of 'pre-expressivity' in some detail.
15. The logic used in these paragraphs is influenced by Douglas Walton's *Argument Structure: A Pragmatic Theory*. University of Toronto Press, 1996.
16. I had the pleasure of witnessing Pina Bausch's Wuppertal Tanztheater perform a number of works; *Blaubart* (1977), *Café Müller* (1978), *Kontakthof* (1978), *Nelken* (1982), *Viktor* (1986), *Tanzabend II* (1981) and *Auf dem Gebirge hat man ein Geschrei gehört* (1984), as well as Lloyd Newson and DV8's *Strange Fish* (1992), *Enter Achilles* (1995), *The Happiest Day of My Life* (1999) and *Can We Afford This* (2000), during my sixteen years of living and working as a choreographer and performer in Germany and the UK.
17. DV8 Website www.bristol.ac.uk/theatre-collection/explore/live-art/dv8-archive/.
18. DV8 Website www.bristol.ac.uk/theatre-collection/explore/live-art/dv8-archive/.

3

Further Presuppositions and Explorations in Search of a Theory of Practice

Revisiting the hypothesis

> *The continuity of any cultural phenomenon, the praxis of any body of knowledge, involves a string of people not simply learning a set of axioms which someone invented in the past, but also themselves repeating the cognitive breakthrough of its 'inventor' and actually re-inventing the institution itself each time. Any phenomenon–geometry or performance, for example – can be understood and practised only when each new member repeats the original cognitive leap.*
>
> (George 1996: 16–17)

In the quotation above, David George suggests that an important route to claiming the knowledge embedded in any body involves the individual owning a process through its rediscovery, through remembering and/or recognizing something that has already taken place in one form or another, in one body or another, and at some previous moment in time. It is precisely this that makes the choreographic process simultaneously challenging and rewarding. In this chapter, I will explore how my choreographic practice builds on this principle by drawing on two projects, *Shango Meets Ogun* (1998) and *Futurist Equation* (1999). These works were made in an early stage of my academic career as I was trying to place myself within a system that invited me in but, in many ways, was not built to accommodate the work that people like myself were trying to do.

A key part of my role as choreographer and director over the many years of my nomadic career was to create an environment where the challenges of discovering and claiming embodied knowledge could occur. Hence, much of the content generated in the choreographic works I stage originates in a careful observation of the bodies of the performers and an assessment of their potential. Coming from a cultural background that is often markedly different from the performers I work with, individuality and cultural diversity as well as technical training and performance skills are important considerations. I am also interested in what these bodies have to say that they might not have considered and that I might also learn about. This can be challenging work when it comes to generating a vocabulary and movement style that works for the group within the relatively short space of time that we have together on a project. Nevertheless, this is a challenge I enjoy since it brings wonderful surprises as people remember and recognize things about themselves.

One can say that there is a meeting point between my expertise as a choreographer with a particular background, training and incisive skill set, and the power dynamic of being the person who gets to organize the information offered by the dancers to create a unique performance work. Although I have the final say in what corporeal information generated in rehearsal is considered important enough to be presented onstage, those choices are inevitably filtered through the same lenses that make choreographers and their dancers uniquely drawn to one another – even though we might be different as far as gender, culture, training or position is concerned. The cognitive breakthroughs and re-inventions of institutional processes we engage in together become a key part of the work itself.

Cognition requires a body with the capacity to perceive the world through the senses and to act thoughtfully using a higher reasoning power. Higher reasoning, in turn, involves the coordination of the entire nervous system, not just the head brain.[1] The performer should also be able to use short- and long-term memories and to learn from their experiences. Finally, he, she or they should be willing to develop and use non-verbal as well as verbal forms for communicating intent. The creation and subsequent performance of a choreographic work is the result of all these processes; it is the ability to move skilfully and artfully through space and time with intent. As I have argued elsewhere, the very notion of embodied knowledge also assumes that the body in question has a biological substrate and, crucially, is the manifestation of an extensive evolutionary process. The choreographic investigation, therefore, intersects with a broader ongoing developmental process, however insignificant that intersection might seem. In this way, choreography becomes a unique opportunity to experience the trajectories of bodies in space and time as they seek to fulfil their potential.

In his early explorations of a species biological development, German naturalist Ernst Haeckel argued for the notion of ontogeny recapitulating phylogeny[2]; the idea that the stages an embryo undergoes during development essentially replays the species past evolutionary forms. This attempt to formulate a 'biogenetic law' (Haeckel in Barnes 2014) was further explored by American psychologist G. S. Hall in what he called 'biogenetic recapitulation theory' (1904). Both Haeckel and Hall claimed in their separate research that species repeat their entire evolutionary processes from conception and birth up to the present state of species development. Although this theory was subsequently disproved – primarily through the work of

Karl Ernst von Baer (1792–1876) and that of Charles Darwin (1809–82) – some useful scientific discoveries in the fields of embryology and evolutionary theory, respectively, have since clarified the issues.

Some of these clarifications came through Darwin's use of von Baer's work on embryological development to formulate his evolutionary theory, which proved that today's perfectly distinct forms descended from a single parent-form (Darwin 1869) that underwent numerous changes over millennia. The point here is that Haeckel oversimplified a theory primarily because of the lack of scientific data at the time. What I wish to emphasize here, however, is that some recapitulation does occur, not in the sense that Haeckel meant it, but in terms of certain sequences, stages and narratives that organisms go through in their development. My point here is that the development of a choreographic signature, i.e. an identifiable style that examines related themes through inter and transdisciplinary methods, is much like the evolutionary process, in that it allows for significant variations from an initial input. And since these signatures take years to develop, artistic ideas, therefore, need time to mature. Looking back at my own work, I see definitive developmental steps that led to the four major projects outlined in Chapters 4, 5, 6 and 7. Within these four projects, there were also thematic concerns that could be traced back to an original set of interests outlined in Chapter 1 in the section 'Will the artist please stand up?'.

As a contemporary choreographer, I am interested in exploring how performers, as a group working on a very specific thematic, can exercise creative agency despite being to some degree genetically and culturally pre-programmed. I am also interested in how an audience sees and interprets this information from their own pre-programming. To me, the success of a choreographic work is demonstrated in the strong responses that audiences have toward it, either for or against. In his book *Innate: How the Wiring of Our Brains Shapes Who We Are* (2018), Kevin Mitchell argues that 'the way our individual brains get wired depends not just on our genetic makeup, but also on how the program of our development happens to play out' (2018: 9). More specifically, he claims that much of the variation that happens does so because of how these DNA instructions are carried out in real life. In other words, 'both genetic and developmental variation contribute to innate differences in people's natures', and 'the environments and experiences we each have and the way our brains react to them are largely *driven by our innate traits*' (Mitchell 2018: 9–11, original emphasis). This means that although we are to a certain extent pre-programmed, there is a great deal of freedom and degrees of agency in how that script is played out.

To facilitate this process, I employ a great deal of structured improvisation in the studio. This involves giving specific instructions to performers on the use of movement phrases, spatial parameters in relation to body parts, objects in the space and textual materials that are introduced. The performers are then allowed 'free' rein to explore these parameters. Just as people are driven by innate traits that can have very different outcomes in an evolutionary sense, the choreographic work develops through the diverse inputs of the performers within certain limits. The diverse cultural backgrounds of the performers also add complexity to the work. However, beneath this desire to explore the complexity and to give the performers a degree of agency is always the larger goal of finding out how these structures of experience play out in the performance of the work in front of an audience. And by this, I mean what kinds of possibilities can emerge from these interactions. At this point, it might be useful to review and restate some of my definitions of the term performance outlined earlier and to demonstrate how these are articulated in the two early works I am introducing here:

1. Performance is a multi-levelled activity that human beings engage in to make sense of themselves and to establish a meaningful relationship with the world around them.
2. Performance allows us to explore different roles and personalities that comprise what we often think of as a single stable identity.
3. Because there are levels of consciousness that exist in 'domains' or 'dimensions' that have different behaviours or operational characteristics, these behaviours can appear to be contradictory. Hence, a strategy is needed to understand how and why this complexity works the way it does *before* we attempt to change anything about it.
4. History, as it individually or collectively unfolds, is a dynamic process that accounts for people's actions in space/time. Thus, understanding history and the architecture of its processes is an important aspect of performance – in other words, understanding how cortical and cartographic maps are created and how they have evolved historically.
5. Exploring these maps through choreography and performance is a method for cultivating embodied knowing and hence understanding what 'being' in the world entails.
6. Bringing artistic practices into a transdisciplinary discourse with science and technology, cultural, colonial and post-colonial studies and philosophy, is a useful strategy for understanding the complex dimensions that the term performance evokes.
7. A theory of practice that benefits from this type of exploration has the potential to transform our understanding of and relationship to the world we live in.

If we think of performance as the ability to act with some degree of agency within a system that is organized – technologically or organically – an interesting transdisciplinary perspective emerges. As choreographer William Forsythe once claimed, 'choreography is about organization [...] either one is organizing the body, or [...] organizing bodies with other bodies, or a body with other bodies in an environment that is organized' (Spier 2005: 352). Forsythe was referring to the fact that choreography is a system in which choreographers and dancers are conscious individuals with some agency or power to determine how that system operates and to potentially change its structure if necessary. I am suggesting that artistic and scientific perspectives on performance share some common ground in how the terms agency and hence power are defined.

Agency is associated with ideas of conscious awareness and the ability to act purposefully in human beings within a system. In the case of technology, the term performance refers to the efficient and optimized operations of computing systems, and hence the term agency has quite a different meaning. In one case, we have a conscious individual with the power to act wilfully and in another that power is limited to slavishly following a set of mechanical or algorithmic rules. However, a certain anthropomorphism occurs, on the one hand, and mechanization, on the other hand, when we 'humanise' the technological systems we create, which itself makes for an interesting link with ideas concerning agency and power that are fundamental to both modern and ancient or Indigenous societies. To examine how this anthropomorphism is relevant to a transdisciplinary examination of performance and to introduce an idea that is common in certain circles that we human beings are little more than sophisticated machines, I will now present the two artistic productions mentioned earlier. *Shango Meets Ogun* (1998) and *Futurist Equation* (1999) bring into stark relief some of the ideas on agency, and by extension how power is exercised within systems and across institutions.

Shango Meets Ogun[3]

Shango Meets Ogun (1998) and *Futurist Equation* (1999) were part of the second phase of my PaR investigations.[4] The first work was a collaborative effort between fellow diasporic artist/scholar Olugbenga Taiwo (Olu), electronic soundscape designer Guy Marshall and myself.[5] It was also our contribution to PSi5,[6] which was organized by Richard Gough and Heike Roms at the University of Aberystwyth in Wales. The second work was my contribution to the International Conference/Symposium *Homo orthopedicus: L'appréhension du corps à l'époque moderniste/The modernist body*, an event organized by Nathalie Roelens and Wanda Strauven at the Museum of Contemporary Art (MuHKA) in Antwerp, Belgium.[7] *Shango Meets Ogun* explored relationships between the human and the divine within the context of a traditional West African ontology that had its own belief systems and representational aesthetics, while *Futurist Equation* examined the relationship between the human and the machine within the context of a Futurist aesthetic that emerged from a Europe in the midst of a Second Industrial Revolution and an impending world war.

Shango Meets Ogun was concerned with how inherited West African practices – built on the notion that the human was connected to the divine and that the actions of one affected the other – were still present in the lives of contemporary Diasporic Africans. Olu and I shared a West-African ancestral past, an interest in its mythic figures or deities and in how practices that were designed to summon those deities were still prevalent throughout the diaspora. Guy Marshall, our White British sound designer, shared our interest in the power of interactive sound and motion capture technologies in live performance contexts. In *Shango Meets Ogun*, Shango the god of thunder (performed by myself) and Ogun the god of Iron (performed by Olu) meet to enact a ritual encounter as a painful reminder of their individual pasts and to consider how a different future might be shaped. To better understand how this Afro-futurist narrative relates to issues of memory within a theory of practice, to extend that to an investigation of how embodiment and disembodiment could be considered acts of performance and to link both to an exploration of agency in human and non-human systems, it is necessary to go into some detail about the cultural context of the work.

Historically, Shango was the fourth king of the traditional Yoruba kingdom of Oyo in Nigeria. He was a human being who became the God of thunder and lightning after his transformation to the divine status of *Orisha*.[8] It is said that the deposed king hung himself in remorse for his Earthly misdeeds, although the legend also claims that his body was never found. Shango's hubris was the abuse of power, but apparently his ultimate sacrifice created a gateway that led to his divine transformation. Ogun, on the other hand, was already an Orisha – the God of Iron – who forged tremendous weapons of war. In the Ifa creation myth, Ogun was sent down to Earth to assist human beings, unlike Shango who made his way up to 'heaven' through personal sacrifice (Figure 3.1). Ogun's hubris emerged from his inability to balance his powers, and his tragedy was his forgetfulness of the task he was sent to perform (Soyinka in Eze 1998).

Nigerian playwright and poet Wole Soyinka problematises the notion of psychic displacement embedded in these two personages – and consequently their migration throughout the African diaspora – in his essay 'The Fourth Stage: Through the Mysteries of Ogun to the Origin of Yoruba Tragedy' (Eze 1998). Soyinka claims that the tragedy of Ogun stems from his forgetfulness; he does not realize where or who he is, while Shango's was his disregard for his people and his irresponsibility as a human being and ruler of a kingdom. Soyinka argues that the means to address these shortcomings must come through the recognition of what he calls

FIGURE 3.1: Olugbenga Taiwo and Henry Daniel in *Shango Meets Ogun*.

'certain areas of depth-experience' (Eze 1998: 440). Since these experiences are not satisfactorily explained by conventional aesthetic theories or by mainstream science, Soyinka argues that contemporary peoples return to their own Indigenous sources for guidance.

He also claims that traditional Yoruba tragedy is based on this 'anguish of [...] severance' or 'fragmentation of essence from self' (Eze 1998: 440). Soyinka hints that we need to practice spanning the bridge between these different realms of reality to repair this severance and become whole once more. He argues that without such rigorous remembering and recognizing practices, the result can only be painful and unnecessary suffering.

In an inherited West African socio-cultural and philosophical framework, the idea of a 'life-cycle' is represented as the movement of entities across boundaries that separate different worlds. These worlds are those of (1) the living, (2) the unborn and (3) the ancestors (Katrak 1986: 43). At the entrance to these worlds stands the trickster Eshu, the two-faced Orisha who plays terrible tricks on human beings. Eshu is the guardian of the threshold between the physical and spiritual realms and hence holds access to the vital life force the Yoruba call 'ase' or 'ashe'. Amongst the psyches of the Yoruba people and their diasporic communities is a deeply embedded idea that human beings are connected to other entities that exist in spaces outside what we consider the everyday. Although these entities obey entirely different rules than ours, their influence extends to all aspects of our everyday lives, entering our worlds when summoned through special rites and ritual actions.

Different West African groups may practice variations of this tripartite division of the world into dimensions of existence, but the underlying pattern is the same: different intelligences with particular responsibilities inhabit three physical and conceptual spaces, each with their own rules. To realize their own responsibilities, these intelligences from 'above' descend and interact with human beings from time to time, and even though movements between worlds are possible, fixed protocols and specific rituals govern each one. Human beings may aspire to 'ascend' to these higher spaces, but they can only get there through the benevolence of those intelligences from 'above', who sometimes prove to be quite fickle.

Avatars of these divine entities may travel between worlds, but they must first be summoned by human beings with symbolic ritual offerings and gifts. The format of these rituals must be strictly followed, and in the case of the African diaspora, one can find them practiced in the *Candomblé* of Brazil, the *Shango* religion of Trinidad, the *Santeria* of Cuba and the *Voudou* of Haiti. In these ceremonies, the devotee's body is 'mounted' by an agent or *Orisha* who allows that individual special insight, and through the intercession of these agents the individual accesses knowledge from the ancestral plane, eventually sharing this information with their communities (Soyinka 1976; Katrak 1986).

Although parallels can be found in other cultures (in Greco-Roman mythology and among Indigenous peoples across the Americas, for example), they differ in their formats in each case. Shango, for example, resembles Jupiter or Zeus as the God of thunder, and Ogun the Roman Vulcan or Greek Hephaistos, God of iron and the forge. Both are associated with cyberspace in a more contemporary context, where iconic and symbolic tools merge with powerful archetypes to form psychological realities operating at both conscious and unconscious levels. African slaves in the New World were instrumental in inserting their own deities into the Christian ideological framework, thus creating a new and complex hybrid system that was meant to appease as well as confound their White slave masters. But all of these actions were part of a complex survival strategy of a group to keep its humanity when they were collectively treated as non-human. And how does a group maintain its belief system, its way of being in and understanding the world, when a totally alien system is forcefully and violently imposed on it? These works bring into stark relief the contrasts in how different cultures understand relationships between the human, the non-human and the technological and consequently how respect, or lack thereof, is afforded. The psychological implications of this hybridization are so immense that it is not difficult to see how popular media culture seizes upon these tropes.

A case in point is *The Black Panther* film (2018), by American film director, producer and screenwriter Ryan Kyle Coogler, where the main character is framed after an Afro-centric figure in the Marvel Comic series. Here the borders between reality, fantasy and a people's traditional spiritual belief system appear to have converged. In this film, the rules of engagement that permit humans, spirits and Gods to interact with each other also allow contemporary people, with the assistance of digital technologies, to create new realities. The phenomenal world is so complexly layered in this Afrofuturist scenario that movement between these different dimensionalities becomes easy to imagine. However, the film demonstrates that the price one pays for the right to exist within any part of that complexity involves an exchange of resources that is designed to maintain the balance between these different dimensionalities. Thus, through films like *The Black Panther*, a conceptual link is created between the mythical narratives of the past and our so-called civilized modern perspectives.

This example of how the human and the divine interact allows us to imagine how relationships between embodiment and disembodiment occur within West African and diasporic contexts. From there, the idea of 'performing disembodiment' or 'performing memory' from human and non-human perspectives does not seem so far-fetched after all. To assume that we have left these so-called primitive beliefs and their practices behind is to deceive ourselves. Whether as futuristic projections or as Indigenous rituals, Shango, Ogun and all the other West African Orishas persist as concepts that continue to influence people's lives today. However, one can argue that such beliefs also assist those who do not share such practices, or who exist outside its epistemological and ontological frames, to characterize them as primitive.

At the time of choreographing *Shango Meets Ogun*, Olu and I were the only two Black lecturers in a theatre and performance department at a respectable British academic institution. We had previously been the only two Black graduate students in another respectable British dance institution. In an interesting discussion we had about our respective pasts,[9] we spoke about our inherited West African religious/ritual traditions and the difficulty of making work in that tradition within these institutions. Somewhere in that discussion, he mentioned that he felt an affinity with the deity Ogun. And because of the island I came from and the diasporic ritual practices that still existed there, I chose the role of Shango.[10] At that moment, we conceived the idea to choreograph a work together that explored our own meeting as the recognition of an encounter between Shango and Ogun.

This choreographic work was therefore a performative encounter between two people who shared similar ancestries, but who also differed in their immediate backgrounds and experiences. Since neither of us had been to West Africa at that point, we relied on our connections to the diasporic community and our experiences of the culture from its hybridized contexts. More importantly perhaps, our knowledge of those rituals was so mixed up with our Christian religious education and our intellectual university training, that any sense of having a pure cultural experience from a West African perspective was questionable. We, therefore, decided to explore how much of that experience could be found in our bodies through heredity and through our individual experiences of African dances and live drumming. In doing so, we chose to use technology to create an interactive ultrasonic motion capture environment. Our technology designer Guy Marshall programmed a spatial architecture of invisible ultrasonic beams (vibrations inaudible to human ears) that gave us some agency in determining when, how and what kinds of sounds were triggered within a dynamically shifting set of spatial and temporal coordinates. Together with Olu's expert drumming, I remember having very distinct sensations from our performances of interacting with my human dancing partner as well as being attentive to the energies that were represented as invisible beams of sound. An attentiveness to and awareness of the invisible was thus highlighted by and practiced through the technological medium.[11]

Shango Meets Ogun presented the concept of embodiment in a dynamic and mutual relationship with disembodiment, and in so doing referenced a Tibetan Buddhist teaching I mentioned earlier, which claimed that 'the various instances of consciousness we experience come into being because of the presence of preceding instances of consciousness' (The Dalai Lama 2005: 132). This teaching claims that consciousness does not die with the body but is transformed through that body and can enter other bodies after the previous body's demise. And since the quality of one's consciousness determines the nature of one's thinking, it is theoretically possible that someone could inherit fully formed thoughts via these transformations. Of course, this does not mean that one is fully aware of these thoughts, but the more important point here is that they can influence how the individual conducts his, her or their lives.

Shango Meets Ogun was an attempt to stage a series of expert actions that could actively and productively engage contemporary audiences with questions of embodiment and disembodiment. The work was also a problematization of the popular turn towards the body and notions of embodied knowledge that was at the forefront of performance studies in the academy at the time. My position then, as now, is that since the body is, ontologically speaking, the place where the issue of embodiment – and by default disembodiment – is grounded, dance and choreography must also be prepared to respond to the idea of disembodying practices. I further argue that with these explorations, it is possible to understand more about our own evolutionary past.

Performing disembodiment

To better understand what I mean by the term *performing disembodiment*, it is necessary to first define these constitutive terms. To *embody* implies giving something a physical presence or incarnation in the molecular world of matter. To *perform* would then mean staging this presence through a practice, in this case choreography and dance. If we consider the primary act of performance as the body becoming conscious of its own selfhood as an individual entity, *disembodiment* must then be a movement of that consciousness out of the body to engage with whatever exists outside it but is at the same time connected to it. As such, I define *embodied cognition* as the process of becoming aware of and consciously directing or redirecting the different levels of consciousness, i.e. cortical and spatial maps, that constitute the individual's bodily presence in space/time. Such a definition reminds one of certain Buddhist and Hindu teachings that matter in its subtlest form, i.e. *prana,* is a vital energy that is inseparable from consciousness; the two being different aspects of an indivisible reality (Gyatso 2005). *Prana* is the aspect of mobility, dynamism and cohesion, while consciousness is the aspect of cognition and the capacity for reflective thinking.

According to the Guhyasamaja tantra, when a world system comes into being, we are witnessing the play of its energy and consciousness as a reality. Because of the indivisibility of consciousness and this vital energy, there is a profound and intimate correlation between the elements in our bodies and those in the outside world. The claim of Tibetan Buddhism is that this subtle connection can be discerned by individuals who have attained a high level of spiritual realization, and, consequently, perceptive abilities (Gyatso 2005). Performing embodiment can therefore be thought of as the ability of mind – or what Damasio describes as the ability of the individual, as the owner of a nervous system that is literally distributed throughout the body – to claim the knowledge that is synthesized from the information that flows throughout that same body as it interacts with its environment (Damasio 2010). Disembodiment then becomes the ability of that conscious self to utilize the body's resources to go beyond its obvious physical limitations.

Thus, if energy is the subtlest form of matter and is inseparable from consciousness, then energy/consciousness is indeed coexistent with what is outside the physical body. If we understand that there are different types of matter, and hence different kinds of bodies, then embodiment is the process of this energy/consciousness coming into human bodies – a process that causes us to forget. Conversely, disembodiment can be seen as a movement towards a consciousness that is radically different from the one we are accustomed to in the everyday world. These two forms of the conscious self are quite different entities, existing in very different space/times. The strategies that I am attempting to articulate throughout this book can therefore be perceived as techniques to become aware of the energetic links between these selves, between the cortical, the cartographic and the cosmological; practices that were arguably common to Indigenous groups prior to New World colonization.[12] In these practices, the human body becomes the place for the gradual appearance and disappearance of the *human* self as that self seeks a different manifestation, or incarnation if you will. But this latter is another issue entirely, which nevertheless begs the question of how it is possible to retain the memory of an individual existence beyond the life of the physical body, or even in sleep for that matter. I believe that this question is at the heart of those rituals of transformation practiced across the African Diaspora and throughout New World Indigenous cultures.

Shango Meets Ogun was not intended as a performance of disembodiment as practiced in rituals throughout that diaspora. It was more of an experiment to discover how much it was possible to reimagine the nature and intention of such practices. Although I witnessed some extraordinary performances of possession in the Caribbean, I was never able to achieve those states myself. If possession is the process of emptying and being filled by something beyond one's everyday conscious self, then it is indeed a disembodying practice. Nevertheless, what I personally was able to achieve was a sense of needing to let go of the rational mind in order to experience anything near transformation. In this respect, *Shango Meets Ogun* both failed and succeeded; it failed to achieve a complete letting go, but it succeeded to a degree in letting some things go, things that allowed us as performers to experience a degree of knowledge about ourselves and our shared past. And this came through a combination of the ritualistic live drumming sequences from my collaborator Olu, the invisible beams of sound and motion-capture technology that our collaborator Guy had changed at will during our performances, and the sense that we were performing a modern-day ritual of re-cognition. And this ritual became an opportunity to play with and perhaps experience a different relationship with ourselves.

Some of the questions we were exploring in *Shango Meet Ogun* were also being examined by another audience of modern scientists and Buddhist monks in the presence of Tenzin Gyatso, the 14th Dalai Lama, at the XIV Annual Mind and Life Conference convened in Dharamshala, India in 2007. In a conversation concerning the fundamental difference of opinion between Buddhism and modern science about the nature of mind, Dr Evan Thompson (then professor of philosophy at the University of Toronto) argued that although both Buddhism and modern mind/brain science agreed that subjective mental phenomena exist and that first-person experiences provide ways of accessing them, these two institutions had very different conceptions of the underlying nature of such phenomena. Mainstream science claims that there is no consciousness outside our biological nature; or put another way, consciousness is not possible outside the human body. Gyatso, on the other hand, argued that pure *Mind* is not reducible to neurological and biochemical activity. Gyatso argued that Vajrayana Buddhism teachings say there is no fundamental division between *Mind* and matter and that both are different aspects of a non-dual reality. This raises the following question: what kind of disembodied presence is possible and how could such a presence be apprehended? I believe Olu and I experienced different kinds of presence through the several performances we had of *Shango Meets Ogun*. It is difficult to explain precisely what that was, but putting it in very simple terms, I personally felt that I had re-discovered a part of myself that I had forgotten and therefore became much more aware of its connections to other parts of my life.

Futurist Equation[13]

As I mentioned before, both *Shango Meets Ogun* and *Futurist Equation* had features that could be perceived as contrasting cultural approaches to agency in human and non-human systems. These approaches addressed ideas about who qualifies as human and how they should be treated within a particular socio-cultural framework. The two works also explored how cultural memories transform over time; following in one case the trauma of a transatlantic journey and the brutal experience of slavery, and in another, the transition from the ancient to the modern and the promises that such a transformation held for a Western European way of life. Both works also featured culturally specific approaches to the body in performance and utilized digital technologies to support their arguments. *Futurist Equation* did this through the lens of a Futurist ideology *a la* F. T. Marinetti and his colleagues.

Marinetti launched Futurism as an artistic movement from Paris on 20 February 1909, and his publishing of the 'Founding and Manifesto of Futurism' – in French and in the daily newspaper *Le Figaro* – was one of a series of performance acts that was to establish his own reputation and that of Futurism as one of the most notorious and controversial Modernist movements. At that point, the group consisted predominantly of men: Umberto Boccioni, Carlo Carrà and Luigi Russolo, joined later by Giacomo Balla, and Gino Severini as a corresponding member. A tremendously aggressive, provocative, political, propagandist and disruptive energy characterized their work. Truly avant-garde in concept and execution, Futurism was an attempt to reorganize art and society around technology and the machine ethic, in many ways anticipating the twentieth-century's digital revolution and the continuing debate on the nature of human consciousness and machine agency. Marinetti argued that the artist's duty was to use art for radical political action. Through a novel expressive treatment of mechanization, this new art would anticipate the digital revolution and technological development as a valid part of its concerns.

Although he himself had no practical experience of the bourgeoning field of Modern Dance, Marinetti took an extremely critical review of Isadora Duncan's work in his 1917 *Manifesto of the Futurist Dance*. My own choreography took its title from his 'equation' at the beginning of that manifesto while playing on definitions of modernity as (1) a condition of change, (2) a state of constant upheaval and revolution and (3) a reference to a specific artistic period and mode of thinking in history. I also imagined that modernity could be seen as (4) a process that artists go through in the development of an individual aesthetic, which requires them to experience or engage with Marinetti's three points as states of being that one encounters and must deal with in the development of one's artistic career. Therefore, I used this work as an opportunity to explore Marinetti's intention and his idea of modernity using my own methods. In this way, I imagined I could recognise the thematic of macho ideology, fascist politics, anti-feminist ideologies, misogyny and issues of cultural exclusion that were inherent in Futurism as a movement. And as I mentioned earlier, this and other works were made at a stage of my academic career when I was trying to locate myself within a system that made little attempt to really understand the ontological and epistemological complexity of some of the ideas I personally was interested in. My objective was therefore to try and introduce some of that complexity and ways of thinking into a Western European context.

Marinetti's 'Founding and Manifesto of Futurism' and his 'Manifesto of the Futurist Dance' were two examples of an aesthetic that prompted me to respond through my own choreography. The latter manifesto begins as follows and contains the above-mentioned equation:

> Once the glorious Italian ballet was dead and buried, there began in Europe stylisations of savage dances, elegant versions of exotic dances, modernizations of ancient dances. Parisian red pepper + the crest + the shield + the lance + ecstasy before idols that no longer have any meaning + the rippling thighs of Montmartre = traditionalist erotic anachronisms for foreigners.
>
> (Marinetti in Flint 1972: 137–41)[14]

Marinetti was of course decrying what he felt were forms of dance that were either dead or dying and needed to be revived and/or reinvented for the modernist age, an age that sought to embrace the ideas and aesthetics of an extended Industrial Revolution. The manifesto continues: 'We Futurists prefer Louie Fuller and the "cakewalk" of the Negroes (utilisation of electric light and mechanisms)'[15] (Marinetti in Flint 1972: 137–41).

This last quote puts the experiments of Louie Fuller – a White American actress and dancer – and the cakewalk dance 'of the Negroes' in an interesting perspective with the equation in the first quote. The new lighting technologies Fuller utilized in her work and the 'exotic dances' of foreigners seemed to appeal to the Futurist ideology Marinetti was developing. The question I raise here is: what exactly is it that Marinetti is comparing in his manifesto for a Futurist dance? Since the Cakewalk was a dance transformed by African slaves from its original White American slave master context where it had a subversive dimension – caricaturing the actions of slave owners – that slave owners themselves failed to recognize (Pugh 2015) and Fuller's dance an exploration of new lighting technologies for the performance stage, the comparison seems tantalizing. Sweeney and Marsh (2013) offer an interesting explanation in their monograph *Afromodernisms: Paris, Harlem and the Avant-Garde*.

They propose that Marinetti must have been swayed by the 'cakewalk mania' that engulfed Paris between 1900 and 1903, and saw this and Fuller's dances as producing 'a combination of the perceived energy of an African body with the mechanical inventions of modernity [and] the metaphor of "technological primitivism" that jazz was soon to embody in Europe' (Sweeney and Marsh 2013: 47–48). Here the 'negro' represented the 'primitive energy' that the Futurists so loved and saw as energizing what they considered the stale traditions of European art. Sweeney and Marsh also suggest that 'Marinetti saw in the cakewalk dances the potential process of preparation for the fusion of man and non-human, in other words, the machine' (Sweeney and Marsh 2013: 47).

Given the energy and excitement that accompanied the exhibits of African Art at the infamous *Exposition Universelle* (November 1900) in Paris, and the launch of the Futurist movement in Europe just over eight years later (February 1909), it is not difficult to appreciate Sweeney and Marsh's inferences. Black culture and the Black body, as articulated in visual art, music and dance, functioned as an intoxicating stimulant as well as an object of fear and loathing for some Europeans. Given that this view of the Black body and culture arose precisely because of ongoing colonialism and the legacy of the slave trade which so profoundly dehumanized Black bodies, embracing primitive art but not colonized people is completely within the logic of White Supremacy. The notion that the negro represented the 'non-human' is disturbing, but the history of its 'discovery' in Africa and mass transportation and enslavement across the Americas is nothing less than tragic given that the same thematic seems to be repeated throughout successive centuries. Thus begins an interesting relationship between Modernism as a movement that involved art, dance, science and technology, and the exclusion of the Black body in serious discussions about what it means to be human and who is allowed to participate in the shaping of that humanity.

I choreographed *Futurist Equation* while living in Europe, still actively performing in my own works, studying for a Ph.D. and teaching full-time at what is now Winchester University. This work was thus an early effort to locate myself within a discourse on the modernist body, its history and its relationship to the avant-garde, keeping in mind that much of this discourse either ignored or diminished contributions that bodies like mine made to the canon of Western knowledge. Like Fuller, I was also interested in incorporating new media technologies into my works as a means of extending their conceptual and performative dimensions. The notion of a machine-human interface, and with it the question of what constitutes the human, the non-human and the machine provided, to my mind, an appropriate challenge. I was able to see clearly how issues of humanity, intelligence, progress and developing technologies could engage with a Eurocentric view of the negro as a primitive and savage other, as non-human and hence machine-like within the context of Modernism. Because of those views, Black bodies had historically been valuable only as labour for the benefit of those who considered themselves superior in a hierarchy of beings.

One of my first questions about engaging with the ideas in these manifestos was how serious Marinetti really was about the statements in his *Manifesto of the Futurist Dance*. Did he actually mean what he said or was he just more interested in creating a performative spectacle? I, therefore, began the work by reading extracts of the manifestos in performance and asking the other performers to do the same. The results were astonishing and took us all by surprise, in the sense that it put our bodies in an extremely aggressive stance toward one another and to our audiences. The two male performers; one of them me, found that our bodies acted out the intention in the words of the text toward the two female performers that was aggressive to the point of violence (Figures 3.2–3.4).

They were so full of vitriol that reading them infused us with that same sense of aggressive power. How much of this was due to the language and how much to the nature of our individual bodies is questionable, since, as far as I knew, these manifestos were not originally written in English nor for bodies like mine.

FIGURE 3.2: Lee Bamford, Diane Sowter and Henry Daniel in *Futurist Equation*.

FIGURE 3.3: Lee Bamford and Diane Sowter in *Futurist Equation*.

FIGURE 3.4: Sally Woodham and Henry Daniel in *Futurist Equation*.

But I was not convinced that a shift in language and in the bodies that uttered those languages could alone produce such radical attitudes in our bodies. The gestures in Figures 3.2–3.4 show some of these attitudes.

We had similar responses reading excerpts from Marinetti's 'Dance of the Shrapnel' to *The Manifesto of Futurist Dance*. Although I did not choreograph 'Dance of the Shrapnel' nor use the text in my choreography, the body movements described in the manifesto below tell their own story. For example, the movements in the text could be described as static, sharp and jagged rather than flowing, and with an energy that was dynamic and violent; quite typical of Futurism as a movement. Compare movements three and four below described in Marinetti's 'Dance of the Shrapnel':

> Movement 3: With the hands (wearing very long silver thimbles) raised and open, as high as possible, give the proud, blessed, silvery explosion of the shrapnel in its paaaak. The danseuse will hold up a sign printed in blue: Long to the left. Then she will hold up printed in silver: Don't slip on the ice. Synovitis.
>
> Movement 4: With the whole body vibrating, the hips weaving, and the arms making swimming motions, give the

> waves and flux and reflux and concentric or eccentric motions
> of echoes in ravines, in open fields and up the slopes of
> mountains. The danseuse will hold up a sign painted in black:
> Water duty; another in black: Mess duty; still another in black:
> The mules, the mail.
>
> (Marinetti 1991: 147)

Clearly, the vocabulary here is intentional. In fact, the aim is to represent the scene as shockingly as possible, in line with the desire to articulate a revolutionary politics. Yet there is some sensuality in this violent carnage, a physicality that contradicts itself through the rich and expressive use of language; at one moment humanly 'vibrating' and 'weaving' and at another machine-like in its instructions. The entire objective seemed to be an attempt to create a future that was of the machine, but of a machine that was controlled by 'man' for 'his' exclusive use.

In the *Manifesto of the Futurist Dance*, Marinetti argues that Duncan never managed to project anything but 'the most complex feelings of desperate nostalgia, of spasmodic sensuality and cheerfulness, childishly feminine' (Marinetti 1917). In contrast, the 'Feminist Manifesto' (1918) of avant-garde poet and artist Mina Loy, a.k.a. Mina Gertrude Lowy, could be seen as a feminist response to Marinetti's manifesto. Loy advised women to look to themselves to discover who they were rather than seek recognition from men trapped in rigid definitions of gender roles (Loy 1982). Although she was briefly involved with the Futurist movement,[16] Loy had little sympathy for Marinetti's attitude to women, and her poems sought to transform the Futurist idea of the dynamic mechanized body into a symbol of female creativity (Loy 1982). This human/machine/gender/creative art dynamic is extremely instructive considering that the movement itself was called Futurism, as a vision of a White Supremacist future.

It could be said that Marinetti and many of the Futurists were equally disdainful of other artists, regardless of their gender, and that every Futurist Manifesto was imbued with the same aggressive, intimidating and declamatory style. Though one might expect this style and aesthetic to be unappealing to women artists, Valentine de Saint-Point, the French writer, art critic and choreographer, did contribute her own voice to the movement, even though she would later abandon Futurism in 1914 before the end of the movement's first stage. Not surprisingly, the Futurists declared in a 1914 Manifesto, *Weights, Measures and Prices of Artistic Genius, Futurist Manifesto of 1914,* that no essential differences exist between a human brain and a machine (Apollonio 1973). This statement anticipated many of the scientific debates concerning machine and human intelligence that would assume prominence later in the twentieth and twenty-first centuries.

Ironically, Futurism also celebrated spirituality in art. For example, Boccioni's notion of 'physical transcendentalism' (Antliff 2000) referred to an object's different mysterious and spiritual aspects, while Bragaglia argued for the 'transcendental nature of the phenomenon of movement' in *Futurist Photodynamism* (1911). In *The Exhibitors to the Public* (1912), Boccioni and fellow signers Carrà, Russolo, Balla and Severini spoke of the simultaneity of states of mind in the work of art. Interestingly, this is where Modernist art and the notion of the 'primitive' that appears in both Cubist and Futurist work connects to African art (Andrea 1995). A case in point being Picasso's *Les Demoiselles d'Avignon* (1907), which depicts women painted with an African influenced aesthetic.[17] My argument here is that, if the purpose of Futurist art was to transform society, then some of the techniques used in that transformation, namely, the linking of mythic space, technological space and cultural space to the body in performance, definitely resonated with ideas from the very people modernity as an aesthetic movement and a way of thinking sought to dehumanize and exclude.

Shango Meets Ogun and *Futurist Equation*, both made within an academic context, were important steps in revisiting the three fundamental principles that guided my interest in performance as an attempt to know a self that was always already multiple and fractured. Those principles are rearticulated here as follows: (1) the use of modulated resistance to generate power in human and non-human systems; (2) the transformation of the body's physical, mental, emotional and psychological states through its own internal chemistry; and (3) a heightened perception of space, time and conscious awareness that is possible through accident but can also be cultivated through practice. While *Shango Meets Ogun* was designed to address some of the ideas embedded in cultural practices inherited from a traditional West African ancestral past, *Futurist Equation* was an opportunity for me to understand what is was like to perform the discourse of the Modernist body at the end of the twentieth century from a Western European perspective.[18] Both works provided an opportunity for me to follow Fanon's and Dussel's directive to challenge some of the assumptions at the base of Western ideas about the Black body (Fanon 1967; Dussel 1996). Notwithstanding, I would adopt and later develop an idea that was at the core of the Futurist ideology in my own creative practice. This was the notion of *simultaneity*, or the linked threads of memories, associations and all the diverse emotions that assail an artist at the moment of creation (Berghaus 2009).

Because of my interest in history and the continuance of certain ideas from the past into our contemporary condition, the concept of simultaneity was extremely relevant to my own research. Viewing it as a construct, i.e. as an overlapping of space/time dimensions, allowed me to explore the idea in my own choreography. I also discovered that this principle could be strategically utilized to allow audience members to invest in the work at hand and to experience it as a phenomenon that potentially had some relevance to their own lives. If I could get that audience to be sufficiently engaged – curious or even confused about what they were seeing – a small door to the unconscious would be opened, allowing a different perspective to enter and perhaps take root. This possibility for making new and interesting connections between different knowledge forms, historical time periods and ideas about reality was an exciting one, even as one engaged in the dance itself as an expert practice (Daniel 2016). This, to me, was an emergent feature of transdisciplinarity.

The futurist/humanist condition

The beginning of the twenty-first century witnessed the enormous effects on society of globalization, new technology and war. Arguably, one could say the same about the beginning of the last century insofar as industrialization, modernization and war influenced people's lives. According to David J. Hawkin, the market, the military, technology and nationalism became 'powers' invested with their own belief systems and orthodoxies and, as such, appeared to have the same supremacy as the old gods of Judaism, Christianity, Islam or Hinduism (Hawkin 2004: 3–4). Hawkin claims that the West's relegation of religion to the past, in favour of a more rational present life dictated by science and technology, has left it blind to the major influence of spirituality on our everyday activities. This, he argues, clouds our perception of some fundamental issues that underpin our social interactions.

I use Hawkin's comments here not as a commentary on religion per se, nor on politics or war, but mostly as a testament to the influence that such systems of thought exert in contemporary society when supported by beliefs that have become equivalent and/or comparable to religion. Marinetti's 1909 *Founding and Manifesto of Futurism,* written a full 80 years prior to Jean François Lyotard's *The Postmodern Condition: A Report on Knowledge* (1984), could be seen as a precursor to Lyotard's exhortation to destabilize an old 'institutional metanarrative' by a sustained effort to create one's own metanarrative. Despite later critiques of Futurism for its exploitation of industrial technologies, the movement nevertheless introduced a provocative idea with its concept of simultaneity. This nonlinear approach to time and space and the practice of juggling multiple domains and personalities might seem like a recipe for chaos to some, but to me it represents a dynamic picture of what the whole would look and feel like if one could consciously experience all that existed in one single moment.

In Lyotard's *The Postmodern Condition*, he claimed that the status of knowledge in any society is altered by technological development and any knowledge that is not immediately translatable into the new paradigm of digital information is in danger of being lost. He also argued that 'The old principle that the acquisition of knowledge is indissociable from the training (*Bildung*) of minds, or even of individuals, is becoming obsolete and will become ever more so' (Lyotard 2004: 3–4). I argue that Lyotard and Marinetti were merely drawing attention to crucial markers of modernity and post-modernity in their own ways. By linking paradigm-shifting events, such as industrialization and later the development of digital computer technology, with the future of knowledge and the course of individual identity and collective social and cultural history, both men challenged us to think about how knowledge could or should be imagined in future societies. Schwab (2017) would later challenge this perspective by arguing that the future would be decided by how power was shared. He asserted that the biggest impact from a twenty-first century revolution would likely come from a single force that he calls 'empowerment' when actors recognize that they are part of 'a distributed power system that requires more collaborative forms of interaction to succeed' (Schwab 2017: 28). In other words, unless we begin to see all peoples as human and all life as part of a distributed and densely connected system designed to produce and transform energy as power, which must be shared, the entire system is endangered.

Although the Futurists correctly recognized industrialization and the development of new technologies as crucial to the future of Europe, their approach to change was framed very much in the familiar masculist, sexist and White Supremacist ideology reminiscent of the so-called 'Age of Discovery' that wreaked havoc on so many New World peoples. Marinetti's original manifesto began by proclaiming man's [*sic*] use of new communication technologies as a means to hurl 'the lance of his spirit across the Earth, along the circle of its orbit'.[19] He also recommended destroying 'museums' and 'libraries' while fighting 'feminism'; he glorified the fruits of industrialism, extolled the power of trains and locomotives and compared bridges that span rivers to 'giant gymnasts'.[20]

I argue that this sense of unbridled power always accompanies riding the crest of the wave of change, inevitably convincing its riders that there is no need for restraint. Consequently, the type of art that emerges from these situations necessarily utilizes many of the materials, processes, ideas and inconsistencies that generated and maintained what I have elsewhere called The Futurist Condition (Daniel in Chytraeus-Auerbach and Maag 2016). Perhaps the artist, the politician and the religious fanatic equally understands that to put themselves forward as instruments of change is to be immersed in such a condition, i.e. simultaneously existing in an 'old' world while trying to project a radically different 'new' one which is still far from becoming a reality. Europe manipulated the trajectory of change at that particular time in its history to their benefit – discrediting other people's beliefs, fundamentally misunderstanding ideas embedded in other cultures, stealing people's resources and plundering their artefacts.[21] In short, taking away their power.

Thus Euro-modernity, or the idea of modernity as a process where Europe generated and controlled the processes that modernized the world and brought it out of its ancient and primitive habits, became a 'global phenomenon whose underlying grammar was coloniality', a coloniality that was also 'the condition of possibility for the centrality and power of the West' (Bragato and Gordon 2018: 5). The West (i.e. Europe and North America) assumed that holding the reins of humanity's future was its God-given 'right', but only for the privileged few who controlled the development of industrial and technological change. All other people were to be used as labour and as steppingstones to achieving those dreams. *Shango Meets Ogun* and *Futurist Equation* provided different lenses through which the concept of the modern, and Modernism in general, could be imagined. They explored different visions of the future through their respective racial, cultural and historical legacies. One could argue that the perspectives of both these cultures deserve to be seen and heard, but history has not allowed for this. Rather, one group with racial and cultural prejudices became dominant, enslaving countless numbers of others, imposing their ideas and institutions by force, and deliberately manipulating others into believing that their ideas were worth lesser than.

Re-cognising/re-membering

The human body is uniquely designed to maintain a 'steady-state' that keeps it homeostatically balanced and ensures that it can survive within certain operating limits (Cannon 1939, 1963). Like all mechanical and biological systems, the body achieves this with the help of a process called negative feedback. With negative feedback, some of a system's output is applied to its initial input location (Wiener 1948) which helps to stabilize that system's operations. In the case of the human body, this occurs in temperature regulation for example, where the production of sweat is the product of the body overheating but also the cause of its ability to cool down. What all of this means is that knowing the operational architecture of a system is important to ensure that it stays in balance and remains healthy up to and beyond what we consider to be its normal operating parameters. And as we know, subtle changes in temperature, illumination, magnetic fields and minute amounts of impurity in atoms cause enormous increases in electrical conductivity within bodies.

Because I work with live performance in technologically mediated spaces, I tend to think of the interactions between the human performers and the technological systems as taking place within a much larger frame of reference. Thus, the choreographic work can be seen as a type of organism that has mechanical and conscious agents working together to achieve a very different kind of homeostatic balance. I argue that working in such an environment provides the human performer with a unique opportunity to know where the limits and borders of their own mechanical nature lie and hence where a conscious agency or human will begin. Here, again, is an opportunity to study the maps that represent our voyages through past, present and potentially future experiences. In short, our memories. Neuroscientist and neurologist Antonio Damasio describes the mapping process in the human brain as follows:

> The distinctive feature of brains such as the one we own is their uncanny ability to create maps. Mapping is essential for sophisticated management, mapping and life management going hand in hand. When the brain makes maps, it informs itself [...]
>
> Maps are constructed when we interact with objects, such as a person, a machine, a place, from the outside of the brain towards its interior. [...]
>
> Maps are also constructed when we recall objects from the inside of our brain's memory banks. The construction of maps never stops even in our sleep, as dreams demonstrate. The human brain maps whatever object sits outside it, whatever action occurs inside it, and all the relationships that objects and actions assume in time and space, relative to each other and to the mother ship known as the organism, sole proprietor of our body, brain, and mind. The human brain is a born cartographer, and the cartography began with the mapping of the body inside which the brain sits.
>
> (Damasio 2010: 63–64)

Essentially, Damasio is saying that the human organism observes and regulates its functions through its own agency, much of which is done without our conscious participation. Note also that his maps are abstract representations of the body's entire experiences mostly stored in the cerebral cortices, which are always in constant dynamic contact with the rest of the body. One could say that the entire human body is a kind of interconnected brain, or that we have three different types of 'brains' that exist in different areas of the body. The information in these maps describes the organism's actions in a world that is dynamic and always changing in response to events operating far outside the body in which the brain is located (Shadmehr and Mussa-Ivaldi 2012). Human beings are thus akin to self-organizing systems that are arranged from within as well as without, which means that our role as seekers after knowledge entails developing practices that allow us to become active participants in these processes.

If these maps contain, as Damasio implies, the history of all our performed actions, then it is logical to say that our entire history is embedded in the archives of our bodies, a history that can be activated and re-activated whenever the body interacts with certain spaces. And since human beings have complex cultural and biological histories that have been developed over extensive periods of time and in different parts of the world, it is fair to say that we carry this information around with us and have daily access to it. The key question, therefore, and the unique challenge for us is: how can we claim this knowledge? If recognising and remembering implies our 'conscious' use of the body's own systems to understand ourselves, a strange kind of game comes into play. And as I mentioned earlier in this book, this entails playing different aspects of a tripartite self against its other selves. However, part of my argument is that this already happens automatically in us. For example, our mind says we must do something about a situation and our emotions become dead set against it, or the body does not possess the physical means to carry out the required task. Or alternatively, our bodies have the resources to do something, but a certain ethical stance prevents us from carrying out the task. Consciously putting oneself into situations where one must make challenging choices generates the potential for knowledge about things that are more important than these simple examples.

To recap, embodied knowing starts with having an experience that has automatically been recorded in maps at different levels, which we can consciously access and use for our benefit. And as I have been arguing, we can cultivate this capacity through practice: dance, choreography and performance being such practices. In this way, the paradox of going in the opposite direction to one's intended destination is articulated as a movement backward to one's origins in order to move forward to one's intended destination. This act of 'return' is necessary for understanding the scope of the territory one is currently traversing or has traversed in the past.

Almost five hundred years after Columbus first presented his case in Seville, Spain, to a group of potential benefactors appointed by the Catholic Monarchs, three men – Tenzin Gyatso, the 14th Dalai Lama; Adam Engle, lawyer and entrepreneur; and biologist/neuroscientist Francisco Varela – founded the Mind and Life Institute to investigate a different set of riches that they felt existed in the overlaps and discontinuities between Western science and Buddhist philosophy and practices. In 1487, five years prior to Columbus' first voyage, the Italian artist Leonardo da Vinci produced a drawing he called *Vetruvian Man* (Figure 3.5) or *L'uomo vitruviano*,[22] a drawing that depicts a man in two superimposed positions with arms and legs apart and inscribed in a circle and square, detailing the ideal human body proportions. Here, the body is not merely an art object, it is a drawing that captures two different kinds of thought processes that were taking place

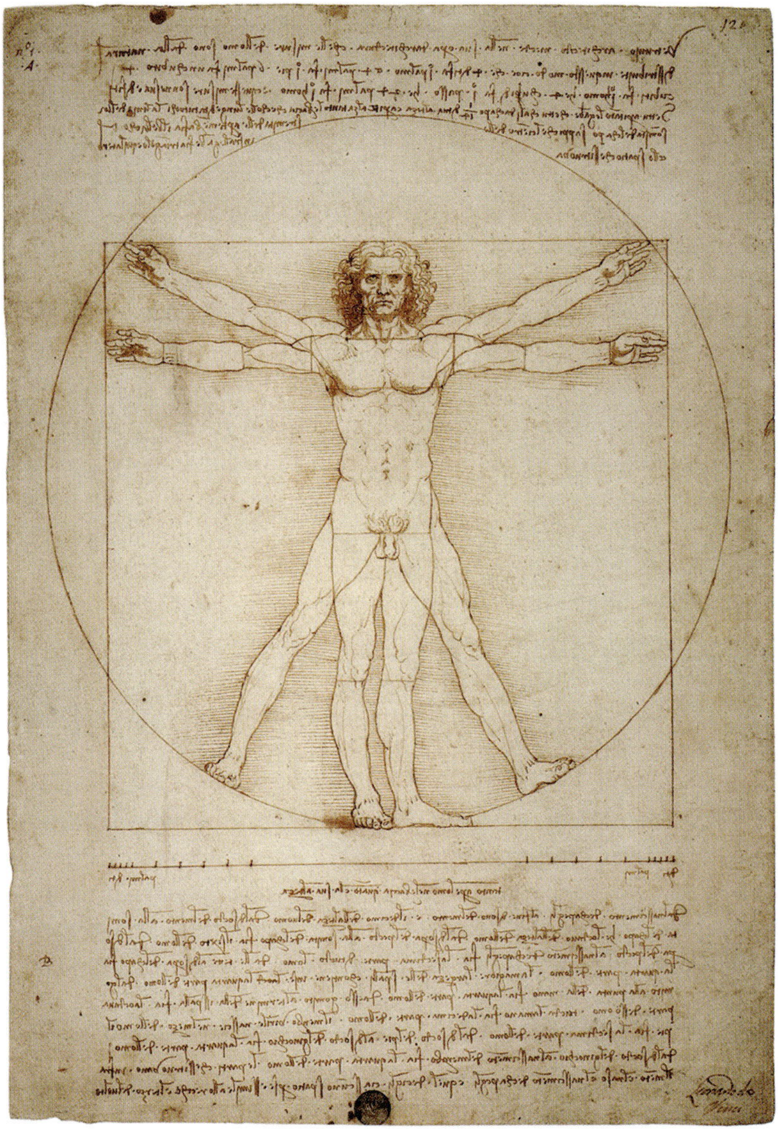

FIGURE 3.5: *Vetruvian Man* by Leonardo da Vinci. *c.*1490. Gallerie dell'Accademia, Venice, Italy.

at the time, thought processes that linked a desire to know more about the human body and its relationship to the external world and another to know more about that world and how it fitted into the larger cosmological scheme. These different knowledge systems were linked, and the desire to know through exploration became a search for power; one was the power to know oneself and the other power to control others.

Varela, Gyatso and Engle may not have been interested in the contributions that art makes to the larger knowledge project or the concept of bodies in performance from the perspectives that I am outlining here, but they did recognize the inadequacy of Western science in one of those knowledge systems, i.e. self-knowledge. Therefore, in 1987, they established the Mind and Life Institute in an attempt to share the different knowledges East and West possessed through objectives that were articulated as follows:

> Whereas science relies on empiricism, technology, 'objective' observation, and analysis, the Dalai Lama, Engle, and Varela were convinced that well-refined contemplative practices and introspective methods could, and should, be used as equal instruments of investigation – instruments that would not only make science itself more humane but also ensure its conclusions were far-reaching. The Mind and Life was formed to bridge this divide and advance progress in human well-being.[23]

Western Europe, in its attempt to connect with a distant east, unwittingly located some of its undiscovered others in the Americas, and after decimating populations in search of wealth and power, forcefully dragged another group from the African continent to serve its colonizing agendas. Five hundred years later, three men from different backgrounds and parts of the world met to realize something that was transdisciplinary in nature. 'East' had now made a journey west to establish connections that were considered crucial for the future of humanity. As a descendent of those who were caught up in those earlier voyages and brought to the New World from the African continent, I share the goal of creating a mediated space between opposing forces that allows one to move to a higher level of thought and action. And although 'East' and 'West' had already met in my Caribbean homeland through the hybrid practices that Africans and Asians brought to the New World and developed there within the cultures of Europe and the Indigenous peoples they encountered,[24] it would require a travelling out of those spaces for me to appreciate the *potpourri* of influences and the philosophical *mezcla* that I had inherited.

That realization came slowly as I travelled and worked in countries on both sides of the Atlantic and eventually to the Pacific. I began to understand what it meant to inhabit a body that was a self-organizing and self-regulating system, one that drew on its surroundings for sustenance and for further development as it created numerous intersecting maps of those experiences in its cortical memory banks. This unfolding map, or rather this unfolding of thought that gave rise to my own cartographic movements, and vice versa, a movement that gave rise to a thought through different spatial coordinates, provided opportunities for me to understand and therefore claim the knowledge that was always in my body but which I never quite comprehended. Given that this body is always creating, maintaining and destroying smaller parts of itself on a daily basis in order to maintain its existence – mirroring the cosmic dance of creation, maintenance and destruction that is fundamental to Hindu religion and philosophy – I began to trust that this complexity, and not rationality according to Barrett (2017), would make it possible for me to be at least the co-architect of my own future experiences. And even though the larger durational dance that Shiva performs plays out in cosmological time, I was convinced that the process operated on a smaller scale within my own body and that recognizing and remembering those processes was crucial to my own becoming.

The lived machine

In this section, I return to the idea of the human as a complex system with different levels of being, one of which I will call 'machine potential' and the other 'human potential' as I argue for the value of the lived experience as a key to how the one transforms into or 'becomes' the other. Some philosophical systems claim that human beings in their natural states are more akin to sophisticated machines (Gurdjieff 1950; Ouspensky 1983).[25] In other words, possessing a human body with a brain does not mean that one has individual free will. We may have degrees of conscious awareness, but that does not mean that we have free will. This of course introduces the question of what *free will* is and whether this gives us special powers to do whatever we wish. While awareness, agency, action and behaviour are all terms used here in relation to performance, the issue of free will introduces another dimension to that term. In his book, *The Astonishing Hypothesis: The Scientific Search for the Soul* (1994), Francis Crick, 1962 Nobel Prize winner (with James Watson and Maurice Wilkins for work on the double-helical structure of DNA), argued that everything we do, all behaviour, could be reduced to the physical operations of the mind-brain, or what I would call 'the machine potential'. 'The scientific belief is that our minds – the behaviour of our brains – can be explained by the interaction of nerve cells (and other cells) and the molecules associated with them' (Crick 1994: 7). He concludes his main argument with the following statement: 'The language of the brain is based on neurons. To understand the brain, you must understand neurons and especially how vast numbers of them act together in parallel' (Crick 1994: 256).

Crick only mentions free will in a postscript, where he claims that it is merely an ability to make decisions (his examples include verbal responses and physical movement actions), which are controlled by a region 'in or near' the brain's 'anterior cingulate sulcus', and 'at or near the higher levels of the motor system' that receives 'many inputs from the higher sensory regions' (Crick 1994: 267). He also implies that the much-celebrated notion of free will is merely a process of decision-making, essentially debunking the idea that free will has any special status in the hierarchy of human agency.

One can of course argue that Crick's claim presents us with a mechanistic view of life, a top-down cognitive view of human 'being'. One can also argue that this view is a practical one based on scientific evidence observed and verified through repeated experiments. The brain gets its information from the body that it helps regulate and that information is acquired through sensing and responding to phenomena in the external world. Control is therefore both internal and external to the body. Since the spinal cord is an extension of the brain, or, more accurately, part of the overall central nervous system that receives and transmits information through the peripheral nervous system, conveying all of this to the head brain (Dowling 1998), it is not difficult to understand Crick's implication that all of human behaviour can be explained by the complex physical operations of its different systems.

However, the question of how aware one is of those operations and hence the ability to make conscious decisions raises some interesting issues about agency, free will and their connections to the issue of performance, what I call here 'the human potential'. Neuroscientists Guilio Tononi and Christof Koch argue that for a system to be aware, or become conscious of itself, it must have specific properties. One of these is complexity, where feedback, interdependence and integration of information is paramount. In 'Consciousness: Here, there and everywhere?' (2015), they propose an Integrated Information Theory (ITT) that positions consciousness as a fundamental property of physical systems.[26] ITT has five key postulates: (1) we have consciousness because we have experiences that we can describe to others; (2) consciousness has a structure because those experiences are structured; (3) experiences are very specific events and thus consciousness is as well; (4) both occur in whole irreducible units and (5) our experiences occur in space/time, have content, and thus can be located.[27]

Their theory also claims that consciousness exists in gradations, proposing an additional five properties that each physical system or entity must have in order to be considered conscious. Conscious entities must have: (1) an intrinsic or cause/effect existence, (2) a structured composition that allows cause/effect operations, (3) contain information that allows one to see or estimate past and/or future states of the system or organism, (4) be fully integrated in that every part must be able to affect as well as be affected by the rest of the system and

(5) must be able to exclude things that it doesn't need for its own survival.[28] Consciousness, according to Tononi and Koch (2015), is all over the body, not simply in the brain or, conversely, our 'brains' are all over the body and not just in the head. Understanding this, to me, is to grasp 'the human potential', in the sense that something begins to change with this knowledge. And what changes is the awareness of the different levels within oneself. Damasio himself has argued via his 'somatic marker hypothesis' (1994), that every one of our reasoned decisions is marked by an emotional element that is generated through the body's sensing systems that begin at the level of the skin (Damasio 1993). And even when we think we are making logical decisions based on a reasoned argument, somatic markers operate covertly throughout our bodies, without coming to consciousness:

> somatic markers are a special instance of feelings generated from secondary emotions. Those emotions and feelings have been connected, by learning, to predicted future outcomes of certain scenarios. When a negative somatic marker is juxtaposed to a future outcome the combination functions as an alarm bell. When a positive somatic marker is juxtaposed instead, it becomes a beacon of incentive.
>
> (Damasio 1994: 174)

The point here is that Crick, Damasio and Tononi all identify aspects of a more comprehensive truth: consciousness is a by-product of complex systems and free will is a higher accomplishment on the consciousness scale. Artificially intelligent computing machines on the other hand may perform extremely well in certain operations but they do not have the necessary amount of levels or layers to qualify for human potential. I argue that what distinguishes us as human beings from intelligent machines might well be the difference in the number of layers within the spectrum that we can access and use to our benefit.

For example, in *Passionate Engines*, Craig DeLancey (2002) argues for an appreciation of the role that emotions play in our mental lives, claiming that a bottom-up view facilitates an autonomous integration of motor control with perception and affect. He is especially critical of the cognitive approach to mind that philosophers like Daniel Dennett propose. Essentially, Dennett argues that the 'mindless' process of Darwinian natural selection is what accounts for the evolution of the human brain, and, by default, human consciousness (1991, 1996a, 1996b, 2013). Unlike Dennett, DeLancey rejects cognitivism in his analyses of mind using instead a version of affect program theory, which explores affects as body states that are motivational; meaning that they produce or induce behaviours in the body (DeLancey 2002: 5). Dennett (1996a) speaks instead of 'intentional systems' and of 'entities' as organizations performing like '*information*-modulated' and '*goal*-seeking systems' (original emphasis). He also refers to an 'intentional stance', which he claims is a 'strategy of interpreting the behaviour of an entity (person, animal, artefact, whatever) by treating it *as if* it were a rational agent' that governs its 'choice' of 'action' by a 'consideration' of its 'beliefs' and 'desires' (all quotes taken from Dennett 1996a: 26–27).

In a resonant mode, Rebecca Kukla argues that Dennett's intentional stance is not just an intellectual attitude, but rather 'collections of concrete strategies for coping with objects and coordinating with others'. And these same strategies ready the body 'for action and world engagement' (Kukla, in Huebner 2018: 5).[29] Dennett's intentionality thus accommodates the notion of a living machine/human interface while DeLancey's perspective is concerned more with a biology and a rationality of the emotions. Both address intentionality as a product of the behaviour of extremely complex systems. While I agree that complexity is the environment that creates 'agency' in human and non-human systems, no one seems to address where the higher register of the consciousness spectrum lies or what its possibilities and/or accomplishments are.

The Austrian physicist Anton Zeilinger once claimed that 'Maybe knowing [...] maybe knowledge is as fundamental, or even more fundamental than reality' (Zeilinger 2007).[30] Zeilinger was speaking to a gathering of Tibetan monks, Western scientists and humanist scholars at one of the Mind and Life Conferences in Dharamsala, India and referring to the strange reality exposed by the famous double-slit experiment. First devised by Thomas Young in 1803, this experiment challenged the existing knowledge about the behaviour of elementary particles and thus went on to create a fundamental shift in how reality was understood.[31] What Zeilinger probably meant was that it might be more useful to apply the knowledge we have to create something rather than to try and explain it to others who may not appreciate its nuanced complexity.

Performing consciousness

As we have learnt, the human body is a complex organism that utilizes feedback, interdependence and integration of information to maintain a healthy steady-state that ensures its survival. According to Tononi and Koch (2015), these are the prerequisites for conscious self-awareness. I have also argued that this constant and dynamic internal activity is akin to an ongoing dance where the body creates, maintains and destroys smaller parts of itself on a daily basis in order to maintain its overall existence. The role of the choreographer, as the force behind the creation of new dances, is to find ways of feeding the organism that is the choreographic work. The food for this kind of creativity is new impressions (Gurdjieff 1950; Ouspensky 1983).

Dance, choreography and performance require the cultivation of an awareness that goes beyond the movement expertise that dancers train so hard to acquire. A capacity for seeing the world as an extended performance research lab or stage is needed (Shakespeare 1623).[32] In my own research, choreography functions as a strategic organization and reorganization of bodies in space/time to generate new understandings of how maps are formed inside us and how we influence that formation through our own movements through the geographic territory. In this way, the dance becomes a dynamic engagement with the totality of one's being in space/time that allows us to understand the mechanisms of map-making up to and beyond the cortical level. To quote Damasio again: 'Because [...] brain maps are the substrate of mental images, map-making brains have the power of literally introducing the body as content into the mind process. Thanks to the brain, the body becomes a natural topic of the mind' (Damasio 2010: 95).

In this theory of practice, dance, choreography and performance come together in the service of an emergent self. Emergent in the sense that human beings are collections of identities and configurations of disconnected experiences and memories that must be integrated. The performance then becomes a deliberate attempt to recognise and remember connections that have been disconnected, forgotten or in some way rendered inoperable. The unindividuated or indivisible self is the ultimate result of this process, and by unindividuated and indivisible I am suggesting an integrated state that takes into account the ideas in the three quotations at the head of the prologue to this publication. Here, the body appears to *think*, the mind to *feel*, the emotions to *move* and vice versa. This self is the result of a body in dynamic balance, a body that *thinks*, *feels* and *moves* as an integrated unit, able to communicate across different levels of existence.

Merleau-Ponty's reiteration of Husserl's claim that the body reveals itself to the world and to itself through the intersection of an external tactile sensation and an internal kinaesthetic one becomes useful here: the 'lived body', he argues, exists in the spaces between the two, and just as we experience it, we reveal it to others (Merleau-Ponty 1962). In other words, the felt and the perceived co-exist in this 'lived-body' as a system of experienced movements (Welton 1998: 47–48). In the below-listed points, Welton proposes four steps to an Husserlian analysis of the materiality of the lived-body, steps that I utilize in my own creative practices with movement and with digital technologies.

1. In our direct and immediate awareness of the body, we know it primarily through the various tactile sensations involved in any activity of touching

something. In fact, Husserl's argument is that a subject that had only vision would never know the body as lived-body.

2. One of the unique traits of tactile sensations is that they are given as having a location in the lived-body. Their location is not a series of discrete points but a field.
3. The field of sensations is experienced as functionally dependent upon a real order of circumstances and events. Each significant change in things and the actions of things upon the surface of the physical body produces a change in the field of sensations according to a scheme of conditional dependency, an 'if-then' scheme.
4. Since changes on the surface of the body are experienced as changes in the field of sensations having that location, the lived body is manifested as material.

(Welton 1998: 47–48)

According to this analysis, the 'lived body' takes on the dimensions of a complex and dynamically changing map, the topography of which is determined by what we touch and/or are touched by. This body has cortical and cartographic coordinates, meaning that it is connected to the extensive memory resources in the cerebral cortex created by virtue of our unfolding physical movements in and through space and time. Many ancient cultures were also aware of cosmological correlates in these maps,[33] as they relied on the movements of those 'heavenly bodies' for the regulation of their lives, their institutions, their cultural forms and when necessary, moving their dwellings to other locations. It is as if one was always listening to the Universe's thoughts as it manifested through the actions of its numerous 'bodies', or physical systems. Therefore, key relationships between geographic maps, individual body maps and cosmological maps were recognized and consciously utilized. The human body thus became the place where the 'beyond' was visible as it intervened in the everyday, and to understand the one it was necessary to observe and correlate it with the other.

I believe that a key reason early Modern Dance pioneers drew on foreign, exotic, Aboriginal and ancient cultural movement practices was precisely because they felt there was something unique about how the body was perceived, conceptualized and utilized in those cultures. However, those same foreign, exotic, Indigenous and Aboriginal art forms subsequently suffered a form of cultural appropriation enabled by colonization, where they were exploited for information that could be used to establish Western dance forms, to mystify audiences and performers alike, even as those forms were considered inferior, i.e. regional, tribal, ethnic, folk and world, rather than sacred rituals performed for very specific reasons. Choreographers, performers and intellectuals alike, including those critical of this practice, did not fail to notice the benefits that these 'enhancements' to their practices brought, even though many failed to acknowledge it.

Early writings by Maxine Sheets-Johnstone (1980) and Sondra Fraleigh (1987), for example, felt that some of the ideas expressed by Husserl (1960, 1969) and Merleau-Ponty (1962, 1969) responded to a need in Western European and North American dance research communities to draw on philosophies that more readily embraced the dancer's instinctive kinaesthetic intelligence. Long-time dance critic for the *New York Times* John Martin (1893–1985) used the idea of 'the lived experience' to critique the dramatic narratives and displays of emotional suffering that were prevalent in the dances of the time. So crucial was the idea of the lived experience to dance that when choreographers with a more abstract, deconstructive style created works that distanced themselves from emotional suffering and correspondingly introduced electronic technologies in these works, some of these same writers became sceptical of what was happening to an art form they felt represented the human and/or the humane in us.

As one of those sceptics, John Martin provides a useful historical window into how dance was perceived. Drawing on his concept of 'metakinesis' or 'kinetic transfer' (1965, 1968, 1989),[34] he emphasized how dance served as a bridge between the world of the intellect and that of the tactile emotional body, between what was considered human and humane and what veered off into virtual and/or technological realms more mechanical than human. And since he wrote a great deal on the American Modern Dance pioneers as well as many of the European dance groups that toured the Americas before the Second World War, Martin's analyses played a key role in our understanding of how different approaches to the body and notions of the primitive, the human and the machine became part of early Modern Dance discourse.

Martin was personally impressed by the work of Martha Graham, Doris Humphrey, Jose Limón and Mary Wigman, for example. He described Graham as the 'flood and fire' to Humphrey's 'stream and light' (Martin 1968: 185), thought that Graham had a strength that was 'almost masculine' yet projected a 'wholly feminine mind, intuitive, impressionable, passionate, tempestuous', while writing that Humphrey was 'feminine to the fingertips', even though she thought with 'a logic and an analytical curiosity' that was 'largely masculine' (Martin 1968: 185). Limón – Mexican by birth – he described as 'magnificent [...] with a natural gift for movement'(Martin 1968: 282). This critic had a special place for Wigman, whom he claimed was second in importance only to Isadora Duncan in the history of Modern Dance (Martin 1989: 115–18).

It is not difficult to notice the vocabulary Martin uses to identify with the physicality, organic vibrancy and emotional and intellectual qualities of these artists. He not only cross-genders them with his descriptions, his 'metakinetic transfer' also explains their qualities 'for which words are not adequate' (Martin 1965: 13) and passionately argues for the immediacy of a form that communicates something quite unique from one person to another without actual physical contact. Although he never reviewed some of the Indigenous and very little of the Afro-diasporic dance forms outside the 'Modern Dance' field but which fed these techniques at the time, his understanding of dance as a medium for transferring aesthetic and emotional concepts from one individual to another is nevertheless interesting for the period and from the position it was written. 'There is correlated with kinesis a supposed psychic accompaniment called metakinesis, this correlation growing from the theory that the physical and the psychical are merely two aspects of a single underlying reality' (Martin 1965: 13).

Even though Martin wrote about the 'single underlying reality' that existed between these different approaches, he was often silent or quite critical in his writings about the choreographic work of Merce Cunningham. The latter's choreographic principles and thematic choices seemed diametrically opposed to those he admired in the choreographers mentioned above. Merce Cunningham and his main collaborator John Cage were part of a growing American post-modern dance scene, and the two men were clearly aligned with the spirit of Modernism that was a key influence on American Art of the time (Copeland 2004). These two considered overblown, dramatic narratives and an outpouring of emotions secondary or perhaps even irrelevant to their artistic aims. They were not at all interested in dance as the site for heroic narratives and tragic depictions. Cunningham, for example, was strictly focused on the interactions of bodies and their movement in time and space, and his work, even though extremely funny at times, consistently avoided emotionally laden narratives.

The music of Cunningham's life partner, John Cage, was an additional deterrent to this type of expressivity, drawing on chance operations from an Eastern aesthetic as well as the reconstituting of natural and artificial sounds as opposed to more traditional harmonic and orchestral modes. Cunningham, Cage and their collaborators made concerted attempts to dissociate themselves from the traditional modes of creating and staging theatrical dance, instead leaning towards an aesthetic 'built upon a careful blending of both the current trends of Modern Art in Cage's time, and Cage's interpretation of Asian thought, particularly the teachings of Zen Buddhism and the Chinese classical oracle book, the *I Ching*' (Martin 1976: 1).[35] I believe it was this radical shift in emphasis on how the body was positioned in dance that provoked John Martin's intense scepticism.

Yet another early perspective on this relationship between emotional distancing and associating that I believe marked out an important space for technological intervention in dance was Sondra Fraleigh's *Dance and the Lived Body*, (1987) where she questioned how the term *instrument* was commonly used by dance-makers to describe the role of the body in performance. Fraleigh argued that it produced important subtexts in the work performed, which tended to promote the idea of a separation between the mover's mind and body, and hence an abdication of agency. Drew Leder, in *The Absent Body* (1990), also emphasized this idea of abdication or losing one's relationship to the body. Leder does not write from the perspective of dance or the performing arts, but he is equally critical of what he describes as a cerebrally centred Western intellectual history, from as far back as ancient Greece, which tends towards an institutionally dictated disembodiment (Leder 1990: 3).

It is clear to me that these debates about distancing, disembodiment, tensions between abstraction and emotion, absence and presence in relation to the body, represent a spectrum of opinion about the human, and by default, the non-human or the machine, need redressing. The point here is that the age that produced Rene Descartes and his philosophy of a mind/body dichotomy also produced an industrial revolution and, with it, the idea of the body as a type of machine that obeyed the instructions of the mind. This physical and conceptual rift expressed itself through the intellect's ascendance over a base and stubborn body. The institutionally dictated tendency towards disembodiment that Leder refers to nevertheless continued through much of modern history, denying body practices the value that they deserved. My argument is that when used in a more expansive context, the term *disembodiment* can reveal a great deal about other dance and movement practices that have been marginalized or ignored in the history of Western dance and studies in performance.

Scales and dimensions, movement and sound

In line with my earlier framing of movement as the process of thought unfolding from a consciousness that can exist within as well as outside the body, I use terms such as 'scale' and 'degree' to indicate that there are different stages within the spectrum of that unfolding. This process, in turn, produces a variety of phenomena in and outside bodies, including sound, speech and language that advanced human creativity. The conscious recognition and remembering of these mapping processes then becomes a method for acquiring detailed knowledge about the realities we construct. Sound, speech and language, therefore, play an important role in the architecture of my own creative work. Emerging from movement as breath, or developed from interactions between objects, sound resonates across space and time, and in so doing reveals its dimensions. Since capturing the attention of audiences and engaging them as participants is key to any choreographic or performance strategy, interactions between movement, breath, sound and language become key communicative tools, playing active roles in a typical choreographic session.

One of my musical collaborators once mentioned that it was very easy to compose for the works I created because of the way I articulated my intentions through breath and sound during the rehearsal process.[36] In these sessions, I would also encourage performers to construct and voice their own texts, which were often recorded separately and later combined into the larger sonic score. These recorded texts were then used in studio rehearsals such that the performers could hear themselves speak as they worked through particular movement sequences. In this way, the sound was used to generate additional movement structures that would then contribute to the larger choreographic intention. Although some of the resulting works could be described as abstract, there was always an underlying narrative expressed as a structural coherence between the movements of bodies and the sounds that they created in space. Through affect (drives, motivations, emotions and feelings), audience members could then make connections between what they witnessed onstage and what was embedded in their own memory archives. This form of choreography – drawing on both non-discursive and discursive methods – utilized musical ideas, re-contextualized sound recordings and original as well as borrowed literary texts as performative devices.

Although there is some resonance here with Derrida's (1978, 1998) claim that we create meaning and identity through our interactions with the structures of verbal language, this creative methodology was designed to remind the individual that thought exists before, during and after language. In fact, one could say that it surrounds language. Because of this, I tend to work from the non-discursive to the discursive, where the verbal functions as an emergent entity, emerging from something that exists only as a potential. When manipulated, this potential allows performers and audiences to become aware of something far more important in the interstices between movement, sound and language.

When Bertolt Brecht (1898–1956) used the term *Verfremdung*[37] in his attempt to remind audiences that theatre is a different form of reality, he was essentially using a strategy of disassociation so people could create new cognitive paths for themselves when viewing his work. The concept of *Verfremdung* resonates with other methods used by Futurist, Cubist and Dadaist artists, all of whom had inherently political motives in that they encouraged people to resist the systemic mechanization, institutionalization and automatization of self that could drive them to commit inhumane acts. One could say that, throughout the first decades of the twentieth century, a deliberate use of abstraction, distancing, alienation and fragmentation opened alternate spaces that the programming languages of new technologies in the Information Age have generously exploited. Thus, the emergence of Modern Dance between the nineteenth and twentieth centuries was not a coincidence; new forms of expressivity were exploring notions of identity and self that brought the past into a new relationship with the present as people tried to envision a different future. These developments were all part of a wave of experimentation that was taking place across the arts, especially in relationships between sound, music and language as creative forms.

Arnold Schoenberg (1874–1951), for example, developed his twelve-tone technique as a system of musical composition that demanded new habits of and often distressed early twentieth-century listeners. Kuiper and Newlin, in an entry in the Encyclopaedia Britannica,[38] claimed that Schoenberg's process of 'transcending tonality' could first be observed at the beginning of the last movement of his *Second String Quartet (1907–08)* and was a strategy that changed the tone of Western concert music forever. Ironically, the title of the finale of that work, *Ich fühle Luft von anderen Planeten* – translated as 'I feel air from another planet' from a poem by Stefan George – motivated Kuiper and Newlin to write that this title symbolically represented Schoenberg's breakthrough to a new world of sound.[39] Both Schoenberg's and Brecht's creative strategies allowed audiences to see theatre and hear music differently by shifting their accustomed modes of perception.

In Schoenberg's case, he moved away from the harmonic relationship between notes within the octave and the relationship of one octave to another. The traditional structuring of the octave is shown in Figure 3.6 where we see the doubling of sound vibrations within an ascending octave represented as a movement from a perfect 4th (as a 4/3 relationship), through a perfect 5th (as a 3/2 relationship) within the basic unit of the octave. In the descending octave, however, the former

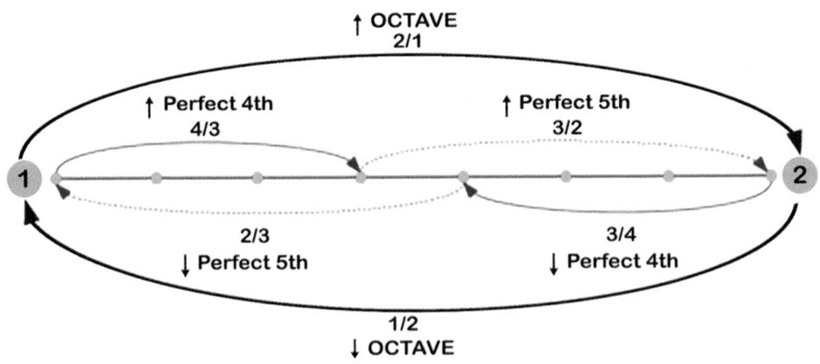

FIGURE 3.6: The 2/3 to 3/4 structure of the octave fourths and fifths.[40]

is represented as a 3/4 relationship and the latter as a 2/3 relationship. Schoenberg questioned this mathematically fixed procedure for doubling and halving sound frequencies, i.e. moving from one level to another, as the only means of creating valid sound compositions. He shattered the tonality of Western music's listening process by exposing the irrational aspects of the transformation of sound vibrations from one level (octave) to another by introducing disharmony – or discomfort – as a hidden component of the transformational process.

In the early nineteenth century, when Schoenberg was composing, similar developments were taking place in scientific disciplines and art forms; abstraction in painting and an exploration of the unconscious in psychoanalysis, for example. These developments pointed to a deepening of awareness and changing perceptions of the world at a time when society was becoming more chaotic – a chaos that would eventually lead to two world wars within the space of three decades. One could say that the changing face of research in disciplines from the arts to the sciences made people more aware of the potentials that existed in the non-conscious, the sub-personal and the pre-reflexive, while introducing the idea that our realities were constructed and institutionalized by processes that necessarily changed over time. The fact is that when these changes occurred people were often ill-prepared to accept them.

In *Walk-About-Timeless* (1995),[41] a work from the first phase of my PaR experiments, I utilized some of Brecht's, Schoenberg's and Derrida's ideas regarding the use of sound, movement and language to create an original theatrical work where the audience could experience a unique involutionary and evolutionary unfolding.[42] By 'involutionary' and 'evolutionary' unfolding I am referring to the capacity that sounds have to develop in octaves whose frequencies double overtime, a doubling that takes place very unevenly within the octave itself before either falling back to its origin or moving to a higher octave. Since this doubling reveals an unevenness, or 'structural discontinuity' with an inherent intermediate 'disharmony' (Figure 3.6), it allowed the composer of *Walk-About-Timeless*, Gareth Giles, a great deal of creative possibilities. For example, in Figure 3.7, the Pythagorean twelve-tone scale descends through a 3/2 ratio to get to the perfect fifth and finds balance through a 4/3 ratio in the perfect fourth. These 'perfect' steps are separated by imperfect ratios that allow the composer as sound designer great freedom to choose new paths to navigate. One can argue that the energetic potentials that exist in these 'imperfect' spaces of the sound octave exist within all natural phenomena, and, as such, provide a conceptual framework that could be utilized across different media.

It is this conceptual framework that I hoped to explore in that work. Figure 3.7 is a mathematical demonstration of the 'logical discontinuity' in the progression of sound vibrations in the twelve-tone scale as a manifestation of energy that moves

Note	Frequency	Ratio	Hz
C	**2.000**	**2/1**	**523.25**
B	1.8750	15/8	496.67
B♭	1.8000	9/5	465.12
A	1.6667	5/3	441.49
A♭	1.6000	8/5	413.42
G	**1.5000**	**3/2**	**392.44**
F#	1. 4063	45/32	372.52
F	**1.3333**	**4/3**	**348.83**
E	1.2500	5/4	331.11
E♭	1.2000	6/5	310.08
D	1.125	9/8	294.33
C#	1.0417	25/34	279.39
C	**1.000**	**1/1**	**261.63**

FIGURE 3.7: Pythagorean scale.[43]

from one level to another, doubling or halving as the case may be, while allowing opportunities for creative intervention in new and perhaps radically different directions. In *Walk-About-Timeless* (1994/1995),[44] the composer utilized the second of Olivier Messiaen's (1909–92) Seven Musical Modes (Figure 3.8)[45] as a formal structuring principle.

This production explored relations between form and content, and consequently between structure and meaning in the creation of an individual movement style; it layered Messiaen's musical logic and his theory of sound vibrations with the Aboriginal Australian idea of creation as a walking journey through time by 'ancestral gods' that caused the physical world to come into being (Turner 1980; Corbally Stourton 1996).

Like Messiaen, I was interested in the use of sound as a source of vibrations that resonated through space, time and the body, creating sympathetic effects in the latter. Using the second of his seven *Modes of Limited Transposition* (Figure 3.8), presented a unique challenge. *Walk-About-Timeless* was composed of four separate sections, each of which could be performed in a different sequence that would be decided prior to the performance.[47] To facilitate an extended investigation, the choreography was produced in three different versions with three different casts with just a single dancer performing in all three versions.

In the choreographic work, the music's harmonic character remains fixed until a note outside the fixed eight notes, C#, D, E, F, G, Ab, Bb and B (Figure 3.9), is introduced. This introduction makes the ear lean towards an imagined key and its resultant harmonic relationship. For example, raising the Ab to A within this mode yields interesting inversions of A Major and D Minor Triads. However, to digress for any length of time puts the composer out of Messiaen's Second Mode.

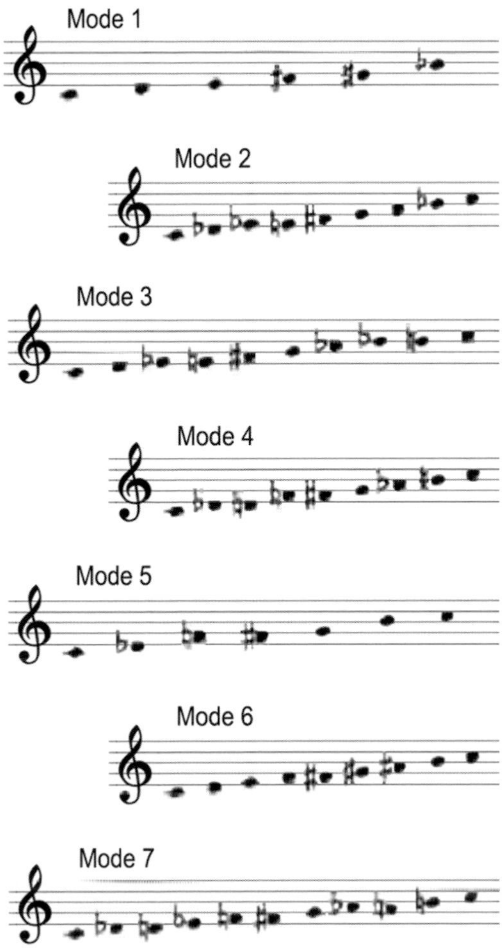

FIGURE 3.8: Messiaen's *Seven Modes of Limited Transposition*.[46]

In order to stay within it, as the rules of that Mode and the basis of the whole compositional structure requires, there is a constant shifting between the formal relationships of tonality and atonality. This results in an air of ambiguity, the harmonic relationships tending to give emotional weight and the atonality a distancing effect to the music.[49]

This idea was explored in a series of shifting structural relationships that utilized different languages (English, French and Japanese), while investigating situations of conflict and the power dynamics that one finds in human relations. This metaphoric Walkabout, in the sense of new 'worlds' being created through the movement interactions of bodies in space/time, engaged with Chatwin's and

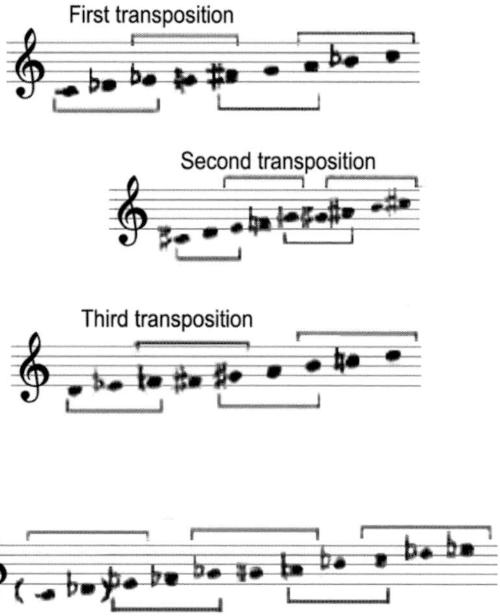

FIGURE 3.9: Messiaen's *Second Mode with Transpositions*.[48]

Turner's writings about how Aboriginal peoples conceive of their intimate relationships with the environment and with each other (Chatwin 1988; Turner 1980; Hume 2002). Messiaen's own efforts to explore notions of spirituality in musical structures, and what he saw as a bond that existed between music and spirituality (Messiaen 1956),[50] was thus brought into a discursive space where notions of creativity were equated with that of an original Creation as expressed through Aboriginal Australian narratives. The result was that the audience knew there was something important happening in the work, but they were never told what the underlying narrative was. There were hints given but no cohesive story except that the movement vocabulary was very organized and quite consistent. In other words, one had to look to the pure movement, to the sounds, the images and how the entire *mise en scéne* was organized for the 'story'.

It must be said here that no attempt was made to access original Australian Aboriginal materials as far as movement or sound resources were concerned. And this was deliberate as I was more interested in the resonances between ideas rather than accurately representing a cultural narrative or appropriating certain cultural practices. However, I did have two Australian dancers in the project who helped me understand the concept I was dealing with and some of the pitfalls that I should avoid.[51] Years later, on a conference research visit to Australia,[52] I would better understand how deeply sensitive such a subject is in that country.

Further conclusions

> *The intelligence of things exists only through what we may call an original fractioning and the comparison of these fractions to one another, which is then only an enumeration of the aspects of Unity.*
>
> (Lawlor 1982: 20)

Some academics have pointed out a trend in Western intellectual history since the ancient Greeks that is prejudiced against body practices as a valid form of knowing (Leder 1990; Foster 1995). In these pages, I've referenced other cultures that recognized and maintained body-centred knowledge practices prior to, and simultaneous with, the development of Western intellectual history. I also suggested that the demise of such practices could have been the result of systemic abuse or prolonged separation between groups who maintained those practices. Working on the premise that at one time or another there were connections between those who created these practices and those who followed them, and that these connections were either lost or ignored for one reason or another, contemporary societies have an obligation to re-establish these connections, considering the importance of these links.

When philosopher and mathematician René Descartes claimed that the things of mind (*res cogitans*), were different from those of body (*res extensa*) (Descartes, trans. by Cottingham 1996a, 1996b), and hence one could not satisfactorily bring the one into a cohesive relationship with the other, he left the Western world with an enormous problem to solve. It is possible that he and others underestimated the importance of the body in understanding the nature of reality and of our being in the world. The term complexity, as used in this book, suggests diverse universes that balance and reflect one another. The idea of the mind-brain as a top-down organizational system is no longer viable. A more practical model is to view bodies as distributed systems with centres around which fundamental functions are managed. The behaviour of these structures is then mapped and remapped in ever-increasing levels of complexity up to and beyond the level of the human. One can therefore say that the human being is directly connected to and completely entangled within a much larger entity that includes all of organic life on Earth. The model adopted in this research perceives individual agency as key within a system that seeks equilibrium. The human body is a unique learning system that perpetuates itself by recording the same information in several places within the organism. Because of this, many of its processes may appear scattered and slow to develop. However, in such a system, complete communication does not break down if one or two sub-systems malfunctions. In fact, the memory of completeness persists while the system strives to restore it through behavioural changes.

To conclude this chapter, I would like to look more deeply at Lawlor's quotation earlier in this section, drawing on the example he uses in his book *Sacred Geometry* (1982) of the Chinese Yin-Yang symbol as a manifestation of the synthesis of opposites (see Figure 3.10). This symbol demonstrates how opposites converge at an interface that appears dual but essentially masks a third principle. In it, a large circle splits into two smaller circles based on dividing the larger circle's diameter into two radii. At first glance, the symbol suggests that the division of Unity is into two equal parts, but this is not true. There is an asymmetrical principle hidden within the symbol that creates proportion and thus enables growth. The ratio of the diameter to the circumference of any circle is $C/D = \pi$ and the circumference of the smaller circles equals $D/2 \times \pi = \pi D/2$. The sum of the circumferences of the two inner circles equals the circumference of the large circle or $2 \times \pi D/2 = \pi D$. Continuing this halving of the smaller circles indefinitely, we discover that the sum of the circumference of the smaller circles will still equal the circumference of the original larger circle. Eventually, a wavy alternating line slightly above and below the original diameter remains, 'illustrating the paradox of the diameter becoming equal to the circumference of the same circle' (Lawlor 1982: 42).

This illustration clearly demonstrates how duality masks itself as unity through a hidden third principle, and although the sum of the circumferences of the smaller circles may appear to be equal to the larger one, essentially, it is not. The hidden tertiary principle resolves the paradox,[54] whilst giving a practical deconstruction of how the logic of the included middle operates. According to Lawlor, this diagram demonstrates that 'at the origin and end all differentiation merges towards Unity' (1982: 42). In expanding, the scale appears as dual, but expanding the scope of one's thinking reveals the mediating principle and a different take on Unity. This paves the way, conceptually at least, for a theory of performance that argues for a mediatory principle that facilitates individual growth towards unity.

This kind of growth, or level change, is not automatic, it requires and depends on individual effort, which brings us back to the overt instruction in David George's quote at the beginning of this chapter. George claims that, 'Any phenomenon – geometry

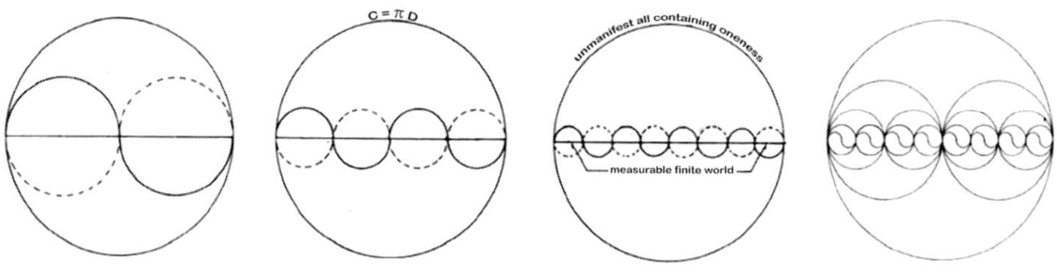

FIGURE 3.10: Taoist symbol.[53]

or performance [...] can be understood and practised only when each new member repeats the original cognitive leap' (George 1996: 16–17). Everyone must 'perform' their own set of actions to achieve the required cognitive breakthrough, and this is only possible with the help of disciplined whole-body practices. As an expert dance practitioner, I see the entire phenomenological world as a choreographic field where creative acts are performed as actions that have the potential to transform some aspect of that world. And as I mentioned in my prologue, if we wish to fully know and understand ourselves and our relationship to the rest of organic life, unique investigative procedures based on sound theories of performance need to be developed. Act II of this volume takes the reader through some of these investigative procedures and displays the diverse range of practical results obtained.

NOTES

1. In Chapter 1, I introduced the idea of 'three different "brains" with degrees of accuracy located throughout the body: brain, spinal cord and peripheral nervous system' in the section titled 'Will the artist please stand up?'.
2. Ontogenesis is the development of an individual organism or anatomical or behavioural feature from the earliest stage to maturity. English Oxford Living Dictionaries, www.lexico.com/definition/phylogenesis.
   Phylogenesis is the evolutionary development and diversification of a species or group of organisms, or of a particular feature of an organism. English Oxford Living Dictionaries, www.en.oxforddictionaries.com/.
3. www.henrydaniel.ca/performance-archive.
4. The first stage occurred as I transitioned from a professional practice to an academic institutional one during my first graduate degree and teaching position at the Laban Centre in London. The second phase began with the commencement of my second graduate degree at Bristol University with teaching positions at the Department of Theatre and Performance at Plymouth University and the School of Arts at the University College Scarborough. The third stage began with my appointment as an assistant professor at Simon Fraser University in Canada.
5. We were all faculty members at King Alfred's College, now Winchester University, at the time.
6. 'Here Be Dragons' – Mapping the Undiscovered Realms of Performance Studies: Boundaries, Hinterlands and Beyond. PSi5, 9–12 April 1999, Aberystwyth, Wales.
7. *'Homo orthopedicus': L'appréhension du corps à l'époque moderniste/The Modernist Body*, Museum van Hedendaagse Kunst Antwerpen/Museum of Contemporary Art Antwerp, Belgium, 7–11 December 1999.
8. An Orisha is a spirit messenger sent by Olodumare, one of the three manifestations of the Supreme Entity or God within the Yoruba religion. As a people, the Yoruba also believe

that these messengers are continually sent to guide human beings and to show them how to live within the larger framework of Creation.

9. He came from a Nigerian family who had emigrated to London, England and I from a Caribbean family from Trinidad in the West Indies.
10. In fact, there is a dance style in Trinidad named after Shango.
11. Charles Kahn once proposed in his *Pythagoras and the Pythagoreans: A Brief History* (2001) that the Pythagorean tradition developed in ancient Greece in the half-century before Christianity fed modern thought through three distinct strands; the first through the occult and the supernatural, the second through transmigration and vegetarianism and the third through the mathematical and musical traditions. Philosophy, biology, mathematics and music therefore provided a fertile base through which many of these ancient beliefs and practices were transformed. Kahn's work suggested that a relationship between the visible and the invisible, the material and the immaterial, the human and the divine, and the artistic to the scientific was funnelled through and shaped by the power of both old and new technologies.
12. The Olmec, Maya, Teotihuacan, Toltec and Aztec are examples of Indigenous groups who actively practiced these ideas.
13. www.henrydaniel.ca/performance-archive.
14. Flint, R. W. (ed.), *F. T. Marinetti: Selected Writings*, with an introduction by R. W. Flint; translated by R. W. Flint and Arthur A. Coppotelli, Farrar, Straus and Giroux, 1972. [I find the Flint/Coppotelli translation smoother and more suited to theatrical speech than Thompson's in the Berghaus edition.]
15. Berghaus, Günter (ed.) *F.T. Marinetti: Critical Writings*, Farrar, Straus and Giroux, 2006, p. 209.
16. Loy showed her paintings in the First International Futurist Art Exhibition in 1914.
17. See www.moma.org/collection/about/conservation/demoiselles/index.html.
18. European Modernism greatly influenced notions of Modern Dance in North American and the rest of the world. *Tanztheater* and Physical Theatre are derived forms that also, in turn, influence North American and the rest of the world. *Futurist Equation* and *Shango Meets Ogun*, as well as all of my other choreographic works cited in this publication, are all attempts to include the Black body and its performative perspectives in these discourses.
19. All quotations from this paragraph are taken from Berghaus, Günter (ed.), *F. T. Marinetti: Critical Writings*, Farrar, Straus and Giroux, 2006, pp. 13–14.
20. All quotations from this paragraph are taken from Berghaus, Günter (ed.), *F. T. Marinetti: Critical Writings*, Farrar, Straus and Giroux, 2006, pp. 13–14.
21. The most typical examples are those of Post-Impressionist painters such as Henri Matisse (1869–1954), Pablo Picasso (1881–1973), Paul Cézanne (1839–1906) and Paul Gaugin (1848–1903).
22. https://en.wikipedia.org/wiki/Vitruvian_Man.
23. www.mindandlife.org/mission/.
24. The indentured Chinese and Indian laborers who came to the Caribbean also brought their cultural beliefs and practices – practices that I grew up reading about, looking at, listening to and often participating in.

25. Gurdjieff, G. I. *Beelzebub's Tales to his Grandson*. Routledge and Kegan Paul, 1950. *In Search of the Miraculous: Fragments of an Unknown Teaching*. Routledge and Kegan Paul, 1983.
26. Tononi, Giulio, and Koch Christof. 'Consciousness: Here, There and Everywhere?', *Philosophical Transactions of the Royal Society of London. Series B, Biological Sciences*, vol. 370, no. 1668, 2015, https://doi.org/10.1098/rstb.2014.0167, www.researchgate.net/publication/274317541ConsciousnessHereThereandEverywhere.
27. Tononi, Giulio, and Koch Christof. 'Consciousness: Here, There and Everywhere?', *Philosophical Transactions of the Royal Society of London. Series B, Biological Sciences*, vol. 370, no. 1668, 2015, https://doi.org/10.1098/rstb.2014.0167.
28. Tononi, Giulio, and Koch Christof. 'Consciousness: Here, There and Everywhere?', *Philosophical Transactions of the Royal Society of London. Series B, Biological Sciences*, vol. 370, no. 1668, 2015, https://doi.org/10.1098/rstb.2014.0167.
29. https://academic-oup-com.proxy.lib.sfu.ca/book/25912/chapter/193634134.
30. 'Mind and Life XIV - Day 1 pm - with the Dalai Lama.' *YouTube*, 9 April 2007, www.youtube.com/watch?v=fO-K13cfJwo. Institute for Quantum Optics and Quantum Information – Vienna (IQOQI-Vienna) of the Austrian Academy of Sciences, www.iqoqi-vienna.at/.
31. This experiment demonstrates how light is both a wave and composed of particles and that the very act of observation and measurement influences the behaviour of these particles at atomic and sub-atomic levels, www.en.wikipedia.org/wiki/Double-slitexperiment.
32. Edward, Blount and William Isaac Jaggard. *Shakespeare's Comedies, Histories, & Tragedies (Shakespeare's First Folio)*. As You Like It, Part II Scene VV, Line 138, 1623.
33. The Maya had a complex calendar based on the movements of the sun, the moon and particularly the planet Venus, which they held in great esteem. This calendar was used to schedule and regulate important events and activities (Aveni 1979).
34. 'Metakinesis' and 'kinetic transfer' have numerous references throughout John Martin's writings on dance.
35. 'The Asian factor in John Cage's aesthetic by Holly Martin: An introduction with a previously unpublished interview from 1976'. vol. 2, BMCM+AC BMC Research Resources, www.blackmountainstudiesjournal.org/volume-iv-9-16/holly-martin-the-asian-factor-in-john-cages-aesthetics/.
36. Martin Gotfrit, with additional material supplied by Albert St Albert Smith, composed the score for *Relatively-Well-Centred* (2000). He also composed scores for *Kafka's Report to the Academy – Response from Dance* (2001) and *Kafka's Report...reproduced* (2016).
37. German for alienating, defamiliarizing or making strange.
38. www.Britannica.com/biography/Arnold-Schoenberg.
39. www.Britannica.com/biography/Arnold-Schoenberg.
40. Image taken from www.sacred-geometry.es/?q=en/content/proportion-musical-scales.

41. *Walk-About-Timeless* explored the Australian Aboriginal idea of creation in space and time as a journey undertaken by the 'gods', and one that they must repeat as an existential act. Daniel, H. *The Force of Experience: A Key Parameter for Dance.* Unpublished MA dissertation, The Laban Centre for Movement and Dance, 1995.
42. Sounds develop in octaves whose frequencies double over time, but this doubling takes place very unevenly within the octave itself before either falling back to its origin or moving to a higher octave.
43. Image taken from https://en.wikipedia.org/wiki/Pythagorean_tuning.
44. Daniel, H. *op cit.* Music for *Walk-About-Timeless* was composed by Gareth Giles. The production premiered at the Riverside Studios, Hammersmith, London, 13 July 1995 and was choreographed and designed by me. The dancers were Mia Atsugi, Louise Chalwell, Sue Harvey, Holly Rook, Amy Whitworth, Chizuko Yoshifuku, Yemi Adenle, Jason Barden, Marco Brénugat and Ben Love. Michael Mannion designed the lighting and Sarah Morris the costumes.
45. Taken from Olivier Messiaen's *The Technique of My Musical Language* translated by John Satterfield, A. Leduc, 1956.
46. 'An examination of the life and musical style of Olivier Messiaen, 1908–1992', 2001, p. 4. Image taken from www.musicteachers.co.uk/resources/messstudy.pdf.
47. This never took place.
48. Henry Daniel, unpublished MA thesis, The Laban Centre, 1995.
49. This never took place.
50. Henry Daniel, unpublished MA thesis, The Laban Centre, 1995.
51. Louise Chalwell and Sue Harvey.
52. 'Body of Knowledge: Art and Embodied Cognition' Conference, Deakin University, Melbourne, 27–29 June, 2019.
53. Image taken from Lawlor, *Sacred Geometry: Philosophy and Practice.* Thames and Hudson, vol. 42, 1983.
54. Compare this with Niels Bohr's *Principle of Complementarity in Quantum Mechanics*, https://faraday.physics.utoronto.ca/PVB/Harrison/Complementarity/CompCopen.html.

ACT 2

4

Transnet

Performing art, performing science, transdisciplinary approaches to performance

Act II of this publication is dedicated to the four multi-year research projects that reflect the ideas we have been discussing in Act I. It is where the theory of practice is staged as artistic works and presented to both academic and general audiences. Each of these projects contains several art works; full-length choreographies, short films and audio/video installations for example and they also became the subject of teaching workshops, conference talks, artistic discussions and peer-reviewed essays. The material generated during these projects constitutes an ongoing mapping process whose final destination is an extensive web-based performance research archive that this book is itself a part of. This archive in turn reflects the unfolding of a complete Performance-as-Research and Artistic Research strategy within a transdisciplinary framework. Transnet functions as a baseline for the three succeeding projects.

In 2003, three years after I arrived in Canada from the UK, I received an external two-year Research Development Initiative (RDI) grant from Social Sciences and Humanities Research Council of Canada (SSHRC) to create a Transdisciplinary Research Network for Performance and Technology (Transnet).[1] Two years later, in June 2005, I staged the concluding event of that research project in a combined conference/workshop/symposium at Simon Fraser University's Burnaby and downtown Vancouver campuses. The overall title of the event was 'Performing Art, Performing Science: Transdisciplinary Approaches to Performance'.[2]

One of Transnet's objectives was to stimulate the founding of a research lab[3] where dance and choreography, in concert with new computer-based technologies, could play a central role in the exploration of a transdisciplinary approach to performance. And since I had been working for several years in both academic and professional dance contexts with some of these technologies, I felt I had the appropriate experience to launch such a project. The overall objective of the RDI program was to support research in its initial stages through the development of new ways of analysing, structuring, integrating and transferring knowledge between the arts, the cultural sector and different scientific disciplines. It was designed to help researchers:

1. Develop new research questions.
2. Explore conceptual and methodological perspectives and directions.
3. Critically analyse and assess research, including its achievements, impacts, strengths and state of development.[4]

This award was the result of a very difficult process between myself and the administrative apparatus at the university, which felt that a much larger Canadian Foundation for Innovation (CFI) grant application I wrote did not have much chance of success at the federal level because of my status as an untenured Assistant Professor who had only recently joined the institution. Although I had an extensive international career as a professional in the field, which included running my own dance company prior to doing an MA and a Ph.D. and holding a permanent tenured position at a British university, I was experiencing the first taste of intellectual bias and the discriminatory politics of academia that would repeat itself throughout my career. And as I would also find out, there was not only a profound mistrust between academics inside the academy and artists in the professional world but also between factions within the academy itself. Nevertheless, I went ahead with a financially smaller two-year application, the result of which was Transnet. Luckily for me, the people I invited to present their research in the form of papers, workshops and panel discussions must have realized that I was not just an assistant professor without tenure, but a recognized artist with international stature who had lately entered their sphere.

Despite my enthusiasm for a new job and country, I had to approach the entire period leading up to the conference very carefully, keeping in mind the common biases that exist across the different disciplinary domains I hoped to engage. Years later, in a provocative talk titled 'Challenges in Formalizing Cognitive Art-Science Research',[5] visiting Dutch cognitive neuroscientist and psychologist Shanti Ganesh would argue that the two most prominent modes of collaboration between artists and scientists consisted of the scientist's interest in 'the artist as a research subject', and the artist's interest in using 'science as a decoration', or as 'lovely images behind a dance'. Freya Vass-Rhee was equally dismissive of such practices in her 2006 paper *Integrating Dance and Cognitive Science: Toward Emancipatory Research* when she claimed that many of these collaborative efforts amounted to no more than a 'fetishization of scientific discourse' (2006: 6).[6] In a gentler but still sceptical mode, Karen Barad (2007) also argued that the general public's fascination with scientific concepts and, more specifically, the subject matter of quantum physics, generated 'all the right questions', brought 'the key issues to the fore' and 'promoted open-mindedness and inquisitiveness', but unfortunately often produced 'unsatisfactory understandings' of the relevant issues (Barad 2007: 6). And this, she claimed, was so because of the notoriously difficult epistemological and ontological terrain that researchers encounter in trying to apply scientific findings outside the initial context of the research.

In spite of such concerns, I felt my objectives had merit: I was interested in finding a deeper and more engaging collaborative experience between artists, media technologists, scientists and cultural workers. And this was so primarily because some of my early work involved challenging and even undermining the operational characteristics of the technological tools I was using. To be clear, the 'undermining' here meant using technological tools in ways that were often antithetical to their design intentions; at times even being deliberately subversive because I felt the technologies themselves were far too primitive, too didactive in their responses to the performative dialogue that my choreographic work sought to engage. However, I must also admit that these early collaborations were not with scientists per se, but more with what I would call media artists and design technologists. Since my early interest in scientific findings came from personal experience of things I could not understand and therefore sought expert opinions of,[7] I felt my approaches to those who were experts in the field seemed justified.

But, in pursuing this approach, I discovered that even within science itself there were different levels of explanation for the phenomena that interested me. And because I was not a scientist, I had to listen carefully to the explanations of those who tried to decipher precisely how their research could be relevant to my artistic context. Following Chalmers' premise, I followed the disciplinary trail from physics to chemistry, from chemistry to biology and psychology before coming right back to the fundamental problem I mentioned in Chapter 1, namely, that of understanding an unusual set of experiences and how these experiences influenced the directions of my artistic practice. Although working with digital and interactive technologies had furthered my understanding of a number of difficult questions I had been asking, I felt that by speaking to and working with other artists and scientists who had more expertise in these areas I could learn a great deal more. Luckily, several of these experts responded to the Transnet conference call, which was framed within the context of the network's description and the grant objectives as outlined below:

> Transnet (Transdisciplinary Network for Performance and Technology) is an international network of artists, scholars, performers, educators, scientists, engineers, and community activists formed to explore notions of performance, especially in the arts and sciences. The network uses a transdisciplinary approach to analyse the

> intersections of diverse disciplines and knowledges and to examine how new research directions can emerge from this confluence. Transnet suggests that performance, of people and of systems, is the primary activity in an exchange across societies and cultures, with new technologies and the human body as common denominators for these exchanges.
>
> Transnet is a place where contemporary art meets contemporary science to redefine notions of performance, and where disciplinary perspectives on the body are challenged. The network operates under the premise that, in an information-oriented age, new knowledge appears to emerge at the intersections of disciplines rather than strictly within them. Its transdisciplinary approach therefore analyses how other knowledges intersect with one's own discipline and how this contact influences both fields of research.[8]

Transnet's objectives:

1. To critically analyse and assess current research, as well as training and production methods for performance, especially movement-based, including their achievements, impacts, strengths and state of development.
2. To develop new research questions and/or proposals, and to investigate new models for collaborative research.
3. To explore new conceptual and methodological perspectives for practice-led research in the arts.
4. To establish and promote new environments that can foster collaboration and intellectual exchange between the arts, sciences and humanities, and among individuals and institutions locally, nationally and internationally.
5. To develop a new Transdisciplinary Research Centre for Performance and Technology.[9]

Significant contributions

Ambitious? Yes! And the event opened with a thought-provoking keynote by Michael Century, a pianist, composer and, at the time, professor of new media and music in the arts department at Rensselaer Polytechnic Institute in the United States. I sought out Century after reading some of his writings on transdisciplinarity, asking him to give the opening keynote. His talk, 'The Historical Décalage: Transdisciplinarity and the *Avant-Garde*'[10] quite articulately laid out some of the main principles of the transdisciplinary approach to research. He stressed the idea that transdisciplinarity, as an entirely new approach to knowledge production, conceptually and practically begins wherever new institutions are formed to explore links between science, art and technology. Century argued that it was during such moments that multidisciplinary cultures were formed and new products created. He also maintained that whenever there were more complex levels of collaboration involved in these ventures, the result was the inevitable creation of new knowledge processes and completely new spaces with jointly defined horizons. This new approach to knowledge production defined transdisciplinarity, something he described as an 'overflow'[11] from the regular disciplinary and multidisciplinary processes.[12] But this overflow brought with it an obligation for involvement in the social realm and a willingness to hand over some control and power to the users of that knowledge.

It was this last point in Century's presentation that, for some reason, struck me as the most interesting – the idea of positioning transdisciplinarity as an institutional commitment to the development of art and technology with an obligation to share the resulting knowledge with society. This, to me, signalled a sharing of the power and control that also came with such knowledge, and to hear it laid out in such a subtle manner made me pause and think about how this was fundamentally different from the historical model I was familiar with. To me, this statement went to the heart of an issue that crossed science and art, and the social and political institutions they were both attached to, while critically commenting on the intentions of those who controlled those institutions. That issue was simply the use of power, and I felt Century's keynote hit the perfect string at the opening of a conference on transdisciplinary approaches to performance.

There were many presentations on that first morning of the Transnet conference, including one from renowned Montreal-based Franco-Congolese dancer, writer, choreographer and teacher of Contemporary West African Dance Zab Maboungou, who described a rather unique approach to cross-cultural collaborations. Zab was the director of the organization Nyata Nyata and its resident dance group Compagnie Danse Nyata Nyata in Montreal for more than three decades, and a professor of philosophy with extensive experience sharing her expertise in traditional and contemporary African dance forms. She outlined an African concept of being in time that was fundamental to her practice as a dance artist and scholar. Although she confessed to being a technological neophyte, Zab was nevertheless a master of African drumming rhythms, working with and through them as part of her teaching philosophy. She explained a dilemma she faced the first time she began working with dancers in the West.[13] Zab admitted finding westerners generally quite agitated when they heard African rhythms, as opposed to Africans who first listened quietly to them before responding. She went on to explain that her manner of handling rhythm – or rather rhythms – was as if they were 'embodied entities' that had the possibility of connecting various elements in time.[14] She further explained that all her efforts in dance consisted in 'trying to create time'.[15]

Zab gave the example of African polyrhythms, which employs a technique of putting two or three conflicting rhythms together. Initially, some of her students apprehended these polyrhythms as dissonant – that is, until she helped them parse those rhythms through her dance sequences. She explained that these rhythms had the capacity to free the body from being bound by the constraints of a limited earthly existence. By understanding, in an embodied manner, that we were complex creatures with the capacity to move in a rhythmically complex manner, the dancer and the musician could engage in the rhythmic interplay that allowed them to experience heightened states of being. This, to me, was a profound philosophical premise insofar as it linked an ancient technology, i.e., the drums, with dance as a method for inhabiting multiple spaces/times. Further, it reintroduced a number of arguments about the links between traditional ritual practices and theatre that were offered by anthropologists such as John Beattie (1977) and Victor Turner (1982) and later strengthened by early performance studies scholars such as Richard Schechner (2019, 1985) and Dwight Conquergood (1989).

At that point in Zab's talk, I could not help recognizing why *Shango Meets Ogun* (1998), a work that I had performed so many times, had played such a crucial role in my thinking about the relationship between issues of embodiment and disembodiment. What began as a somewhat instinctive practice on my part, namely, playing with time in a non-linear way with multiple overlapping sequences, was actually a practice that was used extensively by those in my own ancestral past, and more recently in my Caribbean dance experience. If sensing and moving to different rhythms simultaneously in the body allowed one to perceive space differently, then dancing different rhythmic structures could be thought of as a method for instigating different modalities of being, thinking and, therefore, knowing. Zab herself was used to exploring these ideas with others in her daily teaching and dancing practices. It turned out that I had underestimated, or rather taken for granted my early dance career in the Caribbean, as well as the experiences of working later in New York with African American dancer, choreographer and scholar Pearl Primus.[16] This moment of recognition allowed me to claim a piece of knowledge that had always been in me and which I unconsciously drew on.

Before the end of that first day, New Zealand dancer, choreographer and scholar Dr Carol Brown and her Danish collaborator, architect and computer scientist Dr Mette Ramsgaard Thomsen, introduced additional research that added scope to the idea of performing in multiple dimensions. Brown and Ramsgaard introduced their Art-Science project 'The Changing Room' (2004)[17] as the exploration of 'a new digital ecology', where an anthropomorphic interest in the body in dance gave way to something that was more ecological in scope.[18] That research, Brown explained, involved looking at a number of somatic, movement and body awareness techniques such as Bartenieff,[19] Feldenkrais[20] and Rolfing[21] in relation to digital architectures in virtual environments. The intention, she added, was not one of mimesis, where the 'real' human body was reflected in its 'virtual' copy or vice versa, but rather the exploration of a third space, which she called a 'matrixial space of becoming' that linked the threshold of the dancer's skin with that of the digital realm.[22]

In short, Brown's and Ramsgaard's project attempted to connect different border spaces, which they hoped would affect quite different modes of being. The two researchers were intent on creating a digital morphology that was not mimetic of the human figure, but something which had its own movement logic, its own memories and with an ability to own its own being, so to speak. I found this approach to the dancing body and its interaction with technological space and a virtual reality quite fascinating, very much an experiment to explore the limits of the physical human self and a conceptual approach to notions of embodiment and disembodiment. Brown and Ramsgaard did not use these terms, but I personally saw their work in that light.

Their research process also generated an interesting movement vocabulary that reminded me of the somatic techniques that were so popular among a particular group of practitioners and a style of contemporary dance. Indeed, Brown said that her work drew on some of the techniques mentioned above, which all claimed to explore the myofascial level of attention she was investigating in her performance work. Brown claimed that the work attained a 'hybrid form where, in a sense, architecture became anthropomorphic and choreography architectonic', and where 'transdisciplinarity became transdimensionality'.[23]

I would be reminded of her and Ramsgaard's work when I started The Touched Project (2007–10), which was itself a development of ideas that emerged from a triad of short works: *Out of Body* (2002),[24] *Coloured Bodies* (2004) and *Skin* (2005)[25] (Figures 4.1–4.4). In these works, I was interested in the idea of the human skin as a border zone between the individual and the environment, between biology and technology, and between people whose skin colour was seen as a negative marker of identity. Like Brown, I was interested in exploring an ecology where the digital met the biological and enabled an extension of both in new dimensional forms. *Skin* was my own contribution to the Transnet conference.

Later that year, and quite to my surprise, the research on *Out of Body*, *Coloured Bodies* and *Skin*, which I presented at the Digital Cultures Symposium organized by Johannes Birringer[26] at Nottingham Trent University in the Fall of 2005, just

FIGURE 4.1: Henry Daniel, Courtney Bannon and Albert St Albert Smith in *Skin*.

FIGURE 4.2: Victor Ustarc in *Skin*.

after the Transnet conference, would be described as Afro-futuristic. In truth, I had never thought to label these works in that way, but it became clear to me later why others did so: a Black body performing ideas about the relationship between identity, technology, self and being was certainly suggestive of an 'afro-futurist' ideology. I saw numerous resonances between the work of the artists and scientists at Transnet and my own, but I had not consciously thought of my work in the way that many of them did. I was therefore able to learn a great deal just by recognizing the thematic and conceptual overlaps between my work and those of the Transnet presenters.

A third presentation by scientist, engineer, robotics and artificial intelligence researcher Dr Richard Vaughan addressed work he was doing in his autonomy lab at SFU. Vaughan claimed that the entire corpus of his work was based on a simple premise: that intelligence could be characterized as the effective use of resources. To achieve one's goals, one had to manage available resources to stated aims.[27] To demonstrate his point, he opened the presentation with a cartoon sketch of a robot setting out to do wonderful things in the world, with the caption 'I think! Therefore I am alive! Alive with life, and thought and mind! Sweet consciousness! And immortal soul [...]!'[28] The robot literally gets so wrapped up in its eagerness to explore the world that the electrical plug powering its systems becomes dislodged from the wall and it drops 'dead', so to speak.

Vaughan described his research as dealing with 'the behavioural ecology of synthetic systems', drawing attention to what he described as an interesting oxymoron in the term 'autonomous robot'. He argued that the term was oxymoronic in the sense that *autonomy* meant the ability to self-govern and the term *robot* meant the ability of a machine to automatically carry out specific instructions that it had been programmed to do. Thus, if the term behaviour is what a thing is programmed to do, and we equate the term autonomy with behaviour, were we not conflating two very different issues? At the same time, he pointed out that the behaviour of a rock, or a plant, a cat, or a child, or an adult, all involve quite different abilities, which ultimately depends on what these entities were designed to do, what materials they were made of and how they interacted with what was happening in the surrounding environment. Behaviour, then, was the interaction of all these things, together, and complex behaviour emerged from internal processes that governed things, actions and the environment that an entity found itself in. Therefore, the more complex the environment, the more complex behaviour that could emerge from the same simple programmed rules.[29]

Vaughan then went on to demonstrate how the robots he built, and the environments he constructed to test their behaviours, were able to produce complex and intelligent actions, even though the programmed rules within those machines were quite simple and mechanistic. The key issues for him were that a thing's behaviour is what it did, which, in turn, is determined by how it was constructed, the world it finds itself in, what internal processes are going on inside it and what external processes are taking place outside in the world. Behaviour, or the ability to perform, was the interaction of all these things.

What was most fascinating about this presentation was that Vaughan labelled these performances as *misbehaviour*, meaning that what emerged was not what was specifically programmed, but unintentional. In demonstrating such misbehaviour, he and his graduate student assistant Pouya Bastani put two robots with specially coded programs in the room, programs that allowed them to sense colour, space and direction. From these simple instructions and the observed behaviour of the robots, it soon became clear that there was not a one-to-one correspondence between Vaughan's intentions for the robots, the program that was written to generate their behaviours and what actually happened in the space between the two machines. In other words, unintended behaviour, or misbehaviour as he called it, was the result. The point here is that even with very simple programs, one could get a relatively complex set of behaviours, or artificially choreographed patterns that were determined by the robots themselves and within the limits of the prescribed space. And these patterns would change with each new placement of the robots and/or any obstruction that was introduced into the space.

This presentation not only raised the old issue of agency but also clearly explicated a definition of performance from Vaughan's multidisciplinary training in engineering, cognitive science, computing science and biology, using a transdisciplinary mode of thinking. That definition involved computation, complexity, efficiency and optimization. It also clearly pointed out to the conference audience the enormous difficulties involved in using the terms 'performance' and 'behaviour' in such different contexts. For example, the word *behaviour* is understood quite differently by ethologists in biology who observe animal populations, and by scientists in artificial intelligence research who manipulate code to generate actions in robots. This problem, ironically enough, is at the root of Performance Studies itself as a discipline that historically claims to study performance as behaviour in both human and non-human entities. But my own recognitive moment in Vaughan's talk was that the term 'machine' itself implied the realization of a limited set of behaviours, or, put another way, the ability to explore a limited set of actions that human beings themselves often do not go beyond. In this way, one can say that humans often do behave like machines, even though we are capable of much more than machinic behaviour. Hence, the question that Crick addressed in Chapter 3 returns here: what is agency but decision-making, and is this what we really mean by the concept of free will?

A fifth presentation introducing additional resonant issues was by Dr Stephen Braham,[30] a mathematician and black hole quantum mechanics physicist who worked in computer science and engineering for space exploration. At the time of Transnet, Braham was working on the Haughton-Mars project with NASA on Devon Island in the Canadian High Arctic to prepare for a Mars landing. This site apparently had a Mars-like terrain and Braham's scientific work involved learning to handle that type of geographic environment, as well as building and operating spacesuits, robots, vehicles and instruments for communication with the spacecraft. At the same time, he had to learn how to deal with various politicians, cabinet ministers, documentary film makers, journalists and popular media people who would often misunderstand precisely what the project work was and why the team had to do it there and in that particular manner. Braham titled his presentation 'Dressing up in funny clothes to perform well in engineering and to perform well for the public'.[31]

Since one of the main objectives of Transnet was to build bridges between two main categories of performance, namely, performance as human expression, and performance as the efficient, optimized and computationally complex capacities of technological systems, Braham's presentation was highly relevant in that his scientific work depended on the project's ability to attract billions of dollars of government and public money for space exploration while being accountable to the media and that same public for the spending of those monies. To do this, he and his colleagues had to juggle doing serious scientific work in a barren and hostile Arctic desert environment and communicating with a gaggle of international reporters who comprised almost half of the camp's seventy people. The point was that the scientists not only had to concentrate on doing serious science, they also had to 'dumb it down' to make it palatable for the popular media.

For example, a reporter would ask a scientist to perform a dangerous action several times in order to capture it for the camera – as if that scientist was an actor on a film set – while not fully comprehending the extent of the danger this created in the environment. The scientists had to perform for a public that was partly present, i.e. the reporters and their production teams, and partly absent, i.e. the end user watching a TV set or a cinema screen, or sitting in a government office trying to understand the socio-economic and political implications involved in such work. One could immediately see how important scientific information could become lost, distorted and/or completely misunderstood through this process. Braham's talk highlighted the challenges in living up to Century's principle of sharing knowledge in a transdisciplinary mode, through institutional commitments to develop art and technology and share power and control.

In addition, scientists are understandably sceptical about the ways artists and other humanities scholars interpret and present the results of scientific findings from a non-scientific perspective. For example, in *Fashionable Nonsense: Postmodern Intellectuals' Abuse of Science* (1998), Sokal and Bricmont argued that too many leading academics in philosophy, critical theory and the social sciences in general, use scientific terms incorrectly, and, in doing so, misrepresent some fundamental scientific issues. The challenge for artists like myself, as I see it, is to get to the core of an idea and then try to find ways to make a valid connection to one's own practice, the point being to establish useful lines of communication across domains. This is certainly not an easy task since some specificity is lost by moving information out of its disciplinary frame of reference. However, the point is that if we are truly interested in communicating knowledge that is useful to all, then that effort is surely needed. In fact, Braham confessed that in spite of the media team's methods of capturing what the scientific team was trying to accomplish in their Arctic camp, the resulting documentary film was able to present the essence of that work through a 'rearrangement of the facts, better than we could in a science journal'.[32] In short, the media was able to 'truthfully' communicate an overview of the work being done. The exact details of the scientific knowledge could then be left to the experts to decipher.

I was reminded at that point of a style of communicating information that occurs in Indigenous cultures, in ancient texts, and particularly in the African diasporic context that I am more familiar with. It involves a storyteller or writer speaking in parables. This style of narration is designed specifically to avoid misrepresentation and to compel the reader to think more carefully about the terms being used and their contexts. The narrative invites different levels of interpretation and it is up to the reader or listener to decipher the relevant information embedded in the story. If you get it right immediately, then great, but if not, the parable remains with you until the time is right for understanding.

Scientific and critical modes of writing and speaking are very different in that they try to be as exact as possible, in which case the reader or listener must be acquainted with the entire body of rules and terms of that discourse in order to understand what is being communicated. Little is left to the imagination, or to thinking and speaking as performative acts through which knowledge unfolds. In fact, the aim is precisely to leave the imagination out of the equation. And therein lies the problem: people from outside the particular discourse are prevented from accessing the information due to those disciplinary constructs, and hence 'outsiders' cannot benefit from the information that could be valuable for their own education. In order to decode that resource and translate the information into available knowledge, one must learn the entire vocabulary and terms of reference of that discourse. This not only facilitates the disconnection I spoke of earlier but it also functions as a means of preserving institutional power.

Directly after Braham's talk, a top female researcher in the Department of Molecular Biology and Biochemistry at Simon Fraser University made another unique presentation. Dr Fiona Brinkman, a specialist in pathogen bioinformatics and the development of tools to analyse human and microbe responses to infection, introduced herself by saying that one of the most important things that she did as a researcher was to 'talk to people in different areas in different disciplines and learn what they're doing'.[33] Brinkman confessed to being very excited whenever she found 'something that's applicable to [her] discipline that people haven't thought about before, in [that] discipline'.[34] Now this is someone who was hailed as 'a top young innovator' by the Innovation and Science Council of British Columbia in 2003, was a 2005 Canadian Who's Who, awarded the distinction of being a 'trail-blazer and trendsetter' by Canada's Women's Executive Network in 2009 and by 2018 had become a Fellow of the Royal Society of Canada for her ground-breaking research in biology. For me, Brinkman's attitude epitomized something that is integral to transdisciplinarity as a concept and a practice, namely, curiosity as a mode of investigation and of learning.

Brinkman opened her presentation 'The Dance Between Person and Pathogen' with a declaration claiming that the patterns created by interactions in nature at the molecular level were 'windows into inspiration'. The idea of pathogens performing a dance whose choreography was responsible for infectious diseases developing in the human body provoked much thought on my part, if only because it indicated that a reorganization of systems in the body at a molecular level fundamentally impacted an individual's health and hence their ability to use that body as a learning tool. What was also interesting about Brinkman's talk was that she introduced it by using terminology that suggested a symbiotic link between different disciplinary modes i.e. 'The Dance Between Person and Pathogen'. She followed this by introducing additional terms that could easily be used across disciplines, i.e. 'movement interaction', 'patterns', 'intertwined', 'collection' and 'networks', encouraging the listener to think across disciplines. She continued by introducing the larger context of her research as the fight between microscopic elements in an individual's body that influenced the person's health and well-being, thus demonstrating how delicate the balance between life and death is, proving how bacteria are either bad or good according to how they influence an individual's health, and confirming the unavoidable interplay between 'good' and 'bad' that is mediated by the knowledge and understanding of how these microscopic elements worked in the body's internal environment.

In response to questions about how the vast amount of data being generated by these studies was utilized, Brinkman confessed that biologists were getting increasingly overwhelmed by having to draw on other fields such as physics, mathematics and computer science to assist them in visualizing their data. At the same time, however, she welcomed the potential of using that data in a more immersive way where touch, hearing and other sensory modes could be utilized.

She maintained that there were important discoveries just waiting to be made in data that for the moment was 'just sitting there'.[35] In other words, the problem was getting the right teams of people to act together to address issues that were relevant to their own fields of research. In this last statement, Brinkman confirmed one of the fundamental tenets of transdisciplinarity, namely, the importance of specialists working in cross-disciplinary teams to get things done that no single individual could on their own.

Several experts in quite different disciplinary domains presented their views on performance as a transdisciplinary concept during the three days of the Transnet event, many of them alluding to the fact that valuable knowledge was 'just sitting there' because of an inability to connect bodies of information in a useful manner. This idea of potentially valuable research just waiting to be done was also mentioned in another talk, this time by Steven Brown, whose research involved what he saw as 'the neural, cognitive, anthropological and evolutionary aspects of the arts'. [36] Since Brown was also a classical pianist and an avid tango dancer, his talk on relationships between brain imaging technology and the performing arts, and specifically some of his motion studies work on foot rhythms in the tango, was a wonderful contribution to the discussion on transdisciplinarity as a mode of synthesizing different knowledge forms. The part of the talk that was most revealing and perhaps even disturbing to me, was a short narrative that he shared about a lecture he once gave on the topic of cogitation, which he explained as 'the use of neuroimaging technology to examine the neurocognitive mechanisms underlying artistic production and perception'.[37]

According to Brown, the artists in that particular audience were so interested in the scientific research involving brain scans that they began asking him a number of questions about their creative idiosyncrasies, or as he put it, 'their own unique brand of creativity'. These artists wanted to know why they were the way that they were. Unfortunately, he was unable to help them because, in his work, the important thing in doing these scans of target groups was to identify average behaviour patterns in large populations. In other words, individual behaviour was not that important, or as he described it, it was seen as 'noise' in the general pattern.[38] He then went on to say that research into 'the cognitive neuroscience of individual differences [had] yet to emerge'.[39] As shocked as I was to hear this, I was also inspired by the thought that this could become an important area of future Art-Science research. In fact, Brown's subsequent appointment at MacMaster University and his founding and direction of the NeuroArts Lab there, in conjunction with work being done at the Institute for Music and the Mind and The LIVELab, bore out some of that prescient thinking.

The speakers mentioned above form a mere snapshot of what took place in those three days of talks, scientific and artistic presentations and intense panel discussions. My intention here is primarily to foreground a recurring thematic that always emerges at these gatherings, namely, how experts coming from quite different disciplinary fields are able to make their work relevant to a wider transdisciplinary knowledge framework. Participants learned, first, how different concepts, strategies and investigative procedures applied in other disciplines could impact understanding in one's own field. Second, even though the terms used in another discipline may look and sound familiar, one needs to be careful to determine their specific meaning within the framework of that discipline. Third, it was clear that since different kinds of expertise are needed to flesh out and solve the deeper problems of transdisciplinary research, it is impossible to do that work alone. Lastly, and perhaps most importantly, it was clear that computational technologies, through the collection and analysis of data, could greatly assist in generating solutions, but only if one had regular and sustained access to such technologies.

The question of finding and assembling cross-disciplinary teams in an environment where existing administrative, disciplinary, institutional and political structures were not readily open to change was a difficult one to answer. What became clear to me was that a very different kind of laboratory would be needed to explore my questions and the collaborative projects I was interested in, and I was not sure that such a lab was even possible given my circumstances at the time.

Choreography as transdisciplinary PaR

> *I'm a committed scientist – a neuroscientist who studies the anatomy and function of the brain – and this fact has shaped the way I view behaviour, motivation, and morality for my entire adult life. In my mind, we are machines, albeit machines we don't understand all that well, and I have believed for decades that we have very little control over what we do and who we are. To me, nature (genetics) determines about 80 percent of our personality and behaviour, and nurture (how and in what environment we are raised) only 20 percent.*
>
> *[…]*
>
> *This is the way I have always thought about the brain and behaviour. But this understanding took a stinging, and rather embarrassing, blow starting about 2005, and I continue to reconcile my past belief with my present reality.*
>
> (Fallon 2013: 6–7)

These words are from James Fallon's *The Psychopath Inside* (2003), a fascinating explication of the debate regarding nature versus nurture in the wake of the author's surprising discovery of patterns in his own inherited mental maps. Briefly, Fallon's lab was conducting a study of brain scans of psychopathic murderers, amongst which were mixed scans of some of his own non-psychopathic family members. During that study, researchers discovered an alarming pattern in one of the 'control' scans of low brain function in certain parts of the frontal and temporal lobes, areas commonly associated with self-control and empathy. That scan was of Fallon's own brain. Further studies by him, and others, revealed that he possessed some of the same psychopathic tendencies that his research lab was studying in several criminals and serial murderers. However, for a set of very complex and interesting reasons, Fallon was not himself a criminal, or rather, through both nature and nurture, he had avoided such a fate. But the story is not that simple. Fallon came to understand, by facing some very difficult facts about himself, that he – and all of us – are (1) not simply products of biology, (2) that scientific empiricism can explain only so much as its existing investigative procedures will allow and (3) that particular lived experiences can present us with perplexing dilemmas that reveal the potential of human agency.

While Act II of this book began with a focus on Transnet and its invitation to several scientists and artists to present their work through the lens of performance as a transdisciplinary activity, several of those presentations exposed a set of questions about the nature of consciousness, human agency and knowledge of an individual self that needed further investigation. In many ways, Fallon's experience confirmed something I had been theorizing in my own work: his shock came through the recognition of something within him that, up to that point, was not consciously known but which had long been in the making, something which he unconsciously helped create; a third mediating position that brought with it new possibilities for understanding. Fallon called this the third leg of the stool, a reference to an experience of seeing his mother sitting on a three-legged stool in the garden as he was speaking to her about the tests that revealed his psychopathic characteristics. At that moment, Fallon recognized that it was her nurturing that had prevented him from becoming what his brain structure suggested would be his fate.

In saying that human beings were 'machines we don't understand all that well' (Fallon 2013: 6–7), and then finding out that he did have some agency to become more than a 'machine', or at least a more sophisticated machine with greater agency, the question of how to define precisely the limits of mechanical behaviour and what practices would allow one to act beyond those limits again arises. This question could be put another way: what can human beings do that the best, most sophisticated machines cannot? Fallon's 'reconciling' occurred when he realized that, perhaps unconsciously, he had been developing a new position on something he had previously taken an intractable stance on. One can argue that this was an act of human agency beyond machinic behaviour. After all, Fallon did admit to a history of being 'somewhat selfish', a 'class clown', 'catholic boy of the year', 'hot-headed', 'narcissistic', 'stand-offish', 'high aggression', 'low anxiety', 'care-free or careless', 'single-minded' and 'a booming libertarian'.[40] What this says to me is that *becoming* is a process of self-realization that can start by simply being curious about what surrounds us, even when we are not consciously following a path towards that larger goal. However, what it also says to me is that, once we recognize or remember a particular characteristic, we have an obligation to consciously pursue it to the next stage. This next stage involves re-tracing the steps taken to remember and formulating a coherent framework or theory of practice about the process.

Part of the aim of Transnet was to build on an established history of bringing scientists and artists together at SFU to create a unique research environment at that institution. This history had involved exploring the body in performance with new interactive technologies in virtual environments.[41] My own use of technology up to that point had been without the scientific and engineering expertise that Transnet was designed to attract. Some of these works were made prior to my arrival at SFU and others during my early tenure there. *NU* (1997),[42] *Octo15/97* (1997),[43] *Shango Meets Ogun* (1998), *Futurist Equation* (1999), *Relatively-Well-Centered* (2000),[44] *Out of Body* (2002),[45] *Coloured Bodies* (2004) and *Skin* (2005)[46] explored the varied cultural, psychological and geographical terrain that defines who we are as human beings performing various aspects of ourselves. *Skin,* my contribution to the Transnet conference, was my way of introducing an artistic perspective to Merleau-Ponty's idea that the body reveals itself to the world and to itself through the intersection of an outer tactile sensation and an inner kinaesthetic sensation mediated through the skin (Merleau-Ponty 1962). The version that was shown at Transnet was the third iteration of an ongoing thematic that began as a duet with myself and dancer Courtney Bannon, titled *Coloured Bodies* (2004). In a text created for *Skin* as a dance with six culturally diverse bodies, First Nations performer Lisa Ravensbergen (Figure 4.3) wrote about her own Canadian Indigenous/Settler context:

> I wonder at the skin you live in
> Wide and smooth
> Creases deepen as exhales
> Let me inside, breathe me in so our words, our looks, our touches fill and change
> Making us new
> Being who we are, forgetting who we are meant to be
> All because I believed – because I thought I understood
> It makes me hear the cry that I should be.
>
> (Lisa Ravensbergen)

FIGURE 4.3: Lisa Ravensbergen in *Skin*.

FIGURE 4.4: Courtney Bannon, Henry Daniel, Kyle Toy, Victor Ustare, Lisa Ravensbergen and Summer Thome in *Skin*.

Although *Skin* was not meant as a treatise on Art-Science research per se, it was presented within a forum that encouraged scientists to become familiar with the perspectives, working processes and scholarship of artists (dancers, choreographers, theatre makers, musicians, media artists, etc.) and eventually to collaborate with them on issues that could be mutually beneficial. The piece itself emerged from a teaching workshop with university colleagues Ken Newby and Alexandra Dulic, who at that point were working with a technology that allowed them to 'paint' live bodies on screens positioned above and behind the dancers in a performance space. The dancers were themselves raised on individual platforms during some sequences in the production (see Figure 4.4). The play between technology and ethnology is deliberate, for example, in how windows are literally opened up for discussions about race, nation, colour and gender through the electronic media and the diverse dancing bodies. Working in a country that has a long established policy of multiculturalism that continues to generate controversy, *Skin* showed how artists could engage with issues that were connected to social justice, economic development and ecological responsibility – the three so-called pillars of sustainable development – by simply staging themselves and their ideas in live performance contexts.

Of course, my goal was that future collaborations would go beyond the scientist's interest in the artist as a research subject or the artist's interest in using science as decoration (i.e., lovely images projected behind a dance). In my view, this limited kind of collaboration was not enough to sustain an Art-Science research project. *Skin,* however, drew attention to the richness as well as the challenges of staging these collaborations by utilising a multicultural and multidisciplinary cast of performers with First Nations, Chinese, Filipino, West Indian, European and White North American backgrounds into an environment where dance, music, video, theatre, media art and design, as well as computer programming were brought together. This certainly was an interdisciplinary and even a multidisciplinary collaboration, but, in my opinion, it needed further development to really address some of my transdisciplinary concerns. It was my hope that some of the conference participants would be interested in working with me in that direction.

Century's words regarding transdisciplinarity as a mode that begins wherever new institutions are formed to explore links between science, art and technology again came into view with respect to my goals. But even though I was interested in forming a 'new institution' that could explore collaborative, transdisciplinary projects (provisionally named TransCPT), I remember thinking that it was perhaps more important to create conditions that would result in the necessary 'overflow' that would generate real change. When Eric Kandel argued that science was 'no longer the exclusive domain of scientists' but something that had become 'an integral part of modern life and contemporary culture' (Kandel 2006: xiii), I believe he was extending an invitation to many of us to follow up on that claim. But although I support Kandel's position conceptually, I have doubts about how willing scientists are to venture beyond the boundaries of their disciplines. They would be moving outside a tightly institutionalized system that includes modes of publication, recognition in their field, economic, marketing and business links, and a whole set of other professional benefits that the arts normally cannot compete with. Comparatively speaking, the aim of Transnet was to explore, in conversation with scientists, creative and innovative ways of investigating the production, structuring, mobilization and integration of knowledge within society through dance and other performance activities. And in this it succeeded to a degree I was happy with.

There were significant short-term successes associated with the initiative as well as several long-term ones. Immediate benefits came from the shared knowledge and new collaborations that the event generated. The long-term benefits would become more apparent in the multi-year research projects undertaken in the decade that followed, even though some of these developed in unexpected ways. However, they would build on lessons learned from Transnet while creating their own new directions. The research lab TransCPT never materialized as intended, but a unique conceptual shift emerged with an identity of its own. Put simply, this would build on the idea that the environment we shared with other organic and non-organic systems and entities is itself a laboratory, and perhaps the best one available for such explorations.

NOTES

1. www.henrydaniel.ca/transnet.
2. https://static1.squarespace.com/static/51b3a0efe4b0de8ae9a666f9/t/529e79c2e4b074a-35de1719c/1386117570806/transnet.pdf.
3. Transdisciplinary Research Centre for Performance and Technology (TransCPT).
4. www.sshrc-crsh.gc.ca/funding-financement/programs-programmes/rdi-idr-eng.aspx
5. 22 March 2018 at Simon Fraser University's Goldcorp Centre for the Arts, Vancouver.
6. Continuing Dance Culture Dialogues, *38th Annual Conference of the Congress on Research in Dance*. https://kar.kent.ac.uk/60514/1/Vass-Rhee%202006%20Integrating%20Dance%20CORD%20proceedings.pdf.
7. See Chapter 3 'Will the artist please stand up?'.
8. www.henrydaniel.ca/transnet.
9. www.henrydaniel.ca/transnet.
10. Transnet video archive: Transnet 20050616, Day 1, Conference Tape 1 (Century, M).
11. Transnet video archive: Transnet 20050616, Day 1, Conference Tape 1 (Century, M).
12. Transnet video archive: Transnet 20050616, Day 1, Conference Tape 1 (Century, M).
13. Transnet video archive: Transnet 20050616 Day 1 Conference Tape 3 (Maboungou, Z).
14. Transnet video archive: Transnet 20050616 Day 1 Conference Tape 3 (Maboungou, Z).

15. Transnet video archive: Transnet 20050616 Day 1 Conference Tape 3 (Maboungou, Z).
16. Pearl Primus (1919–94) was a highly respected Caribbean-born American dancer, choreographer and scholar who worked in traditional African dance styles. She travelled widely through West Africa doing research on African dances, introducing many of them to American audiences.
17. www.kadk.dk/en/case/changing-room.
18. Transnet video archive: Transnet 20050616 Day 1 Workshop/Discussion Tape 5 (Brown, C. and Ramsgaard, M.).
19. Irmgard Bartenieff (1900–81) developed her own blend of movement analysis and physiotherapeutic principles after studying with the famous Austro-Hungarian dancer and movement theorist Rudolf Laban.
20. Moshé Feldenkrais (1904–84) was an Israeli movement therapist whose practice attempted to reorganize connections between the brain and body to improve individual health.
21. Ida Rolf (1896–1979) developed a practice called 'rolfing' that involved deep muscle therapy to supposedly realign the body's energy with the earth's gravitational field.
22. Ida Rolf (1896–1979) developed a practice called 'rolfing' that involved deep muscle therapy to supposedly realign the body's energy with the earth's gravitational field.
23. *The Changing Room* (2004) was produced by Carol Brown and Mette Ramsgaard Thomsen with computing scientist Bernard Buxton, www.vimeo.com/80265395.
24. www.henrydaniel.ca/performance-archive.
25. www.henrydaniel.ca/transnet.
26. Birringer was a friend, a key presenter, panelist and provocateur at the Transnet conference.
27. Transnet video archive: Transnet Conference 20050617 Day 2 Tape 3 (Vaughan, R.).
28. Transnet video archive: Transnet Conference 20050617 Day 2 Tape 3 (Vaughan, R.).
29. Transnet video archive: Transnet Conference 20050617 Day 2 Tape 3 (Vaughan, R.).
30. Transnet video archive: Transnet conference. 'Between Earth and Space: Performance in Space Exploration'.
31. Transnet video archive: Transnet conference. 'Between Earth and Space: Performance in Space Exploration'.
32. Transnet video archive: Transnet conference. 'Between Earth and Space: Performance in Space Exploration'.
33. Transnet video archive: 'The Dance Between Person and Pathogen'. Transnet.
34. Transnet video archive: 'The Dance Between Person and Pathogen'. Transnet.
35. Transnet video archive: 'The Dance Between Person and Pathogen'. Transnet.
36. Transnet video archive: 'Brain imaging technology and the performing arts: cogitation, inspiration, incorporation'. Transnet 20050617 Day 2 Conference Tape 1.
37. Transnet video archive: 'Brain imaging technology and the performing arts: cogitation, inspiration, incorporation'. Transnet 20050617 Day 2 Conference Tape 1.
38. Transnet video archive: 'Brain imaging technology and the performing arts: cogitation, inspiration, incorporation'. Transnet 20050617 Day 2 Conference Tape 1.

39. Transnet video archive: 'Brain imaging technology and the performing arts: cogitation, inspiration, incorporation'. Transnet 20050617 Day 2 Conference Tape 1.
40. These are terms that Fallon either uses to describe himself in the book, or are used in interviews with his family, friends and colleagues to describe him, terms that one could say align with psychopathic tendencies.
41. These research projects were headed by Thomas Calvert, then Professor of Computing and Engineering Science at SFU, who was responsible for a host of innovations in dance through the use of technologies by choreographer Merce Cunningham and his New York based Merce Cunningham Dance Company.
42. Premiered 16 January 1997. The Place Theatre in London.
43. The title of this work came from the date of the premiere, i.e., 15 October 1997 at the Watershed in Bristol.
44. Premiered 23 November 2000. SFU Mainstage, Burnaby.
45. Recorded live in Vancouver's CBC Studios on 21 March 2002.
46. Premiered 24–25 February 2005. Telus Theatre, Chan Centre for the Performing Arts, University of British Columbia.

5

New Performance Maps

The Touched Project: Organisation, control and emergence in choreographed performance systems

It became quite apparent after the Transnet gathering that it would be an immense challenge to acquire the material resources to achieve the project's long-term objectives of creating a transdisciplinary research lab, i.e. TransCPT. However, I was able to begin work on some of the research objectives almost immediately with a small SSHRC collaboration grant (Intelligent Dancing Machines 2006–07) with Dr Richard Vaughan, the roboticist who presented at Transnet, and Dr Ted Kirkpatrick, a colleague of Vaughan's working with human computing and haptic interfaces who also attended the event. The three of us would use this grant to do some initial experiments on mutual research interests. We began by arranging a small set of experiments in Vaughan's lab on the behavioural ecology of synthetic systems, using a new set of 'misbehaving' robots (Figure 5.2)[1] and Kirkpatrick's expertise in motion capture technology. The outcome of one of those experiments, *Intelligent Dancing Machines,* was staged at the IRMACS (Interdisciplinary Research in the Mathematical and Computational Sciences) Lecture Theatre at the SFU campus in Burnaby on 10 October 2007, with some of that research eventually making its way into The Touched Project.

Using real-time motion capture, haptics and robotics technologies, our objective was to see how far we could push the idea of a choreographic organism that featured humans and non-humans performing or 'misbehaving' together in a controlled space. Working with just myself as the dancer/choreographer improvising with several robots that were pre-programmed, we looked at what types of formations or choreographic patterns could emerge from different settings. We also examined the data from the motion-sensing technology for hints about what role the actions of the human and non-human agents were playing in the organization and reorganization of those patterns. What was particularly interesting for me was the feeling I got from interacting with these robotic partners. In a few words, it felt more like a mathematical exercise, and any attempt at 'humanising'

FIGURE 5.1: Scheherazaad Cooper and Lily Hsu in *Touched*.

the experience felt odd; it was as if I was a child playing with myself and my toys, trying to anthropomorphize them in some way. Nevertheless, the work with Kirkpatrick and Vaughan was so promising that when I was invited by engineers Dr Ivan Bajic and Dr Jie Liang to work on a new grant, I was extremely excited by the prospect of extending some of this work into a longer-term project.

Bajic's research specialty was in signal processing and machine learning and their applications in image and video processing, coding, communications and multimedia ergonomics, while Liang's was in image and video processing, computer vision and deep learning. We titled our grant application 'Video Coding and Processing for Improved Telepresence Experience in the Performing Arts' and invited Dr Peter Borwein as a Scientific Co-Investigator. Dr Borwein was a Professor of Mathematics and Burnaby Mountain Chair as well as Executive Director of the Centre for Interdisciplinary Research in the Mathematical and Computational Sciences. IRMACS was a unique, interdisciplinary research facility that we hoped to use as a base for some of our collaborative interactions because of its versatile, computationally sophisticated infrastructure that allowed scientists, whose primary laboratory tool is the computer, to work with artists, who needed their expert technical support and state-of-the-art computational, data storage, visualization and communication resources.[2] The application was successful, and The Touched Project was launched in 2007 with three years of joint funding from the Canada Council for the Arts and the National Science and Engineering Research Council (NSERC).

The key scientific objective of this second multi-year research project was to create new tools for a networked dance performance in a *telepresence* environment, which included: 3D video acquisition and compression and interactive 3D display, which could also be utilized in broader settings such as teleconferencing, gaming, TeleHealth, connecting communities, education, surveillance, sightseeing and sports. Since Vaughan and Kirkpatrick had played such an influential role in the early post-Transnet experiments, I felt it was only fair to first recognize and then incorporate their ideas, scientific expertise and technologies into The Touched Project; at least in the initial transitional stage. Thinking back to Ganesh's challenge to the artist to forego using science as a decoration, Vass-Rhee's accusation of the artist's fetishization of scientific discourse, and Barad's claim of unsatisfactory understandings by those trying to apply scientific findings outside the initial context of the research, I felt an urgent need to find an overarching artistic concept that could do justice to the project as a whole. I also felt the need to investigate that overlap or the connective links between performance as human expression, and performance as the efficient, optimized and computationally complex capacities of technological systems.

Given that the idea of *presence* was such a key issue in virtually all live and mediated performance practices, regardless of the discipline (Noë 2012), I suggested this to the scientists as an option. However, to the engineering mind, this seemed a bit too philosophical; my collaborators were more interested in building systems that worked or could work given the time we had to develop and test them. After a great deal more thought, I decided that the terms *organization, control* and *emergence* provided more choreographic scope and fitted quite well with some of the ideas introduced in Transnet. And since these were terms that had a very specific historical contextualization in science,[3] they could easily be applied to the scientific investigations with Vaughan and Kirkpatrick.

The next step was to find a creative connection between the notion of presence and the themes of organization, control and emergence. Since I would be working with dancers and semiautonomous robotic systems as co-performers in a constructed environment, I needed an artistic focus that could accommodate the complexity we would be dealing with. Two popular images came to mind; the first was a detail from Michelangelo's fresco on the ceiling of the Sistine Chapel – *The Hands of God and Adam* (Michelangelo 1508–12) and the second was the previously mentioned dancing form of Lord Shiva in the *Nataraj* (tenth century CE). The fact that these two images were laden with cultural, religious and philosophical meanings, all related to power and control, but were also linked to different dance, performance and cultural traditions, was an important point for me. In this way, I was able to add the element of a higher power, i.e. the cosmological or 'godly' in Shiva, to balance the performance of human beings and complex technological systems.

Michaelango's *The Hands of God and Adam* symbolized the transference of the spark of consciousness from the divine to the human in the Christian religious tradition, while Shiva focused on a key figure in Hindu religion and philosophy that represented the source of all movement in the cosmos. Shiva, the Master of

Dance, was responsible for bringing the world into existence, maintaining it and then destroying it through his – and in our case her – movements (Figure 5.2). Since notions of agency and control were so central to both these images, a conscious decision was made to focus on the conceptual dimensions they alluded to, i.e. that of the divine, the human and the non-human, the last represented by the semi-autonomous robotic systems we were using. The strategy became one of exploring the issue of control in systems, both human and technological, and to investigate how complexity, self-organization and emergence were central to both organic and non-organic systems. The first product of our collaborative efforts was the performance work *Touched* (2008).[4] Figure 5.2 features Scheherazaad Cooper as Shiva, and two images of Lily Hsu – facing her as well as facing away from her – as Shiva's human avatar.

Touched

To satisfy the demands of the scientific research – and to explore the nuanced links between presence and telepresence and between control, complexity,

FIGURE 5.2: Jeanette Kotowich and Cast in *Touched*.

self-organization and emergence at practical, conceptual, scientific and artistic levels – several performance events were staged in different locations across the city of Vancouver. Since control, complexity, self-organisation and emergence had long driven research on the behaviour of systems in the sciences (Nicolis and Prigogine 1977; Prigogine and Stengers 1984), I was convinced that these ideas would be relevant to an investigation of choreography as both an organizing system and as a mapping device for every action that took place within that system as well as its interaction with the external environment. As far as we were aware, few people in dance were doing this type of research at the time.

Of course, the notion of presence has always been a contentious theme in the theatre world. Theatre and media scholar Philip Auslander, for example, devoted an entire volume to exploring the idea of 'liveness' in the context of new digital media presentations (2008b),[5] which, I would argue, is intimately linked with the idea of 'presence' in performance. Auslander even argued that the very concept of 'liveness' irrevocably changes with the advent of new technologies and that it now shares a platform with the term 'mediatized'. The Touched Project was, as a whole, more interested in expanding the use of the term 'presence' beyond liveness and mediatization. I was interested in creating a connection to the Futurist idea of simultaneity as a non-linear approach to time and space and the practice of juggling multiple domains and personalities with the notion of a fractured self that had a distributed presence in multiple locations.

The reader might remember the claim that dancer/choreographer/writer Zab Maboungou made about complex polyphonic rhythms that had the capacity to free the body from the constraints of a limited earthly existence. The question here was how could a choreographic work featuring robotic systems, electronic sound manipulated in an interactive context and sensor-driven motion-capture technology support such an argument? And how could one inspire an audience to imagine that they were truly experiencing being simultaneously located in different space/times beyond a video transaction? With *Touched*, I was also interested in what an audience could experience anew when they had some knowledge of these two popular images and the complex cultural, religious and philosophical systems they were part of. In Figure 5.2, one can see the sixteen small robots – whose programmed patterns the dancers learnt, and on which a basic choreographic script was built – that were let loose in a space with other interactive sound and moving image technologies. In the spirit of Vaughan's Transnet presentation, the goal was to generate and identify emergent forms through an improvisational process that could not be achieved in a more traditional performance context, even as we tried to control or limit the movements of the robots to the parameters of the performance space. The challenge was also to maintain the rehearsal's immediacy, liveness and presence during the subsequent live performance when the dancers

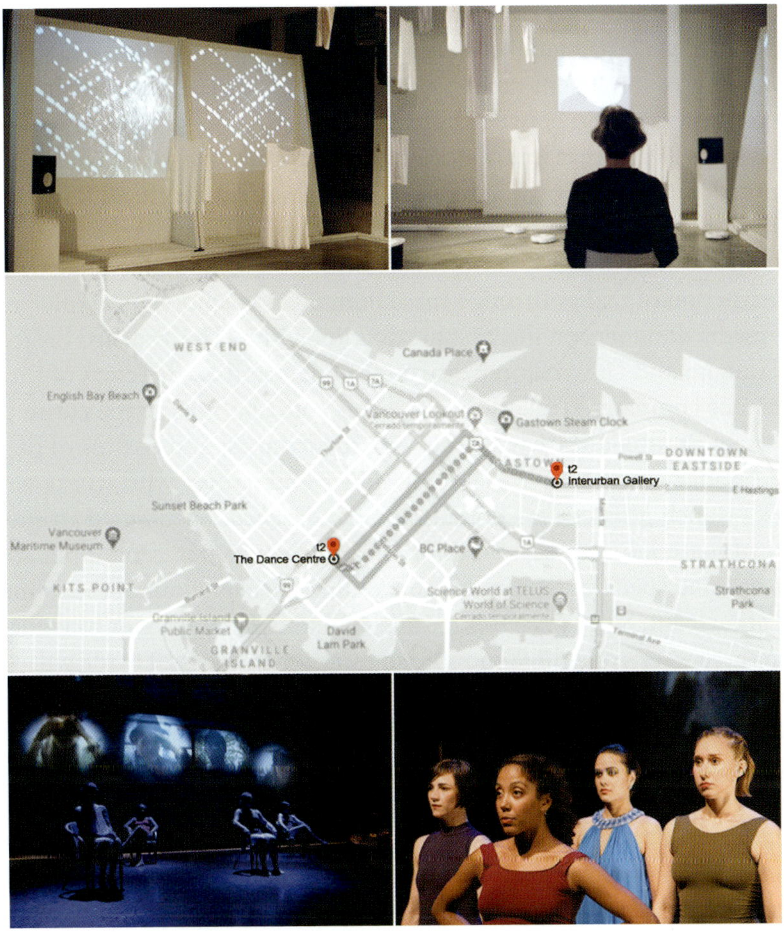

FIGURE 5.3: Brenna McLaud, Livona Ellis, Scheherazaad Cooper and Olivia Shaffer in *t2*.

knew much of what to expect, though they did not know how far the robotic movement script would interrupt, disrupt or disorganize the fixed choreography. As the larger Touched Project progressed and new scenarios became apparent, we challenged ourselves to hold simultaneous performances with separate audiences in different locations across downtown Vancouver, connected through Internet links.

Since the term telepresence itself refers to the experience of being fully present at a live real-world location remote from one's own physical location, we created a set of unique performance environments that would suggest the theatrical notion of multiple presences, geographical as well as psychological. In creating this kind of content, The Touched Project generated some quite unexpected results, not least of all the notion of separate bodies together creating a dynamic but at times invisible and complex set of communicative maps. Each individual work created within the project contributed to a larger 'choreographic organism' where the body functioned as an intelligent medium that received, processed, transformed and transmitted information between humans, the natural environment and technological systems. How that information was interpreted by an audience depended to a great extent on their own imagination. And since we were all aware that the act of perception influences reality (Chopra et al. 2017),[6] *Touched* provided an opportunity for researchers, performers and the viewing public alike to witness the construction of reality through these human and technological interactions.

The media designers on this first production within The Touched Project were Marc Coniglio and Dawn Stoppiello, co-founders and co-directors of the media performance company Troika Ranch.[7] Their contributions to the entire process were very substantial; Marc is a composer, media-artist and creator of the media software Isadora, and Dawn a choreographer and dancer who works with him on Troika Ranch projects. In choreographing *Touched,* I generated an enormous amount of material from several improvisation scores based on input from the performers, and specific instructions concerning the behaviour of the robots from the scientific team. Since my Troika Ranch collaborators were only available for the final three weeks of a three-month semester-long process, I made video files of our rehearsals available to them on a private online site to keep them abreast of developments. For one reason or another – mainly time constraints – they never viewed these files. Hence, when they finally arrived in Vancouver, they knew nothing of what had transpired in the preceding two months. To bring them up to date, I decided to adopt an unusual strategy. I handed them the entire corpus of material I had worked on with my dancers for the past two months, with the instruction to reorganize fifteen minutes of that material for a public preview of work-in-progress. This material consisted of almost an hour of my choreographic investigations.

I remember very clearly Stoppiello's delight when she received the material, mischievously explaining to me a process used by New York choreographer Susan Rethorst. Apparently, Rethorst would invite trusted friends over to her studio to 'wreck' the dance that she had just choreographed.[8] I thought that this was a rather risky thing to do with two people I barely knew. In fact, most choreographers would never hand over their work to another choreographer to quietly witness it being wrecked. However, I believed that the idea was a sound one in the context of the type of research I was doing and my intended outcomes. To have the opportunity to introduce an external, disorderly element into a system that had already attained some degree of equilibrium was a kind of research gift. Also, given the time constraint, I felt it was necessary to invite these two 'outsiders' into the process and allow them to gain their own perspective on what was already constructed, independent of my own interference. This process of re-organisation lasted a full week, at the end of which we presented *Touched* as a work-in-progress at the international Body Spaces: Corporeal Topographies in Literature, Theatre, Dance and the Visual Arts 2008 conference.[9] Following this preview, we returned to the studio to reconstruct the deconstructed choreography, a process that involved revisiting material that had been discarded and explaining the intent behind its creation as well as creating new material with the expertise that Coniglio and Stoppiello and the rest of the research team possessed. This new dramaturgical approach meant that some new agendas had to be worked out. What emerged at the premiere just over two weeks later was an entirely new choreographic organism that featured its own set of surprises.[10]

The entire process of creating *Touched* revealed the kinds of concessions artists and scientists must make if they are truly interested in a more expansive type of collaborative process across disciplinary lines. Everyone had to rein in some aspect of their egos, which is not easy in an environment where artistic and scientific collaborators already have highly successful careers and do not need to prove themselves. These individuals must also be open to things that were not planned, to accommodate ideas that they might not have had or pursued on their own, as well as pursue those unplanned or undesirable possibilities as emergent concepts. *Touched* was the first work that emerged within the Touched Project. Four others followed: *t2*, *t2_echo*, *Imprint* and *Imprint II*, with the short documentary film *Beyond Boxes* (2011)[11] completing the series. Bajic, Liang, Vaughan, Kirkpatrick and myself worked on the first two, and the base research team of Bajic and Liang and myself with other invited guest artists on the final two. All five works explored notions of presence, complexity, self-organisation and emergence in choreographic systems, each having a different approach to the thematic.[12]

t2

t2 (2009)[13] introduced the fully built 'computerised brains' that were intended for *Touched*, but which could not be completed for the premiere of that first work. In Figures 5.3–5.5, one can get a sense of what the interacting bodies and the technologies in the different spaces looked like. The work took its audience virtually from one location in the city to another, with two of the dancers physically changing locations during a single performance, demonstrating to the audience that the two spaces and the people in them were performing live and that these audiences were not viewing some pre-recorded video event.

The two locations were the Interurban Gallery (Figure 5.3), an old tram relay station on the Downtown East Side of Vancouver that was converted into a

FIGURE 5.4: Chengxin Wei in *t2*.

FIGURE 5.5: Livona Ellis, Scheherazaad Cooper, Chengxin Wei, Olivia Shaffer and Neelamjit Dhillon in *t2*.

volunteer-based community art space, and the Scotia Bank Dance Centre (Figures 5.3–5.5), a renovated commercial structure that became a prominent centre for contemporary dance in Vancouver. Like so many other cities, the terms 'uptown' and 'downtown' were loaded with economic, political, socio-cultural and aesthetic implications. In Vancouver, the Downtown East Side (DTES) neighbourhood currently has a high degree of homelessness and drug use, and the Interurban Gallery was designed to 'engage the community in a welcoming and inclusive live art space and to increase cultural tenure for those who have been rejected at the entrance of most galleries in the city'.[14] The Dance Centre, on the other hand, is a space where one could find much of Vancouver's professional dance community at work; the Centre's stated goal being one of supporting 'the development of a vibrant dance scene in BC' and increasing the profile of dance 'by providing resources and services for the dance profession [and] presenting public performances and events'. All of this while operating as 'one of Canada's flagship dance facilities'.[15]

I think the differences between the roles of both institutions are clear – their goals, how they locate themselves in a community and the histories associated with the buildings they occupied. Part of my reason for choosing these sites, therefore, was not just availability, but also my interest in seeing how audiences in both locations would respond to the work I was presenting. What I had not given much thought to was how working in these two locations would affect my own behaviour. To begin with, the difference in locations visibly affected the way I moved through the surrounding spaces and interacted with the people reminded me of the vastly different environments I worked in, from small inadequately equipped halls in small villages with their unsophisticated audiences to technologically advanced international stages in large cities with extremely rich patrons. The local community in the DTES was quite varied, but the area also had a dense population of poor, homeless and drug-addicted individuals whose presence gave a distinct – and for non-residents – a discomforting feeling. In many ways, I quickly adapted to the pace of those who were 'native' to the area, the manner in which they moved about the streets, the spaces that were available or unavailable to me, while trying to be as inconspicuous as possible. Fitting in was not easy at first, but as someone who had experienced similar locations in many different countries, I quickly adapted to it.

The uptown environment of the Dance Centre was also quite varied but clearly different from the Interurban Gallery in several ways. One could say its patrons were more discerning as far as exposure to the arts was concerned. In fact, a couple of 'unusual guests' I invited from the DTES felt extremely uncomfortable entering the Dance Centre, as did those who saw them and considered them completely out of place. At the Interurban, there was no formal seating for the audience so those who saw the show did so from the street. At this downtown location, audiences saw a solo male dancer in skin coloured 'tights' performing in a gallery space while interacting with media images from another performance that was obviously taking place in a different location. This must have been quite a sight in the early evening. After completing his performance, the dancer got dressed and headed uptown on foot. A few minutes after his departure, a single costumed female dancer arrived in a taxi and started another solo performance in the space. After her dance, she also returned to the uptown location. As far as the downtown audience was concerned, the two locations were obviously linked to each other and to the people in the projected media images inside the building, but how and why must have been a question for some. To complicate matters, this passer-by audience could sometimes see themselves in the performance space inside because of the camera installed on the outside of the Interurban Gallery building. They were part of the event, but they did not know why. As far as they were concerned, it could well have been some sort of sophisticated surveillance strategy.

During the entire sequence of events, audiences in both locations could see – in a technologically mediated way – what was taking place in both spaces as well as what took place on the journey between them via the live video feed. However, after the live performance was over, both audiences were invited to enter the downtown space and to share opinions on the relevance of what they previously witnessed. The effect of this dramaturgy was that the uptown audience experienced a somewhat typical live, mediated and relatively continuous performance, while the downtown audience experienced something like a discontinuous live art or performance art installation. The uptown audience had a single evening event with the option to visit the downtown location in the days afterward, while the downtown audience experienced some aspects of that uptown event in addition to interactive media and movement material created specifically for the downtown space. The Interurban live-art video art installation ran for just under two weeks while the Dance Centre event lasted two evenings (11–12 July 2009). In the gallery, a complex *mise-en-scène* included additional robotic technologies, cameras capturing and manipulating their movements, the dancers' costumes hanging in the space and specially created videos of these dancers moving on the constructed screens. Figures 5.3 and 5.4 show the scenes from the two locations and a small map of the areas in a single image.

The amount of work done in *t2* was tremendous, and the lessons learned about how one could engage with notions of presence and telepresence no less so. Also, how complexity, self-organisation and emergence could open up entirely new dimensions of creative work in dance encouraged me to explore these ideas in additional spaces. Judging from the people I was able to speak to in both locations, it appeared that the unusual nature of the performances was precisely their attraction. The issue of meaning or what the underlying narrative was seemed less important to the audience; they made their own connections and assumptions. As far as they were concerned, it was a live event designed to make them aware of creative possibilities for dance and new media, and there was in it a transparency that both 'located' and 'dislocated', as well as 'oriented' and 'disoriented' them. They saw familiar and unfamiliar events inside as well as outside buildings they were familiar with, but which gave them a new perspective on the locations as well as the buildings themselves. Was this what the Futurists were thinking of with their concept of *simultaneity*?

t2_echo

I was soon able to mount another production with four dancers, a violinist and a media designer when I was invited to present some of my research at the 'Interactive Futures '09 Stereo'[16] conference at the old Emily Carr University of Art and Design (ECUAD) Granville Island location. I welcomed this opportunity to work briefly with the guest media designer Christian Ziegler and violinist Julie Sun Lee in a compartmentalized gallery space where the audience could sit or stand wherever they wanted throughout the performance, but also to utilize a more traditional performance space in the same building on a different floor where a different audience could sit. The Interactive Futures '09 Stereo conference event was advertised as follows:

> The word 'stereo' usually refers to two-channel sound or stereoscopic 3D. For IF'09: Stereo, we are showcasing work and research that specifically experiments with the perceptual event that occurs from symmetrical sources (2 eyes, 2 ears, 2 data streams). IF'09: Stereo has invited media artists, designers, researchers and filmmakers experimenting with: stereographic projection; illusionary sound and vision; and methods of co-location (ways of simultaneously mapping and representing more than one location).[17]

The way the spaces were set up at ECUAD presented an interesting challenge; dancers were able to communicate with each other (1) by being fully visible to each other in the same space, (2) by being in the same space but only partially visible to each other and (3) and by being in completely different spaces but able to see some version of each other virtually (Figure 5.6–5.7). *t2_echo* (2009)[18] was therefore a continuation of my experiments to explore complementary and contradictory actions within a Futurist-style drama that took place in different locations within a single building or different but related events in separate spaces.

FIGURE 5.6: Chengxin Wei, Tara Dyberg, Brenna McLaud and Donald Taruc in *t2_echo*.

FIGURE 5.7: Chengxin Wei, Tara Dyberg, Donald Taruc and Brenna McLaud in *t2_echo*.

However, *t2_echo* was nowhere as dramatic as any of Marinetti's works,[19] or my own *Futurist Equation* (1999). This experimental performance could be seen as tame in comparison; conceived as a minor expression of simultaneous events in human life within a fast-developing West Coast city. The dancers and musicians in *t2_echo* constantly changed locations and costumes during the 40-minute performance, with the art works in the gallery as their backdrop, and with the images of their fellow dancers in other spaces. Here the term 'echo' was more about how the dancers used the movement vocabulary in both spaces and how the technology was able to accentuate the movements resonance, i.e. speed up, slow down, multiply, discolour or simply 'drag' the images. *t2_echo* drew on both modernist and post-modernist aesthetic dimensions in its statement about the influence of new digital technologies on the process of live art making. What became clear to me as the choreographer was how an entire process, and a sense of meaning, could be disrupted by certain staging decisions and particular dramaturgical choices. This insight would prompt me to shift directions with respect to the content of my next two works on the project, *Imprint* (2010)[20] and *Imprint II* (2010).[21]

Imprint

The first of these next productions, *Imprint* (2010), was an interdisciplinary work created for a Celebration of Creativity and launch of the new Museum of Anthropology (MoA) at the University of British Columbia in 2010 (Figures 5.8–5.11). The second, *Imprint II* (2010), the concluding work of the series, was a site-specific work for dancers, large music ensemble and telepresence technology that explored the resonance of cultural artefacts and stories as transmitted from place to place, time to time and person to person. *Imprint II* involved a complex collaborative process between MoA curator Jill Baird, Gwawaenuk First Nation Chief Robert Joseph, First Nations carver/artist/singer and dancer William Wasdan, and the Turning Point Ensemble, a music ensemble directed by my colleague Professor Owen Underhill. *Imprint* responded to and extrapolated on Kwak'wala language and Kwakwaka'wakw artwork – as well as other First Nations artworks – that resided in the public gallery and private archives at MoA as the performers tried to re-articulate the space with new music, dance and telepresence technologies (Figures 5.8–5.11).

The creative process for *Imprint* had some interesting ethical challenges. In a part of the country where no treaties were signed regarding the ownership of land, and with a people who suffered decades of exploitation, abuse and denigration by European settler colonizers, the issue of who is allowed to present or attempt to re-articulate the museum setting of First Nations artworks, and hence

FIGURE 5.8: Chief William Wasden, Henry Daniel and Chief Robert Joseph in *Imprint*.

FIGURE 5.9: William Wasden, Brenna McLaud and Henry Daniel in *Imprint*.

its relevance to a contemporary society was a very sensitive one. For example, Chief Robert Joseph, a leading voice and hereditary chief of the Gwawaenuk First Nation in BC, and the founder, with his daughter Karen, of Reconciliation Canada, was quite sceptical of the attempts by two non-Indigenous artists, Owen

FIGURE 5.10: Tara Dyberg in *Imprint*.

FIGURE 5.11: Tara Dyberg, Thoenn Glover, Brenna McLaud and Michelle Cheung; Henry Daniel and Tara Dyberg in *Imprint*.

Underhill and myself, to 'introduce' the complex works on display in the Museum of Anthropology in a technologically mediated setting.

In fact, we had to convince him that our intention was not to represent what was there, but to demonstrate our appreciation for being allowed to share the lands that these cultures had shaped; lands that were taken from his Indigenous ancestors so many years before. In my case, the intention was to try to understand precisely what the artefacts in the Museum of Anthropology meant, as I attempted to choreograph and dance with a group of other 'alien' bodies around them (Burt 1998). In short, my research question was; how can a body sense the information in these artifacts, the people who made them, and the lands they occupied for thousands of years?

To be able to understand, in an embodied manner, the nature of these artefacts, I felt I had to be with them in different modes of performance. Hence, with the permission of the curator, the dancers and I were able to gain access to the space after hours when no one was there, both at night and during daylight hours, outside as well as inside the various collections and the building itself. In fact, I would spend hours walking the area just thinking about how that land, and the people who occupied it, may have looked so many years ago.

As I was going through these actions, I clearly remembered a conversation I had with an Indigenous artist who recommended that I read the publication *Feasting with Cannibals* (Walens 1981) to get a more informed perspective on the Northwest Coast Indigenous cultures. This book explained a great deal about how coastal Indigenous peoples viewed their relationship to the land, and to the visible and invisible beings that shared it with them. Some of that information resonated with another knowledge system I encountered on my first extended stay in Germany in 1980.[22] Both stressed the importance of a reciprocal 'feeding' between human beings, organic life and something that was higher than both on the scale of being. These teachings also stressed that such processes were crucial for the balance between these different worlds and the forms of life that existed within them.

Also, in both knowledge systems, the role of human beings was to help maintain the existence of the phenomenal world through their awareness and affirmation of it. In this way, the everyday human 'self' sustained a higher level of consciousness, and impressions were the nourishment for these 'higher' forms just as food, water and air were for 'lower' forms (Ouspensky 1983: 186–94). I took these teachings to mean that impressions, generated through a conscious awareness of the world around us, were as important for the existence of our creative life as food, air and water were to our physical bodies.[23]

Many of the images we found in the Museum of Anthropology were symbolic mouths of creatures carved into huge totem poles or represented as individual art works. Taking care of the land and its produce, killing animals for food and eating the products of the land where more than survival strategies, they were fundamental ritual forms that celebrated being part of a larger whole and contributing to a balanced maintenance of that whole. This was all done in the full knowledge that, at some point, one would have to sacrifice oneself to that larger entity to fully become an enduring part of it. I did not hesitate to use these images of an all-consuming mouth in *Imprint II*, which followed the MoA production.

At the premiere of *Imprint,* I remember quite vividly the power of Indigenous ritual performance when chief Joseph, in full regalia, did a short welcoming dance for the audience. I also remembered why I insisted that chief Wasden take part in the formal choreography I created for the other four dancers and myself. I believe that both these chiefs eventually recognized the sincerity of our intentions in trying to understand and pay our respects to their cultural traditions. These experiences – particular the ones that informed my understanding of the relationship between ethics and aesthetics in different cultural contexts, the role of the individual within a larger group or system and the nature of communication between different levels within any system – would become important in staging the final work of the series.

Imprint II

Imprint II (2010)[24] was part of an inaugural set of events to celebrate the opening of the new School for the Contemporary Arts (SCA) in the DTES (Downtown East Side), a part of the city that had an unenviable reputation for economic and social despair, drugs, prostitution, homelessness and mental illness, but which was slowly being transformed by a process of gentrification. Therefore, this work took some of that thematic into consideration during the creative process. The DTES was once a thriving cultural and economic centre in Vancouver, and perhaps, hundreds as well as thousands of years before that, a place where Indigenous tribes lived, exchanging gifts and other cultural artefacts with other groups along the extensive west coast and inland territories. The descendants of these same Indigenous peoples formed a substantial part of the destitute ones living in this area: the mentally ill, the addicts, the homeless, the prostitutes and the ones in economic and social despair. Although *Imprint II* could not and was not in any way an attempt to represent this situation, it was made in full knowledge that this was the larger background on which our performances were being staged.

Touched and *Imprint II* were definitely the two most complex works in The Touched Project in terms of their production values. They were also created before and after a move by SFU's School for Contemporary Arts (SCA) into a downtown location, a newly renovated state-of-the-art building just three city blocks away from the community gallery where the *t2* live art/performance art installation had taken place. *Imprint II* incorporated several texts from the performers as well as photo and video images referencing the area that the SCA sought to embed itself in. I was also able to engage a number of artist/researchers who had contributed to the earlier works and to consolidate many of the ideas proposed at the Transnet event five years earlier. Arguably, my approach to this endeavour could be summed up by the statement that complexity, self-organization and emergence were not only inherent in the evolutionary processes of nature and fundamental to how individuals and societies function but could also assist in the creation of complex choreographic works. My hope was that we could provoke some reconfiguration of settler cortical maps during these performance works with an awareness of those who occupied and tended the lands thousands of years ago as well as in recent times, and with knowledge of the inequitable appropriation of those lands. Too many cortical links had become disorganized through the settler/colonizing process and far too many of the native population seemed lost as they wandered through the spaces of the city (Brand 2001).

I chose to stage *Imprint II* as a dance performance as well as a live art installation. When the audience entered the building where the theatre was located[25] prior to the 8:00 p.m. show time, they encountered a live art/performance art installation in the Audain Gallery on the ground floor. A cast of seven performers occupied the space, five against the walls and two within and upon a box in the centre. Just before 8 p.m., the five performers seated against the walls would leave the space, one by one, to go two floors down to the Fei and Milton Wong Theatre where the live performance was to take place. The two centrally located dancers remained in the gallery. Audience members collected their tickets at the box office and observed the action in the Audain Gallery space, then proceeded to the theatre for the scheduled stage performance. As the house lights went down, they became aware that the five performers on stage, each in one of the additional five boxes, were the same ones they had encountered in the gallery, but who had left, one by one to go to this new location. The audience also became aware that video images projected onto these additional boxes were of the two dancers who remained in the gallery (Figure 5.12). There was therefore no doubt that this was a live interactive event taking place between the two spaces.

A few moments after the lights dimmed, the audience also became aware that a sixth performer had entered the space (making a total of eight performers altogether) in 'street clothes' that were markedly different from the other performers' costumes (Figure 5.13). As the performance progressed, it became clear that some form of separation or forgetting of identities had taken place and the unfolding choreography was a tacit remembering of a previous state of unity. This unfolding was also taking place through a strategic rearrangement of the set design and

FIGURE 5.12: Samantha Jane-Gray, Felicia Lau and Cai Glover in *Imprint II*.

FIGURE 5.13: Felicia Lau, Matthew Waldie and Owen Underhill and The Turning Point Ensemble in *Imprint II*.

the placement of the musicians' bodies, as well as through costume changes by the performers in the boxes and encounters with the newly introduced sixth performer. At different times in the choreography, the two remaining dancers from the gallery would enter the theatre space, the first wearing an outfit similar to the everyday clothes that the other dancers had, in the meantime, changed into (Figure 5.14). The second dancer, who never changed her initial costume, would enter the space in the final minutes of the hour-long production, after the rest of the cast had changed back into their initial costumes from the beginning of the show.

The same construct also played out in the music, which began with only the conductor onstage directing a small section of the orchestra located in the lighting gallery high above the audience. These musicians were later integrated into the full ensemble, who were initially offstage, but later came onstage to join the conductor. With the audience seated on three sides of the performance space and the orchestra completing the square on the fourth, performers and audience had the feeling of being enclosed by or enclosing the action. One could say that the choreography was composed of an intact group of eight performers who had willingly separated from their group to fulfil some sort of task, who forgot what the task was on separation, but who later reunited after remembering a previous state.

Imprint II was about remembering and recognizing what was once an original unity. It was a conceptual depiction of aspects of a united self, consciously separating and later reuniting, thus remembering a previous state that was physically, psychologically and geographically located. The work was able to achieve different degrees of success; those controlling the action from off-stage, i.e. the media artists and scientists were thrilled that the technologies worked and that audiences were enthusiastic about what they had seen. The performers on-stage felt that they had created a temporary community during the entire staging process. The

FIGURE 5.14: Samantha Jane-Gray and cast with The Turning Point Ensemble in *Imprint II*.

dance audiences were surprised to see the range of technologies in dialogue with traditional cultural beliefs and the scenographic staging within a contemporary dance context, even though many were unaware of exactly how and what types of technologies were being used. As to what it all meant, there were several different interpretations that included a melding of modern and ancient rituals to how one discovers oneself within an existing community.

Like *t2* and *t2_echo*, many enjoyed the multi-sensory media experience of the event and felt that it was very much in the realm of the 'experimental' or the 'post-modern'. All in all, the project bore out my suspicions that in a transdisciplinary project, not everyone might recognize the different levels of information available and be curious enough to enquire further about what they had witnessed. Nevertheless, I found that those who were curious enough to open themselves to the information that was available were able to make a great deal of sense of the intention behind the work and to enquire further about it.

Embodied choreographic knowing

Embodied choreographic knowing can be described as a state that choreographers try to inspire in audiences witnessing their works. After an intense process where the material is developed with a cast of performers and collaborators, where a great deal of observation and assessment of that material takes place over many rehearsals and where decisions are made based on what the team sees, intuits or anticipates happening, the hope is that individual audience members have an embodied experience of the performers' intentions. If movement is the process of a single thought or several thoughts unfolding, then that unfolding generates numerous kinaesthetic, emotional, mental and psychological states in the bodies it encounters. The requirements for embodied knowing are fulfilled through these acts of performance and/or 'co-performative witnessing' (Conquergood 1985; Madison 2007) that involve what D. Soyini Madison describes as 'a shared temporality, bodies on the line, soundscapes of power, dialogic inter-animation, political action, and matters of the heart' (Madison 2007: 827).

A major objective of The Touched Project was to promote the idea of embodied choreographic knowing as a model that works alongside the theory of practice this book promotes. Hence, the entire project was designed to function as a system with a structure and logic of its own, as an exploration of a world that is akin to a thermodynamic system seeking equilibrium or resolution in its engagement with external forces. The external forces being everything that it came into contact with, including audiences. These inputs were vital to completing a process that started in the choreographer's mind, was shared with collaborators who sometimes had different opinions, and was explored in studio rehearsals with performers before being presented onstage to an invited audience. The project thus exposed a great deal about how control, and hence power, works in any system that seeks equilibrium. By seeking equilibrium, I mean attempting to resolve any type of opposition or competing forces – from contrasting opinions within a team trying to find a common voice to different opinions among audience members about what they thought was happening in the performance they had witnessed. It is this entire dynamic activity between people and technological systems, and between those with different degrees of agency within those systems.

Ilya Prigogine, Nobel Prize laureate for his work on thermodynamic processes, and collaborator William Schieve confirmed that over time 'an isolated system, whatever its nature, will approach thermodynamic equilibrium, a state characterized by the maximum value of entropy, that is, of "disorder"' (Prigogine and Allen in Schieve and Allen 1982: 5). They also proved that such a system, if it were 'subjected only to weak flows of energy or matter, so that it remains only slightly out of equilibrium, adopts a steady-state which corresponds to minimum entropy production'.[26] Schieve and Allen argue that social and biological systems follow the same processes as physical, chemical and technological systems, i.e. they operate far from equilibrium, with a great deal of non-linear behaviour, and in doing so display 'a rich variety of self-organizing behaviors' (Prigogine and Allen in Schieve and Allen 1982: 7). Applied to the larger multi-year Touched Project, this meant that although there were multiple individual works as well as opinions about those works that were coherent in themselves, one needed to look at the larger macroscopic pattern beyond the individual works in order to appreciate the value of the entire process as artistic research. In other words, my PaR strategy for The Touched Project was to organize it as a larger entity that could not be properly defined by any single one of the individual works that comprised it, but whose abstract core could be ascertained from any one of the individual parts.

The Touched Project was for me a unique opportunity to explore alternative approaches to Art-Science collaboration while using technology as a platform to address some of the concerns articulated by Ganesh, Vass-Rhee and Barad. It began by investigating notions of performance as the efficient and optimized use of motion tracking technologies and autonomous robotic systems and as human beings expressing the innate knowledge in their bodies through theatrical staging. One can say that it ended with the realization that the roles human beings and machines perform are very different, but that they form part of a larger system in which it is important to know precisely what those roles are. While the project invited computing scientists to think of their work as contributions to a larger choreographic organism, it also asked artists to consider themselves as part of an extended network where these technologies played a key role in how their work could be perceived.

Touched, *t2*, *t2_echo*, *Imprint* and *Imprint II* were instalments in a kind of ritual theatre where the human body and the technological machine operated as self-sustaining systems, with each sustained by the other in a kind of evolutionary movement; evolutionary in the sense of contributing to something greater than itself. The project also investigated the key question of how to define performance; I was personally interested in a definition that went beyond the efficient, optimized operations of a digitally programmed system and the expressive articulation of biological bodies in a process of becoming. I sought to realize a world that was being created on the spot and always for the first time, with part of my task being to convince the performers to help me do so. They, in turn, had to convince audiences that they were entering a structure through their own initiative. And to remind my audience of choreographer William Forsythe's statements, 'choreography is about organization [...] either one is organizing the body, or [...] organizing bodies with other bodies, or a body with other bodies in an environment that is organized' (Gardiner 1996).[27] This, he argued, was 'the challenge of choreography at the end of the twentieth century'.[28]

I would add here that choreography in the twenty-first century, for me at least, was about cultivating greater and more complex forms of awareness, about giving performers and audiences alike more opportunities to exercise their perceptive capacities, and to re-member and re-cognise the knowledge that exists in their own bodies as they sought to enhance it. Theorists such as Elizabeth Grosz and Patrice Pavis have argued that audiences are inherently capable of sensing the structures of a work in a deeply embodied manner. The 'spectator's body' (Pavis 2003: 127–30) and its 'psychic corporeality' (Grosz 1994: 181) are still crucial concepts for understanding contemporary performances. The Touched Project was part of an ongoing attempt to create a new framework for this kind of work. As part of a larger entity that strove to bring scientists, performers and audiences together as witnesses to new material interfaces between technology, the body and our phenomenal environment, this project became a ground breaker for my choreographic ideas in terms of the articulation of an intricate, complex and methodical process for extracting knowledge from bodies – human and otherwise – and representing them in increasingly new ways.

NOTES

1. These were automated commercial vacuum cleaners (Roombas) that Vaughan set about building new computer interfaces for, i.e. new brains.
2. www.irmacs.ca/.

3. Much of the work on organization, control and emergence was done by Russian-born Ilya Prigogine, who received the 1977 Nobel Prize in Chemistry for his work in the area of thermodynamic systems. Prigogine discovered that the importation and dissipation of energy into chemical systems could result in the emergence of new structures due to internal self-reorganization (Nicolis and Prigogine 1977).
4. www.henrydaniel.ca/the-touched-project/#touched.
5. Auslander, Philip. *Liveness: Performance in a Mediatized Culture*. 2nd ed., Routledge, 2008b.
6. This idea forms the basis of the Copenhagen model of quantum mechanics.
7. www.troikaranch.org/.
8. Stoppiello used the phrase ‘how to wreck a dance’ to describe a process that American choreographer Susan Rethorst first utilised when deconstructing and then reconstructing a dance. Rethorst also invited trusted artists to do the ‘wrecking’.
9. ‘Body Spaces: Corporeal Topographies in Literature, Theatre, Dance and the Visual Arts’. 15 March 2008, Dorothy Somerset Studio Theatre, UBC, Vancouver, Canada. https://project.arts.ubc.ca/bodyspaces/.
10. Premiered 3 April 2008, SFU Mainstage Theatre, Burnaby, BC, Canada.
11. www.henrydaniel.ca/the-touched-project/#beyondboxes.
12. The Touched Project is the first to be articulated in the web-based Performance Archive.
13. www.henrydaniel.ca/the-touched-project/#t2. Premiered 11 July 2009, Scotia Bank Dance Centre, Vancouver, BC, Canada.
14. www.phs.ca/project/interurban-art-gallery/.
15. www.thedancecentre.ca/about-us/.
16. http://if2009.ecuad.ca/; www.connect.ecuad.ca/node/3626.
17. www.connect.ecuad.ca/node/3626.
18. www.henrydaniel.ca/the-touched-project/#echo. Premiered Saturday 21 November 2009, Concourse Gallery and Intersections Digital Studio, ECUAD, Vancouver, BC, Canada.
19. In May 1914, Marinetti performed his sound poem *Zang Toumb Toumb* at the Doré Gallery in London. Part of this performance involved using hammers to imitate gunfire, blackboards to sketch his ideas, and instructing the painter C.R.W. Nevinson – who was in an adjoining room – to repeatedly strike two large drums to simulate cannons. This instruction was done through a telephone Marinetti had installed on stage (Tisdall and Bozzola 1978; Warden 2015).
20. www.henrydaniel.ca/the-touched-project/#imprinti. Premiered 23 January 2010 at the UBC Museum of Anthropology, Vancouver, BC, Canada.
21. Premiered 17–20 June 2010 at SFU Woodward’s, Vancouver, BC, Canada.
22. This was the work of Armenian born mystic Georges Ivanovich Gurdjief and that of the Russian esotericist P.D. Ouspensky who introduced it to many in the West.
23. The Kwakiutl peoples on the Northwest coast of British Columbia, for example, believe that the world is full of intelligent sentient beings, with and without visible material forms,

which are all linked by a chain of reciprocal feeding (Walens 1981: 12). Life is thus a cyclical process where individuals are what they eat and become what they are eaten by.

24. www.henrydaniel.ca/the-touched-project/#imprintii, Premiered at SFU Woodward's, 17–20 June, 2010, Vancouver, BC, Canada.
25. The Goldcorp Centre for the Arts, SFU.
26. The Goldcorp Centre for the Arts, SFU.
27. BBC re-broadcast of a taped interview with choreographer William Forsythe, 1996.
28. BBC re-broadcast of a taped interview with choreographer William Forsythe, 1996.

6

Going West to Find East

Choreographing from the underside

Theories or ideas, no matter how lofty, are not immune from historical circumstance: the latter often discloses what otherwise is left unsaid.

(Dallmayr 2004: 1)[1]

[T]he large-scale accumulation of unpaid land, unpaid labor, and overall wealth expropriated by Western Europe from non-European peoples, which was to lay the basis of its global expansion from the fifteenth century onwards, was carried out within the order of truth and the self-evident order of consciousness, of a creed-specific conception of what it was to be human – which, because a monotheistic conception, could not conceive of an Other to what it experienced as being human, and therefore an Other to its truth, its notion of freedom.

(Wynter 2003: 291–92)

Rather as Ginés de Sepulveda in the sixteenth century Spanish debates over treatment of the Amerindians argued that violence was justified to bring them into civilization, so generations of psychologists have defined the lives of those 'others' as needing description, administration, treatment, therapy, correction, not as an autonomous scientific enterprise, but as part of the overall administrative state that polices the deviant Other, protecting the accumulation regimes that the state guarantees for Capital.

(Burton and Flores Osorio 2011: 29)[2]

Project Barca: New Architectures of Memory and Identity (2011–14) was the multi-year initiative that immediately succeeded The Touched Project. Its artistic title was Project Barca: Going West to Find East/Going East to Find West, and it continued the development of a set of ideas begun with Transnet and continued with The Touched Project. Like Transnet, Project Barca was funded by SSHRC. Unlike both Transnet and The Touched Project, however, it concerned itself less with collaborations between scientists and artists to develop new technologies for their mutual benefit, and more with the social, cultural and political issues that the two had exposed through their examination of agency and power as properties of systems of organization. In classic transdisciplinary research mode, Project Barca focused its investigative lens on notions of identity and belonging in relation to structures of power. Since knowledge of any kind is also associated with access to social, cultural and political power; I was interested in how the European urge to adventure, to discover, to take possession of and to colonize what they found in their path during the so-called Age of Discovery would inevitably determine how new cortical and cartographic maps were thereafter structured.

In his *Archives of Flesh* (2016), Robert Reid-Pharr cites Jamaican writer Sylvia Wynter's argument that the key 'ideological, discursive, and aesthetic structures [...] put in place post-1492 at the service of modes of capital accumulation' were the same ones that either barred Black people from the entrance into contemporary versions of these same structures or made it extremely difficult for them to enter (Reid-Pharr 2016: 12). Reid-Pharr's argument traces Columbus's voyages and Spanish colonial history as essential elements in the colonization of knowledge, which attempted to force the entirety of Black culture, philosophy, critical thought and modes of being into a physically, psychically, mentally and emotionally pre-determined mould created in the White man's image (Reid-Pharr 2016). Though this analysis was easy for me to understand, exploring its implications as a Black choreographer/scholar presented some unique challenges in a research environment where I was confronted with overwhelmingly White bodies in studios, lecture rooms and across the University's administrative apparatus. This was especially difficult given that, beginning with *Imprint II*, I was no longer performing in my own choreographic works. Nevertheless, living on the west coast of Canada would give me the opportunity to work with an interesting diversity of bodies in the creation of original works for Project Barca.

The seeds for this project were sown during a trip to Barcelona, Spain in the summer of 2010. I was reminded of the many times I had been to that city but was never able to stay long enough to fully appreciate the richness of its history and culture, its relationship to the rest of Spain and the role that both city and country played in the colonization of the New World. My first visit to Spain was more than two decades earlier as a member of the José Limón Dance Company, performing in Madrid and Barcelona. This was followed by several stints as an independent choreographer and teacher to places further north such as Zaragoza in Aragon and as far south as Lanzarote in the offshore Canary Islands. During each of these visits, and particularly to the city of Barcelona, I became increasingly fascinated with a historical contextualization of what I was seeing and experiencing.

At first, I thought the lure had something to do with my distant knowledge of the place from a Caribbean-oriented British education. After all, we were taught *ad nauseam* that Columbus discovered Trinidad – the island I was born on – during his third voyage in 1498 and gave it its name from the three peaks he saw to the south-east of the island. Also, since Trinidad & Tobago had been occupied by Spain, France and Britain at various times, their three languages – with Latin as a fourth – were foundational to my secondary school education. We were obliged to learn geography as well as the literary, social and political histories of these countries. Additionally, in my early career as an actor and dancer, I performed in Caribbean playwright Derek Walcott's original 1974 production of *The Joker of Seville* that was based on Tirso de Molina's 1630 classic *El burlador de Sevilla*. I remember admiring Walcott's ability to create a powerful sense of cultural hybridity that celebrated our 'creole-ness' in his works. This Trinidadian *creole* Spanish, French and English mixture gave us song, dance, music and language that allowed us to experience a unique relationship to these cultures, often forgetting that we were neither British, French nor Spanish, but descendants of colonized Africans who were now 'West Indians'.

Nevertheless, on that fateful holiday in Barcelona, I decided that I would find a way to look more deeply into Spain and its culture. On my return to Vancouver, after long consideration, I decided that whatever imagined connection I had to this place and to these people could only be found by being there and interacting more closely with them. I applied for a three-year research grant to 'design a new intellectual framework for research/creation in choreographic practice that deploys and foregrounds intersections of difference, and to produce the full-length multidisciplinary performance work *Barca* within that framework'.[3] *Barca* would explore a range of ideas contained within the phrase 'going west to find east' by first inverting it, and later playing on the inherent paradox of going in either direction to find the other.

Using the Spanish and Portuguese term for small boat, *barca*, the research would embark on a journey of exploration, utilizing comprehensive new research/creation methods that questioned the very platforms utilized to disseminate results, i.e. live performances, mixed media installations, film documentation, academic and mixed-mode writings, etc. Most importantly, the research would position contemporary choreographic practice at the centre of a scholarly investigation of the following question: How can embodied personal and collective memories be shaped into new architectures of identity and belonging in the form of innovative performance works that speak to wider sections of society?[4] My throw of the dice was successful, and I received the award; the production would allow me time to examine 'how new roles could be formed and performed against a backdrop of strong local, Indigenous, and multiple intersecting identities' (Daniel 2011).[5]

I chose the autonomous region of Catalunya and the city of Barcelona as a base and was extremely fortunate to find a dance studio in the city that I could work from while travelling across the country. After receiving the SSHRC funds, I held a first exploratory workshop with the base research team to search for performers for a Vancouver production; the plan being to do a separate work on each side of the Atlantic. I had not at the time imagined that I would later do a third production that combined material from these two. In this way, I was later able to construct an encounter between descendants of (1) Asians who were the objects of the European quest for power and influence in 'the Orient', (2) those from Europe who instigated and implemented those explorations, (3) those who were discovered in the so-called New World as a result of those quests and (4) those who were engaged as labour to cultivate the agricultural and industrial riches that were discovered in the Americas and later developed in Europe.

My three main collaborators on the research grant were Dr Rita Dhamoon, at the time a Professor in the Department of Political Science at the University of the Fraser Valley, whose research was on identity/difference politics, culture, critical views on multiculturalism, race-thinking and racism, feminism and gender, and democracy; Dr Olena Hankivsky, a Professor in the Public Policy Program at Simon Fraser University (SFU) and founder and director of the Institute for Intersectionality Research and Policy; and Professor Owen Underhill, a prolific composer, co-artistic director and conductor of the Turning Point Ensemble, former artistic director of Vancouver New Music, and at the time Director of the School for the Contemporary Arts at SFU. Since I had previously worked with Professor Underhill on The Touched Project, he was familiar with some of my choreographic research strategies. With Dhamoon and Hankivsky, however, the process began with that day-long workshop for us to get acquainted with each other's work in a studio-based research context. Hankivsky had been instrumental in helping me in her former role as Research Grant Facilitator at SFU with the initial framing of the grant application. She, therefore, had a clear sense of my theoretical objectives and could make suggestions concerning how those objectives could be enhanced by an intersectional framing. It was also she who suggested Professor Dhamoon as a collaborator as they had previously worked together on other projects. Both these women had extensive research experience in theories of intersectionality and their knowledge helped frame that first workshop and later the production itself.[6]

After that initial workshop, I began my search for dancers and research assistants for the first production from within the School for the Contemporary Arts. In our first rehearsal, I issued a challenge to the dancers to trace their family ancestries from 3 August 1492 to the present (Spring 2012) – a span of exactly five hundred and twenty years. I also gave them the freedom to choose any time frame within that larger period to concentrate on. They could be as concise or as expansive as they felt they needed to be but had to use strict historical reference points to orient themselves and their future audiences. The results of the performers' efforts were a fascinating set of personal narratives that would be used as the basis for an entire evening-length production.

To be clear, I did not expect nor require everyone to have at hand or to reproduce accurate information regarding their family ancestry within the given time span. Rather, the issue was to see how such a difficult question could be creatively approached by a group of young people with diverse cultural heritages. I was therefore interested in seeing what would emerge when someone, anyone, considered the implications that such a question posed. Could genuine stories or specific memories of important events emerge? And would the dancers fall into the trap of inventing stories of things that never took place, or of people that never existed? The type of truths, half-truths and even fictions that could surface was anyone's guess. This same question would be asked in one form or another in each successive work within the Project Barca series. Eventually, the content of several choreographic works, gallery installations, short films and site-specific performances, created and performed by an international cast in separate productions made in Spain, Canada and the United States, would be built on source material that emerged from this simple provocation. And in creating these works, I was truly struck by the nature of the probability equation that presented itself; how many of these stories, remembered or created by the performers, were recognized by audience members, and what further memories of stories told to these audiences by friends, family and strangers could be triggered during our performances?

Most of the rehearsals for these works were recorded, a practice that had become fundamental to my research strategy at that point. In The Touched Project, I was able to produce one short documentary film, a gallery installation, and five live performances on site-specific and traditional proscenium stages,[7] including visiting lectures, conference talks and published essays.[8] In Project Barca, I would increase this production volume by revisiting, reorganizing and diversifying the source material to create significantly more artistic and intellectual products. The research was thus able to position contemporary choreographic practice at the centre of a scholarly investigation that asked the following key question: How could embodied personal and collective memories be shaped into new artistic and intellectual products? In this way, I was able to design a creative methodology that began with the performer's texts and improvised sequences based on movement material and related thematic ideas from the extended research team.

Haikai, Encounters *and* Here Be Dragons (Stage I Creative Preview)

The first three outcomes of this initial exploration were (1) *Haikai* (2012), a live performance with gamelan orchestra; (2) the installation *Encounters* (2012), an 8-channel audio and 4-channel video installation and (3) *Here Be Dragons (Stage I Creative Preview)*, a live preview of the material generated for the production of *Barca* to that point. *Haikai* premiered on 20 May 2012 at the Goldcorp Centre for the Arts in Vancouver, and the other two works on 29 May and 1 June 2012 respectively at the same location. These three works were very different treatments of the material emerging from my question to the dancers to trace their family ancestries over the specified period. The first, *Haikai*, was put together for an invitation from Jon Siddal, founder and director of Gamelan Si Pawit of Vancouver, to perform at his music festival. Siddal had been looking for a 'gifted SFU choreographer/dancer'[9] who would be excited by his project and I responded to his call.

Haikai was inspired by John Cage's composition and the Japanese poetic form, both of the same name. Cage's work was also chosen for this concert because the year 2012 was the hundredth anniversary of his birth. Siddal had initially approached Cage in 1985, more than 25 years earlier, to visit his Toronto-based gamelan group. Their meeting resulted in Cage composing *Haikai* in 1986 for Siddal's Evergreen Club gamelan ensemble.[10] I accepted Siddal's invitation to perform the material generated to that point in my research for a number of reasons: first, I was excited to work with the gamelan orchestra and with music by Cage specially made for such an ensemble; second, this was an opportunity for me to explore some of the practices outlined in the Chinese oracle book the *I Ching*, which inspired Cage's works. One of these practices was to 'listen' to what was being 'said' by the environment and try to remove one's own intention from the creative equation. This of course was extremely difficult since there was already an intention behind the material generated up to that point. However, I felt that Cage's 'chance' approach to composition would be a useful way for me to play with that material simply as an 'abstract' movement score. Third, I relished the opportunity to perform the existing material using a musical form I had no previous experience with, but which was part of an aesthetic I had always been curious about. And since an important part of my choreographic strategy was working in silence or with the voiced texts of the performers themselves, having a musical score that was created for a completely different context was a challenge I could not turn down. The result of the experiment was a work with a very meditative feel, which offered quite a different take on the notion of going west to find east and going east to find west. This kind of unplanned event was always a challenge that I relished in an otherwise focused research project. And since my academic collaborators had warned me to be careful about any conceptualization and use of the terms 'West' and 'East' *a la* Said (1978), I though this might be a way to provoke people's perception of both.

Encounters, the 8-channel audio and 4-channel video installation, and *Here Be Dragons (Stage I Creative Preview)*, the live preview of the entire corpus of material generated to that point, benefitted immensely from this experiment. *Haikai* did not utilize any of the performers' texts, which of course gave the work some of its abstract feel. However, *Here Be Dragons* (*Stage I Creative Preview*) had a definite narrative form that was structured in such a manner that the audience could follow the performers' stories within strict temporal frames of reference. *Encounters* explored both strategies; the work featured four video screens, three with two performers on each screen and one with three performers, making a total of nine performers within four screens. Three screens were projected side by side on one long wall, with the fourth screen with three performers occupying an opposite wall. Both sound and video channels were looped. The eight channels of sound were asynchronous with the videos, which meant that one had to closely follow the script in order to decipher which performer was speaking which text. And since all four videos had different lengths, the texts never occurred in the same section of the videos in each cycle.

Three short films, three full-length performance works and two more gallery installations followed *Haikai*, *Encounters* and *Here Be Dragons* (*Stage I Creative Preview*). These works were made in different countries and with an increasingly diversified international group of performers, designers, technical staff and audiences.[11] This creative journey would link my two bases – the city of Barcelona, Spain, an 'Old World' city at the edge of the Mediterranean; and Vancouver, Canada, a fast-growing metropolis located on the Pacific NorthWest at the far edge of the so-called 'New World' – with a third location in the USA: the city of Davis, a 'University town' and agricultural community just outside Sacramento, the state capital of California. This geographical configuration was the result of both rigorous planning and some luck. While the first two productions involving Canada and Spain were planned, the third came as a result of an invitation from Professor Lynette Hunter – then Distinguished Professor of the History of Rhetoric and Performance at UC Davis – for me to be the 2014 Granada Artist-in-Residence in the Department of Theatre and Dance. Since many members of the three-country cast were born outside Canada, Spain and the United States and had migrated to these countries for various reasons from work to study, I had the unique opportunity to learn about and stage a fascinating set of embodied cortical and cartographic maps. Given that PaR was the vehicle through which I was conducting my trans-Atlantic journey of rediscovery and its trans-Pacific connections, building and navigating such a vehicle was a special undertaking. The first international stop with this small *barca* would of course be the Iberian Peninsula itself.

Barca: el otro lado

There are several important sites and key reference points in Spain, and the Iberian Peninsula in general, that I felt a need to visit for the research. However, Barcelona, a major city on the edge of the Mediterranean, was the most convenient for me to use as a base. This city has a wonderfully diverse population, is very strong in its support for the arts and, luckily for me, has several schools with a good reputation for contemporary dance training and performance. I was fortunate to get a recommendation that allowed me to locate my research at AREA DANSA,[12] – one of these dance institutions – while travelling across the country. Since this second stage of Project Barca required several visits back to Vancouver, I was able to maintain some continuity between the work in Spain and in Canada. I arranged for one of my graduate research assistants, Lara Abadir, to travel with me to Spain for some of the time, and I hired another assistant in Barcelona, Rakel Ezpeleta, who could speak Catalan, Spanish, French, English and Euskara, the Basque language. These two women greatly facilitated the work of researching and collecting information, rehearsing dancers, filming the material and eventually assisting in the production of the evening length work *Barca: el otro lado* (2012), and two short films *Implicados* (2012) and *Voces del Vacio* (2012).[13] Although the research involved some extensive travelling throughout Catalunya, to the south in places such as Córdoba, Sevilla, Granada, Huelva (Palos de la Frontera) and Antequera in Andalusia, and to Vitoria-Gastciz in the Basque Country in the north-west, all of the rehearsals and performances were done in the city and province of Barcelona.

I mentioned earlier that I visited other cities on previous visits to Spain but never for more than a two-week stint. This extended visit, therefore, allowed me to accumulate detailed and nuanced information about specific locations over a five-month period. For example, the trip to Andalusia produced valuable information that I felt no book or scholarly article could provide. The dances I saw, the music I heard, the street culture I witnessed, the formal and informal concerts I attended, and the entire influence of the three cultures (*Las Tres Culturas*) of Judaism, Christianity and Islam that was available in the architecture, the artefacts, the cities and countryside as well as in the bodies I encountered contributed to my understanding of the place in all its complexity. It was a daunting experience, for example, to visit the Archivo General De Indias in Seville (The General Archive of the Indies) and compare that to what I saw in the Museo de la Inquisitión (Museum of the Inquisition) in Córdoba, or the confusing experience of being stopped from kneeling to take a picture in *La Mezquita* (The Great Mosque of Córdoba) to that of being joined by four North African guest workers at the only table left in the Plaza Comandante Ramón Franco in Palos de la Frontera.

The artefacts in the *Synagoga* across the street from the *Casa de Sefarad* in the Jewish Quarter of Córdoba, the Alhambra and the Albaicín in Granada – the last Moorish stronghold in Spain – and the quasi reification of Columbus in almost every plaza or public building in Huelva and Palos de la Frontera; all of these provided valuable information that influenced the choreographic script that was *Barca: el otro lado*. On many occasions, I had a curious feeling that I was virtually reliving, throughout my body, the memories of a specific time and place. At other times, I had conversations with strangers that brought memories of different events in the past into a space in the present. Two short examples will suffice here.

Sitting in the Plaza Comandante Ramón Franco in Palos de la Frontera, at the north-west end of which is a statue of Martín Alonso Pinzón (the Captain of *La Pinta*), brother of Francisco Martín (the Master of *La Pinta*) and Vicente Yáñez Pinzón (the Captain of *La Niña*),[14] I was joined by a group of men, *trabajadores inmigrantes* or guest workers from Morocco, Tunisia and Algeria (Figure 6.1). During our conversation, they shared some of their experiences of being guest workers from a foreign country that had contributed so much to the development of a country that was now treating them so badly. This was in 2012, at the beginning of the Syrian conflict when the death rate for those trying to get to Europe via the Mediterranean was increasing exponentially. I particularly remember our discussion about the fickle nature of Spanish memory insofar as an appreciation for the immense contributions that Islam, the Moors and North African countries made to Spanish culture. One did not have to dig deeply to find such evidence, and there was certainly no need to convince me, as I had already witnessed it as an outsider.

In the second example, I learned about the history of cultural occupation embedded in the walls of the *Synagoga* in Córdoba's Jewish Quarter. According to interpretive documents displayed in the building, the *Synagoga* was built in 1315 and is the oldest preserved synagogue in Andalusia, and one of three left in Spain. I had seen the other two many years before on a day trip to Toledo, while performing in Madrid. In 1492, the *Synagoga* was converted into a hermitage with the house used as a hospital for hydrophobic people.[15] Later renovations converted it into a Christian Chapel until one day in 1885, mortar fell off one of the walls and the Hebrew texts written underneath were discovered. The building was then declared a National Monument.[16] Visiting these buildings and artefacts from previous centuries was a unique experience that would substantially influence the staging of *Barca: el otro lado* and eventually *Here Be Dragons/Non Plus Ultra (HBD/NPU, 2013)*.

These examples show how the complex cultural history of the Iberian Peninsula – its series of invasions, tense co-existences and intolerances, and desire to exercise total power and control would influence how events unfolded an ocean away in a new world. When the defeated Muhammad XII, Boabdil, handed over the keys to the city of Granada on 2 January 1492 to the Catholic monarchs Isabella

FIGURE 6.1: Plaza Comandante Ramón Franco in Palos de la Frontera, Andalusia, Spain. The author is second from the viewer's right in this image.

and Ferdinand, that action marked a key turning point for what would become the country of Spain. First of all, it gave Isabella and Ferdinand an enormous foothold in the south. It was also the beginning of the final stage in the exodus of non-converted Moors, Muslims and Arabs from the peninsula, after more than seven hundred years of occupation. On that same battlefield in Granada, Columbus signed a contract to go West in search of wealth and political influence for his new employers. The day before he sailed, an edict requiring all non-converted Jews to leave the country expired, leaving them with no option but to convert if they wished to stay. Finally, rules were established that laid the groundwork for the Spanish Empire and for the later enslavement of millions of Africans. It is not difficult to imagine the turmoil: some doors were opening while others slammed shut, masses of people were leaving at the same time but for different reasons and in different directions. South, East and North-East were refuges for some, while West became an adventure and/or the beginning of a nightmare for others.

The artistic team of *Barca: el otro lado* was composed of eight dancers, four musicians, one actress, three multimedia artists, two filmmakers and one lighting designer, all of whom were instrumental in the creation and staging of the work. The performers I auditioned, interviewed and eventually selected to work with me on *Barca: el otro lado* were all given the same task as those for *Here Be Dragons (Stage I Creative Preview)* in Vancouver earlier in the year. The context was of course quite different. Although these new performers were all resident in the city of Barcelona, many of them were not born there, and some not even in Spain. Thus, the responses to the question of ancestry were so varied, rich and imaginative that it was not difficult to create the two additional short films from the material gathered. Below are two short examples of texts the performers created and which I used as a baseline to choreograph individual sections within the larger work. I called this particular dance the colonization duet, in that the two dancers take turns invading each other's personal spaces and manipulating each other's bodies. The texts below in Spanish, and translated into English, speak for themselves.

Sections I and II are for a mixed duet between performers Sara Martín and Joahn Volmar (Figure 6.2), while Section III is for the male performer Ángel Zotes who subsequently replaced Volmar in the duet with Martin (Figure 6.3). Since the two men had quite different stories, ways of moving and very different bodies, stylistic and movement changes were made in the second version of the duet. The change in the identity of the male partner in texts I and III significantly shifts the tone of the work. The sentences and phrases in texts I and II should be read alternately as if the performers were having a conversation. After this, the reader should read the texts in II and III as a different conversation, except that the female's story is the same.

> I
>
> Spanish: Mi nombre es Sara Martínez Fernández Calvo Rodriguez Rubio Árias Martínez Rey. Soy de Madrid, pero mi familia viene de Galicia. Mi último apellido, bueno, uno de los últimos, Árias, también viene de Galicia, desde sus inicios. Estuve buscando por [...] gente que se apellidara Árias o que empezara a tener el nombre de Árias y [...] fueron personajes principales en la conquista de América. Ellos fueron allí y también algunos regresaron. En América podemos encontrar ríos y ciudades que tienen el nombre de Árias.
>
> (Sara Martín)

FIGURE 6.2: Joahn Volmar and Sara Martín in *Barca: el otro lado*.

FIGURE 6.3: Ángel Zotes and Sara Martín in *Barca: el otro lado*.

English Translation: My name is Sara Martínez Fernández Calvo Rodriguez Rubio Árias Martínez Rey. I'm from Madrid, but my family comes from Galicia. My last name, well, one of the last ones, Árias, also comes from Galicia. From the very beginning, I was looking for people whose last name was Árias, or that they would have that name [...] and [...] they were main characters in the conquest of America. They went there [...] and many of them came back. In America we can find rivers and towns called Árias.

II

Spanish: Me llamo Joahn Volmar López. Mi padre nació en la Guayana francesa, de madre nativa y de padre neoyorquino. Mi madre nació en Argelia, de padres españoles. En 1498, 6 años después de su salida de España, Colón descubrió mi país y lo denominó "la tierra de los parias". Grabado en las memorias, este nombre representa la historia de mi país: una tierra de presos europeos y un sitio de deportados africanos negros, ancestros de mi abuela.

(Joahn Volmar)

English Translation: My name is Joahn Volmar López. My father was born in French Guiana, of a native mother and a New Yorker father. My mother was born in Algeria, of Spanish parents. In 1498, six years after his departure from Spain, Columbus discovered my country and called it "the land of the outcasts." Engraved in their memories, this name represents the history of my country: a land of European prisoners and a site for black African deportees, my grandmother's ancestors.

(Joahn Volmar)

III

Spanish: Ángel Zotes Ramos, de Laguna de Negrillos, León.
Zotes, apellido tomado de un pueblo cercano por los judíos conversos.
Ramos, apellido tomado de la naturaleza por los musulmanes conversos.
Convertir, reconvertir, requeteconvertir y más reconversión.
Todo se repite.
Siembra de desconfianza entre vecinos y amigos. Mentiras impresas para la identidad y el orgullo.
Lo único que crecen son muros. Y las pilas bautismales no descansan.

(Ángel Zotes)

English Translation: Ángel Zotes Ramos, from Laguna de Negrillos, León. Zotes, name of a town taken as a surname by converted Jews. Ramos, term from nature taken as a surname by converted Muslims. Conversion. Reconversion. Re-reconversion [...] and more conversion.
Everything repeats itself. Mistrust seeds among friends and neighbours. Lies printed on identity and pride. The only things that grow are walls. And the baptism polls are always busy.

(Ángel Zotes)

Another incident that precipitated the choreography in an early part of the dance occurred in the main hall of *La Mezquita* in Cordoba, a complex piece of architecture that is also called Cathedral of Our Lady of the Assumption. Officially this building is a cathedral, but it actually incorporates two structures, a mosque and a cathedral, built at different times and reflecting the historic cultural shifts that took place in that part of the country. As I mentioned earlier, I had knelt down on my way to a lying position to take a wide-angled shot of the beautifully decorated ceiling in the mosque part of the building when I was immediately accosted by one of the security guards. At first, I was baffled and somewhat irked by his attitude since there were many other people taking pictures from all different angles. However, at that moment, I vaguely remembered something I had read in my earlier research.

It had noted that on 31 March 2010, half a dozen members of a large group (over 100) of Muslim tourists from Austria had begun praying in *La Mezquita*, in defiance of the ban on Muslim prayers in the building.[17] This led to a fight between guards and those praying. Though half the building is designed as a mosque, it is not designated as such in the city regulations, and hence cannot be used for daily prayers. In the moment of my confrontation with the guard, my body recognized that I was experiencing something that may have happened to so many others in different contexts. But now it was happening to me, a middle-aged Black man about to kneel in the Great Mosque of Córdoba. This experience made such an impression on me that it would make its way into *Barca: el otro lado* in the form of a male solo that morphed into a male duet, a male quintet and back into a duet (Figure 6.4).

As I mentioned earlier, my objective with the production was not in any way an attempt to represent historic facts, but to give myself, and others, an opportunity to recognize and remember the complex information that is embodied in the spaces through which our bodies moved – both then and now, to recognize what those bodies encountered during those movements, and the memories that were

FIGURE 6.4: Ángel Zotes and Ireneu Tranis in *Barca: el otro lado*.

released in them because of these actions. Whether as lived experiences or as staged actions, I argue that valuable information can be gleaned from these experiences as they are re-cognized and re-membered through the medium of performance. And it is precisely through these performances that we can all begin to rethink, reorganize and rechoreograph the roles that those in power have unfortunately assigned to many of us.

A barca: *Reaching back to go forward*

Between 9 April and 12 April 1999, the fifth iteration of the annual Performance Studies International (PSi5) conference convened in Aberystwyth, Wales, under the provocative title '*Here Be Dragons': Mapping the Undiscovered Realms of Performance Studies: Boundaries, Hinterlands, and Beyond.*[18] The organizers invited 'artists and academics in a variety of disciplines whose interests and concerns converge[d] in the contested and still-evolving areas of live art and performance [to] map the unexplored boundaries and hinterlands' of performance studies.[19] The Call for Papers elaborated as follows:

> As the Performance Studies Conference migrates from North America to Europe for the first time, the conference will create an opportunity for performance studies to encounter its neighbours and relatives – the disciplines that have in the past or may in the future complement and challenge performance studies (Cultural Studies, Human Geography, History, Archaeology, Anthropology, Theatre Studies) as well as the practices of theatre, live art and performance.

PSi5 occurred at a time when PaR as a concept was undergoing a challenging time in UK's higher education system. I was writing my Ph.D. in the Department of Drama: Theatre, Film and Television at Bristol University while working as a full-time lecturer in Theatre and Performance at King Alfred's College, now Winchester University. I also performed *Shango Meets Ogun* at PSi5.[20] Although there was work being done in technological reconstructions of stage design at the time, there was little talk of the performance of computational systems or machine/human interfaces within Performance Studies. In fact, I remember having an exchange with Richard Schechner, one of the leading scholars in the field, two years earlier at the Colston Symposium in Bristol,[21] and he was not at all enthused about the idea. I'm not at all sure he saw my point about performance from the point of view of power as an emergent property of complex systems, human or non-human and that such power manifests itself as a need for control over others through any means possible so I blamed it on my inability to articulate the idea more clearly.

It was this link between the human being and the technological machine, or the human being as a productive machine for state institutions, that I was unable to articulate then. Seeing the power of these institutions, feeling their attraction, and knowing where the ideas to develop and implement them came from, made me always sceptical of those who looked at and treated other human beings as if they were machines to be used as labour.

On 10 January 2013, almost fifteen years later, I premiered *Here Be Dragons – Non Plus Ultra* (*HBD/NPU*) in Vancouver, Canada. *HBD/NPU* combined two prior productions, *Here Be Dragons (Stage I Creative Preview)* and *Barca: el otro lado*,[22] the former with a local cast of Iranian Canadian, Chinese Canadian, Portuguese Canadian, First Nations Métis, Trinidadian Canadian and European Canadians that premiered on 1 June 2012 in Vancouver, and the latter with a local cast of Catalan, Castilian, Basque, French, Algerian/Guyanese and Chilean performers that premiered on 6 November 2012 at Theatre Nau Ivanov in Barcelona. These two original works were made independently of each other. However, for the new recast and combined work, *Here Be Dragons-Non Plus Ultra* (*HBD/NPU*), the performers (Figures 6.3–6.10) would not physically meet until 1 January 2013, ten days before the combined event's premiere.

There was no conscious attempt on my part to connect the proceedings of PSi5 or *Shango Meets Ogun* with Project Barca or *HBD/NPU*. However, in retrospect, the agendas of these separate research events seemed to be fulfilling a set of unconscious or at least not fully worked-out objectives that I had been developing throughout those intervening years. Just as PSi5 'migrated' from North America

FIGURE 6.5: Luciana D'Anunciação in the opening scene from *Here Be Dragons/Non Plus Ultra*.

FIGURE 6.6: Kyle Toy, Karin Kato and Eloi Homier in *Encounters*.

FIGURE 6.7: Thoenn Glover in *Encounters*.

FIGURE 6.8: Ireneu Tranis, Sole Medina, Arash Khakpour and Sara Martín in *Here Be Dragons/Non Plus Ultra*.

to Europe for the first time – the term suggesting a kind of voyage – so too were Project Barca and *HBD/NPU* making their own voyages within the context of movement as a set of personal thoughts unfolding that then gives rise to other

FIGURE 6.9: Dorothea Hayley; Rakel Ezpeleta, Dorothea Hayley and Luciana D'Anunciação and cast; Elisenda Moya and Ireneu Tranis in scenes from *Here Be Dragons/Non Plus Ultra*.

FIGURE 6.10: Thoenn Glover, Arash Khakpour, Sole Medina, Eloi Homier, Sara Martín, Elisenda Moya, Karin Kato, Ángel Zotes Ramos, Laura Calvet-Butzbach, Julia Carr, Ireneu Tranis and Kyle Toy in *Here Be Dragons/Non Plus Ultra*.

kinds of movement. These movements were distinct stages of a transcontinental exploration motivated by a definition of performance as acts of embodiment and disembodiment that people engaged in for the excavation, recovery and analysis of personal and collective memories, i.e. knowledge. This exploration attained a certain level of complexity when I was able to see how human systems, mechanical systems, institutional systems, systems of colonialization and systems of institutional power and control were all part of an even wider systems ecology in which non-Western 'alien bodies' (Burt 1998) with diverse cultural systems, tools and forms of organization became pawns in an uneven game of power. And it would be a combination of the guns, germs and steel, along with Christian colonizing fervour and the growing technological/industrial machine (Diamond 1994; Hawkin 2004) that would contribute to some of this destruction. These colonizing voyages would involve a movement back-and-forth over time as a complex and multidimensional unfolding and enfolding.

My own personal voyage was into a different type of unknown and it came at a time and place that seemed fortuitous as I was living and working in a part of the world (Vancouver) that Columbus was never able to reach. I also had an extended team of artists, scholars, scientists, community activists, visionaries, administrators and policy makers who were willing to assist me. And, with the help of digital technology as creative and conceptual tools, we seemed well equipped for the journey. Many of the countries of the 'East' that were Columbus' original destinations (China, Japan and India) had subsequently become modern socio-political and financial powers that were now successfully challenging the autonomy of the West. The idea of 'Going West to Find East' was therefore met by a counteractive 'Going East to Find West' as those regions sought to define themselves through new forms of engagement. PSi5's agenda was relevant to Project Barca's as they both conceived of performance as a personal and historical journey within the context of individual and collective history. 'Going West' and 'Going East' meant much more than opposing geographical and conceptual positions in search of knowledge of 'self' and 'other'; these concepts represented the dynamics of a mediating principle that would propel both the individual researcher and the discipline of performance studies itself toward new levels.

As mentioned previously, my PaR projects were designed as vehicles, *a barca,* to explore creative and academic interests, and to investigate the boundaries of the academic and professional worlds of dance, theatre, music, live art, new media, film and performance using the extensive toolkit of the artist/scholar. While PSi5 was designed to 'map the unexplored boundaries and hinterlands' of performance studies, much of the work we were concerned with in Project Barca had to do with how to redefine these terms within a decolonial context. The apparent paradox that shaped much of the research and which enabled us to embark on the journey 'going west to find east and going east to find west' had much to do with my own identity as a Caribbean-born artist and academic trained primarily in North American and European institutions and working predominantly within the 'triangular' post-colonized educational trade routes that connected Europe, North America and the Caribbean with countries in the Far East.

It would take me quite a long time to realize that I had already experienced some of that East/West dynamic from growing up in the Caribbean. The people who replaced the African slaves were indentured workers from China and India who brought their languages, customs and other cultural practices with them. These Chinese and East Indians mixed with the European, Black, Amerindian and Creole populations, creating a curious *mezcla*. The inevitable mixing between British, French, Spanish, Portuguese, African and Amerindian that occurred led many of the subsequent generations to go 'West' to find or rediscover 'East' and to go 'East' to find or rediscover 'West'. But most of us were inheritors of journeys our ancestors didn't ask for and never wanted to be a part of (Williams 1961). Thus emerged the need to construct a vehicle, *a barca,* that utilized a conceptual framework built with the timbers of performance studies, guided by practices of embodiment and disembodiment and destined to travel in search of elusive notions of self and being.

As I mentioned before, *HBD/NPU* boasted a team of artistic and academic collaborators with backgrounds in countries as diverse as Italy, France, Algeria, Iran, Chile, French Guiana, Brazil, Mexico, Trinidad and Tobago, Japan, China, Hong Kong and Canada. The issue at the heart of the research was how embodied personal and collective memories could be shaped into new architectures of identity and belonging in the form of innovative performance works that spoke to wider sections of society. As performers coming from both sides of the Atlantic all the way to the Pacific, we were all particularly sensitive to issues experienced on a daily basis by immigrants, aliens, outcasts, self-exiles, illegals and people in general who do not readily 'belong' or 'fit in'. We literally faced both east and west simultaneously (Figure 6.5). Attempts to negotiate the 'I', 'me', 'we', 'you', 'us' and 'them' in communities where space is shared by 'natives' and 'non-natives', 'strangers' and 'estranged' emerged in Project Barca and continued later in Contemporary Nomads (2017–21), the final multi-year project this book deals with.

The structure of the phrase 'going west to find east/going east to find west' thus speaks to the paradox of going in one direction to find the other, of starting out with one intention and ultimately having the opposite of that intention manifest itself, and, more importantly perhaps, understanding that the resolution of this seeming paradox is part of the overall process of fulfilling the original set of objectives. This 'going against', which appears as a necessary step in getting to one's destination, guided me in my explorations. So too did Goffman's (1981) idea of a relationship between the self we protect and the one we present to the public, both of which were poles in the unfolding of new spaces and identities for becoming that I was interested in.

But the Caribbean had already been the fated place, for me, where opposing forces met to generate a new potential. It was also a place I had to leave to realize that potential, a going back to move forward so to speak. Project Barca looked at the descendants of those who left Spain, of those native and Indigenous peoples the Spanish encountered on the journey, and those who followed on subsequent journeys, either by choice or through enslavement, in the belief that everyone who made these 'crossings' became implicated in a journey that called for some kind of resolution.

Based on Bakhtin's argument in *The Dialogic Imagination* (1981), I operated on the idea that the individual is constituted as a subject through the merging of many voices and languages. And, as Goffman argued in *The Presentation of Self in Everyday Life* (1959), I also worked on the idea that these identities were constructed in opposition to what surrounded them. Levinas, in his *Totality and Infinity: An Essay on Exteriority* (1969), claimed that it is especially in the encounter with 'the Other', who is exterior to us and outside the reach of our system of thought, that we are obliged to open up our self-contained identities and feelings of security and at-homeness. He also argued that it is at that point that we often find out who we are.

This became true for me and for many others in the cast; it was the 'others' who were both internal and external to us and in the dynamic and creative conflict that fuelled the drive to become. Each performer in *HBD/NPU* (Figures 6.6–6.10) made an enormous contribution to the work, and my hope was that, as audiences saw the performances, listened to the narratives being voiced and looked at the bodies onstage and onscreen through the vocabularies generated by them, they would reflect on their own circumstances. I also hoped that the performances would encourage a mirroring, or a tacit deconstruction by audience members of the architectures of their own individual pasts, which could then help them understand that their daily activities could also be used as performative re-cognition and re-membering strategies.

In thinking about the contribution that my various research projects made to the idea of PaR, I was pleased with the vehicle that Project Barca was becoming. We were able to demonstrate an understanding of performance as acts of embodiment and disembodiment that people engage in for the excavation, recovery and analysis of personal and collective memories. We were also able to accomplish this through a strategic use of different technologies. In all of the choreographic works, we utilized film, video, sound and other interactive technologies both in the creative studio phase as well as in the live and post-production phases. Since the narratives of the performers in Project Barca did not follow a linear timeline, the editing process gave us an additional opportunity to develop the concept of simultaneity as a non-linear approach to time and space, and to suggest multiple domains of self by presenting multiple presences in different locations. Audiences were never completely sure exactly who and where the 'I', 'we', 'they' and 'us' were located in the complex staging of film and installation works (Figures 6.6–6.10).

In the films, the images of dancers were almost never synchronous with their voices, which opened up a host of issues about how stereotypes were created and maintained in everyday life.[23] For example, when one performer speaks of his Arab ancestors having to leave Spain in 1492 directly after the conquest of Granada, a section of the video installation shows images that are deliberately not aligned with his text, or at least not representative of it. During the narrative of that person's family moving to Vancouver, Canada in 2005, it is mainly other faces that are visible. The same occurs with other performers – their texts are never wholly consistent with the images shown, hence producing a set of overlapping narratives that audiences must exercise some effort to understand. This effort is crucial to claiming the knowledge that exists within the larger structure. With the sound and video files asynchronously looped, the act of reconstruction itself by the audience becomes performative.

> In 1492 my family had to leave Spain
> اجدادم ناگزیر شدند اسپانیا را ترک کنند۱۴۹۲در
> The other option was execution or, worse still, conversion
> راه دیگر پیش رو اعدام بود، یا از ان ناگوارتر، تغییر مذهب
> So we went back to Persia through Africa; Granada to Iran
> اینگونه شد که از قلب آفریقا گذشتیم و به ایران بازگشتیم؛ از گرانادا تا شمال ایران
> The longest way you can ever imagine
> طولانی‌ترین مسیری که هرگز می‌توان متصور شد
> We moved to Vancouver in 2005
> به ونکوور مهاجرت کردیم۲۰۰۵در
> Freedom in the woods of the west!
> در جستجوی آزادی در سرزمین‌های باختر!
>
> (Arash Khakpour)

In the text above, the performer uses a historic moment to imagine a scene from the lives of his ancestors. The expulsion of Islamic peoples from Granada – the last Islamic stronghold in Spain – took place at the same time that Columbus was granted leave to explore the Indies. In fact, the contract for that first voyage of exploration was signed on the battlefield of Granada. Therefore, the account that 'we went back to Persia through Africa; Granada to Iran' is a historic possibility, even though it was only imagined by the performer in question. In this case, a precisely accurate individual story was sacrificed in support of a collective one – subsuming individual identity within a broader collective truth. One could also imagine that the phrase 'in the woods of the west' might contain a deliberate political ambiguity, suggesting the exchange of one form of personal and social containment for another. Who knows what kind of forests were waiting to trick, deceive or ensnare the twenty-first-century migrant?

In another situation, a different performer speaks of her distant relative, the captain of a Norwegian sailing ship who took his young daughter on voyages with him. The dancer comments on this female relative being allowed onboard in the 1850s, an uncanny but apparently true story. Although the audience does not know who this dancer in the video is, the installation asks them to imagine who she could be amongst the other female bodies represented in the four channels of the video.

> In 1492, Columbus left Palos with three ships and ninety men and boys; no women, all stories of men! [...]
>
> September 4th, 1850, Gunder Mauritz Erichsen was born and a tradition of Norwegian sailing ship captains continued. Mauritz shares my September 4th birthday. He took his youngest daughter on a couple of long voyages. She wrote a journal. Finally, a female protagonist! Can you imagine a young girl as an explorer in the 1880's?
>
> (Julia Carr)

In the text above, this performer problematizes the overwhelmingly masculine presence of those early explorations. However, she also draws attention to an anomaly, the presence of a young woman on board a ship full of seasoned male adventurers, to debunk another stereotype.

ambos lados

ambos lados[24] (2013) was a short film that incorporated material from *Here Be Dragons (Stage I Creative Preview), Barca: el otro lado* and *HBD/NPU*,[25] and took it to another level. For example, the performers' stories and dance movements reappeared as a more complex encounter between individuals from different groups on both sides of the Atlantic and around the Pacific. For example, a third performer's story unfolds in the Basque language Euskara, with the English translation following. We never see this narrator in the film *ambos lados*, nor do we hear her text in English, but we do see her and hear some of the text in both English and Basque during the live performance of *HBD/NPU*:

Emakumezkoa, langile klasekoa, abertzalea, ezkertia, artista. Horiek dira nire nortasun markak. Bakoitzak zapalkuntza gradu bat dakar, politikoa, ekonomikoa edo soziala. Nahiz eta batzuetan ezikusiarena egitea hari aurre egitea eta borroka egitea baino errazago gertatu. Eskubide eta justiziaren konkistan sinesten dut. Uko egiten diot lurren, arimen eta gorputzen kolonizazioari. Horregatik, niretzat 1492a lotsa-sinbolo bat da.

Euskaldun bezala Amerikarekin lotura empatikoa dut: nire herriaren historia handia han garatu bait da. Badiote euskal baleontziek Kolon iritsi baino azkoz lehenago ur Kanadiarretan arrantzan egiten zutela. Ohiko portua Terranova zen. Kolonen bidaietan euskaldun asko egon ziren, ontziolak eta nabigatzaileak. Geroago gudari mertzenario batzuk izan ziren ere, Lope de Agirre adibidez, eta misiolari asko (dominikoak, jesuitak, frantziskotarrak [...]).

(Amerikar) indiarren eskubideen aldeko eta kolonizazioren gehiegikeriei uko egin zien lehen legelaria, Francisco de Vitoria, nire hirikoa, izan zen. Berarekin Jende-Eskubidea hasi zen.

XVIII mendetik aurrera, Euskal Herriko jesuitak kanporatu zituztenetik, eta orain dela 40 urte arte, Ameriketaranz emigrazio eta euskal erbeste izugarria gertatu da: gerra karlistetan, gerra zibilan, 40 urteko diktaduran eta okupazioan [...] XX. mendean 150.000 euskaldun baino gehiago erbesteratu ziren Amerikan: Argentinan, Venezuelan, Mexikon [...]

Nire birramona biologikoak emigratu zuen ere. Nire amaren ama adoptatua zen. Dirudienez bere amak, emakume librea -beharbada dantzaria-, haurdun geratu zen herriko gizon ospetsu eta ezkondu batekin. Traba ez egiteko, desagertu behar izan zuen, eta oparitu zioten Amerikarako, itzulerarik gabeko, itsazontzizko bidaia. Haien alaba, nire amona, herrixkan geratu zen, berezko deiturarik gabe.

Emakume bezala emakume guztiekin lotura sentitzen dut.

Rakel bezala, saltsa dantzatuz gozatzen dut.

(Rakel Ezpeleta)

I am a woman, working class, Basque, and left-winged. These are my marks of identity. Each involves some degree of social or political oppression. Although it is sometimes easier to ignore it than to face it and fight against it. I believe in the conquest of rights and justice. I repudiate the colonization of lands, souls and bodies. For this reason, 1492 is a symbol of shame for me.

As a Basque I feel sympathetically linked to the Americas: the great history of my country has developed there. It's said that Basque whalers caught in Canadian waters much earlier than Columbus arrived. A frequent port was Terranova (Newfoundland). There were many Basques involved in the voyage of Columbus; shipyards and sailors. Then, there were some warrior mercenaries, such as Lope de

> Agirre, and many, many missionaries (Dominicans, Franciscans, Jesuits [...]) who built their lives there, with the new people. The first lawyer ever interested in the rights of the Indians and who rejected the excesses committed during colonization was Francisco de Vitoria, from my city. He started the Law of Nations in the XVI century. From the 18th century on, when the Jesuits were expelled from Euskal Herria, and up to four decades ago, Basque exile and avalanches of emigrations to the Americas occurred: Carlist Wars, civil war, 40 years of dictatorship. In the 20th century more than 150,000 Basques exiled into the Americas: Argentina, Venezuela, Mexico [...]
>
> My biological great grandmother also emigrated. The mother of my mother was adopted. Her mother apparently was a free spirit, perhaps a dancer, a woman who got pregnant with an illustrious, married man. She had to go, so that she would not be an inconvenience, she was sent by boat to the Americas, a non-return journey. And the daughter, my grandmother, would stay in town, without her real surname.
>
> As a woman I am attached to all women. As Rakel, I enjoy salsa dancing.
>
> (Rakel Ezpeleta)

The Basque language, *Euskara,* is one of the most unique languages I have ever heard and quite difficult for a foreigner to understand. The speaker in *HBD/NPU* is a talented actress, singer and dancer who is also proud of her ancestry and fierce in defence of her people's history. As with so many of the other texts, the audience is never quite sure how much of her story is true. But this is not as important as the fact that these and other stories are reconstructed versions of historical events being narrated by performers attempting to understand the full extent of what was embodied in their texts within the rehearsal/workshop context in which they were generated. Factually they were true in the sense that such events really did take place. It would take a few chapters or even an entire volume to discuss in detail the various texts that generated the performances, installations and documentary films during Project Barca. These examples draw attention to the multi-dimensional modes of presentation that the material is capable of as well as how the relatively simple video and sound technologies conspire to construct a historical 'truth'. In the case of post fifteenth-century colonisations, the primary technologies that Columbus and other European men utilised to access the New World were ships and weapons – 'guns, germs, and steel' (Diamond 1994).

Columbus' triad of ships, *La Santa Maria*, *La Pinta* and *La Niña* (Figures 6.9 right/front and 6.11) became symbols for the opening up of a New World, for the exploitation and colonization of peoples across the Americas. Throughout

FIGURE 6.11: Janelle Reid, Luciana D'Anunciação and Milton Lim in *Here Be Dragons (Stage I Creative Preview)*.

Project Barca, I tried to exploit this triad of vehicles in a more conceptual manner and with a different set of voyages in mind. For example, the three individuals in Figure 6.11 were used as guides/commentators in *Here Be Dragons (Stage I Creative Preview)*. In HBD/NPU I developed the concept a little further with a new more professional triad that can be seen in right half section of Figure 6.9. These three performers literally introduce the work, were commentators vocally and movement-wise throughout, much as one would do in the style of a documentary film, eventually closing the entire performance as a final full stop at the end of a book. As much as I wanted to keep the initial trio of performers in *Here Be Dragons (Stage I Creative Preview)*, I could not, the main reason being that I wanted a group that that had a different combination of languages, cultures and artistic disciplines that challenged the cast of performers from Barcelona and Vancouver.

The apparent paradox that shaped much of Project Barca's research and enabled us to embark on this journey had much to do with my own belonging to the 'underside' of history as described by scholars such as Dallmayr (2004), Dussel (1996) and Maldonado-Torres (2008), for example. The term 'underside' here referring to geographical regions as much as states of being – the condition of those whose voices are usually left out of history, the colonized, the racialized, women, etc. As performers in search of knowledge of self and opportunities to engage with 'new territories', we choose to design a different kind of vehicle, *a barca*, utilizing a conceptual framework built from the timbers of dance and performance studies, and guided by practices of embodiment and disembodiment.

Isabella's Dream

Isabella's Dream (2014) was the final production in the Project Barca series. As I mentioned before, this work was made possible through a 2014 Granada Artist-in-Residence invitation from Professor Lynette Hunter in the Department of Theatre and Dance at the University of California Davis.[26] The production also marked the third country I was given the opportunity to work in with a diverse group of performers, this time with graduate and undergraduate students. The idea of 'new architectures of memory and identity' became more critical as I was working in a part of the Americas where Spain had a more limited and later influence than in Mesoamerica and South America. But North America had its own set of 'going west' narratives. In fact, the history of the United States and Canada is steeped in stories of extended westward journeys and of many tragic encounters with Native Americans and First Nations cultures, tragic mostly for these Native Americans and First Nations. The terms 'out West' and 'back East' therefore hold great significance for those early settlers who came from Europe to North America as well as their modern descendants. Although I had read a great deal about these experiences and performed in some of the classic American Modern Dance works celebrating them in my early dance career, I made it clear to the cast and crew of *Isabella's Dream* that my goal was not to repeat, retell or glorify these narratives. Rather, the work was more focused on establishing a connection between a complex set of events that continued to resonate in the bodies of contemporary peoples and in the spaces they occupied. *Isabella's Dream* began in the imaginary, in a constructed memory that was informed by history as well as the lived experiences of the descendants of the many who continue to occupy those spaces.

Isabella, La Católica, Queen of Castile and León, is daydreaming about how to acquire the resources she and her husband Ferdinand II of Aragon would need to become a major Christian power on the Iberian Peninsula and in Europe as a whole. Dominated by Arabic and Moorish conquests for centuries, the Christian forces on the Peninsula began an equally long *Reconquista*,[27] or reconquest, to reclaim these lands (Hazard 1975). In a scene that I imagine could well have taken place, she abruptly wakes up from a pre-cognitive dream fuelled by unceasing daytime thoughts about where the resources for this latter stage of the *Reconquista* would come from, as well as repeated requests for an audience from an Italian sailor named Cristóbal Colón.

Now let us imagine another woman, a Mexican *seer* perhaps, on the other side of the world, divining that something terrible was about to happen and that it would be precipitated by the actions of strange men coming from far far away. These men would come in large sailing vessels, clothed in metal armour and carrying weapons never before seen in that part of the world. But these scenes are not being played out in Spain or in Mexico, and the opening lines of this drama outlined below are certainly not those of Queen Isabella or an imaginary Mexican *seer*; they were written and voiced by Joyful Simpson and María de los Ángeles Ceja, Jewish American and Mexican American performers respectively in *Isabella's Dream*. The scenes that unfold begin just after 8.00 p.m. on 22 May 2014 at the University Patio, Nelson Gallery at UC Davis with Isabella's/Joyful's words (Figure 6.12):

> My dress was richly embroidered, fit for a Queen. Yes, I was a Queen. Somewhere in a forest, in a clearing of sorts, a distinguished looking man was laying out something on the ground. He looked very composed, intent on drawing something, a kind of map perhaps. I felt eyes in the darkness at the edge of the forest looking at me. I felt strangely connected to that man and to the unseen eyes looking, searching, undressing, and peering deep inside me. I woke up sweating, terrified, arms clasped around my breasts, as if to protect myself from what was to come.
>
> (Joyful Simpson)

FIGURE 6.12: Joyful Simpson and María de los Ángeles Ceja in *Isabella's Dream*.

And our seer Isabella 'Chabela'/María:

> I saw a woman, a white woman, far away. She was dressed in black and white. She is weeping. She sent a man to find the East, but he found us. Then there came a terrible fire that scorched the forest. In the middle of the fire there was a woman sitting, unharmed. That woman was me. My name is Isabella. But my real name is Chabela.
>
> (María de los Ángeles Ceja)

These two texts open and close the hour-long production of *Isabella's Dream*;[28] the first sets the stage for what unfolds, and the second marks the point where that unfolding ends. What happens in-between the two scenes can be thought of as a coming together of opposing forces or energies to create a third mediating force or energy that would change the course of both countries' histories. Arguably, *Isabella's Dream* was more of a catching up than a beginning; the cast of performers and I were reminding ourselves as well as our audiences of the extent to which our present circumstances had been determined by the actions of those in the past, and that changes in direction were still needed. But such change first requires a fuller understanding of what took place in the past; a proper re-cognising and re-membering before new directions could be built. The unique resources at UC Davis allowed me to recreate a new version of the key motif used in *Barca: el otro lado*. This was a spinal brace that belonged to one of the performers in Barcelona, which was used as a corset and an *armadura* or breastplate armour in *HBD/NPU*.

The head of the costume shop offered me the luxury of a fifteenth century styled Spanish royal dress. Although I eventually got a costume that looked like a cross between Spanish and Elizabethan (Figures 6.12–6.13), I was nevertheless extremely pleased with the design as it added an extra dimension to the coloniality of power that was fundamental to the thematic of *Isabella's Dream*. The dress became a symbol for the shifting nature of power in the New World. In Figure 6.13, the image in the middle of the composition is that of our New World seer, and the four images surrounding her are the four characters who attempt to inhabit the dress as a power motif. The text below is that of the African American performer Mary-Ann Brooks at the bottom left of the composite image.

The performer as herself:

> We lived on the East Coast in a place called Connecticut. In 1492 my father's Cherokee ancestors were also on the East Coast. My mother's and father's African ancestors were probably on the west coast of Africa. I have no way of knowing

FIGURE 6.13: María de los Ángeles Ceja, Joyful Simpson, Tiffany Martin, Mary Anne Brooks and Daniel 'Bear' Davis in *Isabella's Dream*.

> where my mother's European ancestors might have been. I am the only one in my immediate family who went west to what is now called California.
>
> (Mary-Ann Brooks)

Brook's words indicate the rich and complex cultural heritage she inherited; there are at least three cultures with very different belief systems embedded in the body of this one performer. And when she puts on and then later discards the symbolic royal outfit of Isabella – the last of four performers to do so – we understand what is being discarded and why.

The Mexican-American performer in the middle of Figure 6.13 is surrounded by the Jewish-American woman in the top right corner, the Scandinavian-American woman in the bottom right, the African-American woman to the left of her and the Jewish-American male figure in the top left-hand corner of the image. In the production, the character in the top right corner who opens the performance loses the dress in a nightmarish scene that appears to be conjured up by the *seer* figure in the middle. The other three characters each occupy the costume, momentarily shaping it into a different identity. But each of them, for one reason or another, eventually discards the dress and what it stands for. Additional excerpts from the texts of the remaining two performers (the characters at the bottom right and at the top left of the image) are in Figure 6.13. 'Stop! I command you to stop! In the name of the Queen, I command you to stop now!' (Daniel 'Bear' Davis 2014, see Figure 6.14).

FIGURE 6.14: Daniel 'Bear' Davis. The male Jewish-American performer as a Cortes-like character.[29]

The performer as himself:

We talk of the promised land
As if it's a *place* to *arrive* to.
Seeking that perfect finality where something settles, and we know we are finally home.
What if it's that very seeking that keeps us wandering in the desert for decades?
Always looking for the next best thing.
Always yearning for the garden.
The garden in my head is an Eastern European village.
Full of wood and rust and cobblestones.
People are singing. I don't speak the language, but I know the tune.
And I sing along, and I'm swept up in a dancing throng of smiling faces.
It's so tempting to pull out all the weeds and make the garden perfect!
But that music that brings me, finally, home, it grows out of the embrace of hardship.
The joy of the dance is built on the backs of sorrow and loss. We eat bitter greens dipped in saltwater to remember. We eat the garden to bring us home.

(Daniel 'Bear' Davis)

The Scandinavian-American female performer as herself:

Roots, spread out in the mud
And scattered in the sky
We are from so many places
This blood, a blending of streams and rain

Floating in a body
From Norway, lifted his skull and made the sky
Four corners, dwarves, to hold the corners up
North, East, South, West
My family believed in a warrior religion
Ruthlessness, savagery, strength and will
1492 [...] these myths, the gods, fading
Some even stopped believing
Then, from the East, Christianity
One god, unity
A healing god figure
1492 [...] my family stayed [...] centuries passed
My family stayed [...] 1830
Great, great grandmother
Passage west...here
Came, settled [...] passages
Sometimes I dream of Norway
Stones, sea, hills
It lingers in my breath and bone
Perhaps someday I'll go
Retrace the footsteps where the grass grows
Where they danced and sang in circles
Long ago

(Tiffany Martin)

To conclude this chapter, I openly admit that it is impossible to give enough credit to the many performers who participated in *Isabella's Dream*, or the valuable contributions that each individual made to the project as a whole. What Project Barca showed was the complex identities that exist in each one of us and the potential to create new architectures out of them. The richness of the stories, the beauty of the performers sharing their embodied knowledge and their willingness to do this in an honest manner in front of their peers and strangers remains in my memory as well as in the extensive performance archives with material that is continuously being added to the website.[30]

What began as a supposedly spontaneous thought during a trip to Barcelona in the summer of 2010 unfolded as a multi-year project that brought a new level of knowing to dozens of people from across five continents. One can say that that summer in Barcelona was not an accident, and that perhaps it was just one of many reminders that I previously failed to notice. Project Barca was not just the result of seminal work done on Transnet and The Touched Project, it was part of an unfolding that included individual works produced over decades of search in different geographical, psychological and virtual spaces. Following a hypothesis which claimed that human beings are cognitively embodied through their own lived experiences of movement through space and time, I sought to revisit, i.e. re-member and to re-cognize, what had previously taken place by different bodies in different spaces, through acts of performance. Also, following the premise that dance and choreography are the deliberate organization of those movements into coherent and meaningful structures towards a goal of a self in the process of becoming, I am fulfilling a stated thesis that movement is analogous to thought unfolding that then gives rise to other more complex movements that are multi-directional in scope. Hence, the process of staging these works supports the theory of practice that I've taken great pains to set out in previous chapters. Contemporary Nomads, the fourth project in this series, adds a final twist to these efforts.

NOTES

1. *Constellation*, vol. 11, no. 1, 2004, pp. 102–20.
2. *Psychology in Society*. On-line version ISSN 2309-8708. *Print version* ISSN 1015-6046. *Psychology in Society* no. 41, Durban, 2011, https://citeseerx.ist.psu.edu/viewdoc/download?doi=10.1.1.1060.4655&rep=rep1&type=pdf.
3. SSHRC grant application, 2011.
4. www.henrydaniel.ca/project-barca.
5. www.henrydaniel.ca/project-barca.
6. *Here Be Dragons* (*Stage I Creative Preview, 2012*).
7. *Touched*, *t2*, *t2_echo*, *Imprint*, *Imprint II*.
8. www.henrydaniel.ca/the-touched-project.
9. Email communication from 22 September 2011.
10. www.thewholenote.com/index.php/newsroom/beatcolumns-sp-2121861476/choral-world-music/19139-john-cage-master-of-silence.
11. *Voces del Vacio* (2012) was a short film based on material generated in Barcelona, Spain for Project Barca; *Implicados* (2012), was another dance film, also based on material generated in Spain, and *Here Be Dragons (Stage I Creative Preview)* premiered soon after on 1 June 2012 in Studio T at the Goldcorp Centre for the Arts. *Barca – el otro lado* premiered on 6 November 2012 at Theatre Nau Ivanow in Barcelona, while *Here Be Dragons-Non plus ultra* premiered 10–12 January 2013 in Vancouver, BC, at the Fei and Milton Wong Experimental Theatre, Goldcorp Centre for the Arts with a cast of performers from Barcelona and Vancouver. *Isabella's Dream* was done in the United States on an Artistic Residency at the University of California, Davis. It premiered on 22–25 May 2014.
12. None of the research would have been possible without the kindness and generosity of Owner/Director/Manager Sonia Klamburg, www.areadansa.com.

13. Links to these works can be found on my research website at www.henrydaniel.ca
14. These men were part of Columbus' crew on his first voyage to the Caribbean.
15. Since hydrophobia was a symptom of rabies the term was used as a substitute for the disease.
16. This information is clearly written in documentation hung near the entry to the *Synagoga*.
17. www.theguardian.com/world/2010/apr/01/muslim-catholic-mosque-fight?INTCMP=IL-CNETTXT3487; http://soerenkern.com/2013/02/14/spain-ban-remains-muslim-prayer-cathedral/.
18. www.psi-web.org/psi-archive-project/psi-conferences-archive/psi-5/.
19. www.psi-web.org/psi-archive-project/psi-conferences-archive/psi-5/.
20. Program of PSi5, www.psi-web.org/psi-archive-project/psi-conferences-archive/psi-5/.
21. New approaches to theatre studies and performance analysis. 21–3 March 1997, http://guenter-berghaus.com/?page_id=1304.
22. *Barca: The other side.*
23. Short excerpts from the various productions within Project Barca can be seen on the author's website at www.henrydaniel.ca.
24. Spanish for 'both sides' as in Spain and Canada on different sides of the Atlantic.
25. *Barca: the other side*
26. https://arts.ucdavis.edu/seasonal-event/isabellas-dream-granada-artist-henry-daniel.
27. www.britannica.com/event/Reconquista.
28. www.vimeo.com/114213623.
29. Hernan Cortes was a Spanish Conquistador who was primarily responsible for the fall of the Aztec Empire, which eventually established Spanish rule in much of Mesoamerica.
30. www.henrydaniel.ca/.

ACT 3

7

Contemporary Nomads

Nomadism

III
I stared back at the Celotex
ceiling of room 16,
my coat still on, for minutes
as the key warmed my palm-
TV, telephone, maid service,
and a sense of the parking lot
through cinder blocks-homesick
for islands with fringed shores
like the mustard-gold coverlet.
A roach crossed its oceanic
carpet with scurrying oars
to a South that it knew, calm
shallows of crystalline green.
I studied again how glare
dies on a wall, till a complex
neon scribbled its signature.

(Walcott 1987: 105)

The concept of the modern-day nomad has been addressed by numerous writers from quite different perspectives. I draw brief attention to a few of them here as a means of introducing the final multi-year research project in this publication. The feminist scholar Rosi Braidotti once wrote that the nomadism she defended as a theoretical option was also an existential condition that translated into a style of thinking and a mode of writing (Braidotti 2011). Stuart Hall spoke of the complex circular destiny of the New World nomad constantly moving between centre and periphery (1998). Yana Meerzon claimed that there is a kind of nomadic consciousness in those who 'by force or by choice find themselves on other shores, [and] for whom the hardship of exile is both an existential ordeal and an opportunity to exercise their creative abilities, professional competence, and artistic resources' (Meerzon 2012: 2).

In the text of *The Arkansas Testament* (1987), Derek Walcott embodies Meerzon's perspective as we find the already famous but not yet Nobel Laureate poet/playwright staring back at the ceiling of a motel room, homesick for an island home in the Caribbean and poetically musing over the cockroach that scurries across the carpet next to his bed. Braidotti, Meerzon, Hall and Walcott all have something in common: they chose to move away from the places where their most formative experiences took place but were nevertheless still able to maintain important connections to those spaces. Nomadism, migration and exile are all different forms of displacement, but they are also modes of existence that increasingly defines the conditions many of us, for one reason or another, find ourselves living under.

In a 2011 final report sponsored by the British government on global environmental migration changes (Government Office for Science 2011), the 'Prospects for International Migration Governance' (MIGPROSP)[1] project leader Andrew Geddes claimed that one of the challenges posed by migration was not that people will move, but that they will become trapped where they currently live, or conversely, move towards areas of risk rather than away from them. He further asserted that migration should be seen as an adaptation to environmental change. I argue that some of the same issues equivocate migration and what I call contemporary nomadism, with the difference being those in the latter category have more choice and opportunities to move than the former. Therefore, I would consider each one of the above-mentioned writers a contemporary nomad. Every culture, language, art form or identity has its own set of borders, real or imagined, and part of my definition of a contemporary nomad is that such an individual always seeks to defy any border that attempts to contain or limit their creative potential. Therefore, as Meerzon suggests, the successes of these writers could also be seen as modes of entrapment; trapped by frameworks that limit how others see them or how they wish to be seen.

The point here is that researchers concerned with transnational migratory movements, and those concerned with forms of artistic expression share a desire to understand how individual bodies and entire populations are defined by events that compel them to move beyond the borders of their accustomed spaces. In the same way that my thinking process requires a crossing of disciplinary borders, so too does my body require me to cross spatial and geographical borders. Since a key objective of the Contemporary Nomads project was to investigate notions of mapping as a strategic performative device for accumulating knowledge about bodies and the environments through which they move, the cortical and cartographic movements of writers such as those mentioned above speak a great deal about how one negotiates such a condition.

After the experience of Transnet, which invited an international network of artists and scientists to share ideas in the symposium 'Performing Art Performing Science: Trans-disciplinary Approaches to Performance'; The Touched Project, which looked at how power influences behaviour in both human and technological systems; and Project Barca, which examined some of the consequences of a systematic European colonization, it seemed natural to want to look at the more fundamental questions of: (1) why contemporary peoples moved away from their accustomed dwellings and how their modes of thinking manifested performatively in space and time? As a choreographer, these questions are not at all difficult for me to visualize as a research project. In fact, the reader may recall other questions I posed at the beginning of this book when I suggested that embodied knowledge presumes that there are mental, emotional and physical maps generated and stored within the body whose scripts could be staged as unique performance works. At that point, I also asked the question of what happens when these same bodies become displaced from their lived environments. Can new scripts not be written?

Contemporary Nomads was inspired by a set of recurring transnational movements over extended periods of time. I was interested in the concept of return, in the sense of an initial cause whose effects would eventually seek out their origin. I imagined that, starting with a small case study, I could gather enough information to create such a map. The case study would begin with a series of interviews with people – professional and non-professional 'performers' – who were living along or close to two main geographic axes, with Vancouver as the central focus in a map that was constantly being reconfigured. One of these axes ran in an East/West direction connecting Europe, the Americas and the Far East, and the other in a North/South direction connecting Canada and the United States to Mexico, and Central and South America. This of course was an enormous space, but I felt that Vancouver and its unique geographic location and historical past could be an interesting focus for the study.

The process began by setting a few practical goals, practical in the sense that I needed to convince the Federal granting agency to give me the finances to implement the project. Contingent on that funding, I would first begin work with trained performers who were already in or had recently moved to Vancouver from elsewhere in Canada or abroad. Second, I would engage regular bodies who were also Canadian or had recently moved to Vancouver from elsewhere. The third stage would involve a range of bodies outside Canada along both of these two axes as far as my resources would allow. Essentially, I was doing a reverse ethnographic study, one that started with bodies trained in specific dance and theatre performance contexts and later moved on to 'ordinary' people who had no such professional training. The work would involve collecting material; stories or informal conversations with those who were willing to share their experiences with me with regard to five stages of a movement process I envisioned. These stories or informal conversations did not necessarily have to be about migration per se, the point was simply to find out what the term 'contemporary nomad' elicited in people's minds. Below is that envisioning.

1. ***Home*** – beginning with the conditions that one lives under and calls home, but which one also thinks of moving away from.
2. ***The Parting*** – remembering the moment that one decides to leave, and when one begins the actual physical journey.
3. ***The Journey*** – the specific route taken and any event, experience, situation, landscape marker (a mountain, a body of water, a person, a path, a fellow traveller, a spoken word, etc.) or other experience that was unique to or crucial to the journey.
4. ***Arriving…or not*** – the feeling of making it, or conversely not making it, to the desired destination.
5. ***The settlement/return*** – the process of making a new home, and the dream of finding one's way back, i.e. the (im)possibility of return.

Working across different disciplinary platforms, but prominently featuring dance, theatre, live performance and film, the research was designed to investigate these five stages of the traveller's journey – in the broadest sense of that term – seeking to find out how, when and why individuals and populations move from place to place. The more philosophical question underlying the work, i.e. what it means to say that movement is the process of thought unfolding that gives rise to other movements that are more multi-directional, would be the unasked question lying in wait, so to speak. Why move? Can I not stay here and leave things as they are? Where should I go? What are the dangers involved in staying as opposed to leaving? What lies out there? How do I get to my destination? What will I find there and how can I return with the objectives of my search? For the purpose of the research grant, however, the key objectives of the project were stated as follows:

1. To explore some of the large- and small-scale international migration patterns we are currently witnessing through the lens of choreography and performance.
2. To investigate performative body practices at both micro and macro scales to understand how complex economic, socio-political, geo-physical and neuro-biological forces act on human beings so that they are driven to cross difficult borders.

3. To extend my long-term objective of having dance, choreography and performance practices seen as valid research activities within an academic context.
4. To examine the nature of a thought unfolding in space and time through a body.

The core research team – who were also trusted advisers and former collaborators – consisted of people working inside as well as outside of Academia. I first invited Dr Ali Abdi, a Somali-born Canadian and professor of educational studies at the University of British Columbia, to the project. Abdi's research was in citizenship and human rights education, international development education, multi-centric philosophies and methodologies of education, postcolonial studies in education, and social and cultural foundations of education. I also invited Dr Handel Wright, a Sierra Leone born Canadian and professor of cultural studies of education, multiculturalism (critical and comparative) and its alternatives, anti-racism, critical race theory, cosmopolitanism, interculturalism, identity issues (youth, Africana, politics of difference, complexities of identity and identification), comparative and international education issues and postcolonialism and diaspora. These two men had considerable expertise in areas I did not, and in our conversations together, as well as in their academic writings, I was guided towards some very important sources that would be of enormous help to the project as a whole.

Because I needed an experienced filmmaker on the project, I invited my colleague, Canadian and Italian-born Professor Simone Rapisarda to join the research team. Rapisarda's experience as an award-winning filmmaker and educator whose feature-length films challenged the traditional borders between creative and critical practice, and his work and advice on documentary film, oral history and anthropology was seminal to the project. His own films had already garnered accolades at festivals in Locarno, Amsterdam, Vienna, Rotterdam, Ann Arbor, Montreal, Vancouver and Los Angeles, and were part of the permanent collections of museums and galleries such as the MoMA in New York and the National Gallery in Washington DC. As I mentioned previously, his expertise and advice would prove extremely beneficial to the project, particularly in how I would eventually stage the audio-visual installations.

My three non-university-based artistic collaborators were Israeli-born Canadian composer/sound designer Adam Basanta, and two Taiwanese-born Canadians, Sammy and Shanghan Chien, brothers who formed the Chimerik Media Collective. Adam, Sammy and Shanghan were extremely talented artists who had previously worked with me as students on The Touched Project as research assistants and who had gone on to very successful careers in their respective fields. Since all three were now sought-after artists working across Europe, the Americas, Asia and the Middle East, it was indeed a pleasure for me to capitalise on their limited time and valuable expertise as far as the visual media and sound design were concerned. All five collaborators, and myself, were born and spent a substantial amount of time outside of Canada, a fact that enabled us to agree on quite a few base-line issues and possibilities for the direction of the research.

nómadas

The first staged work was *nómadas* (Figures 7.1 and 7.2),[2] a combined live performance and audio-visual installation that positioned Vancouver as a destination, transit point or 'home' at the apex of the two axes I spoke of earlier. And, as per my accustomed research strategy within the University system, I assigned the performers a personal task three months ahead of the first rehearsal date. This task was as follows:

1. How would you define the term 'contemporary nomad' and what would the characteristics of such a person be?

FIGURE 7.1: The *nómadas_the installation* with Kenny León, Katrina Mugume and Montserrat Videla Samper.

2. Write a story about your personal relationship to the term; this could be centred around any of the nine characteristics outlined below or to ones you feel are more relevant to you or your family's situation. What's important is that the text addresses the theme of the production in some direct or indirect way.
3. Be ready to record this information as initial material for movement improvisation.

The nine characteristics referred to above were as follows:

1. An incessant curiosity that drives someone to keep searching for answers about their own existence.
2. A sense of belonging nowhere completely but at the same time having parts of one's identity that are at home in different places.
3. An inability to immerse oneself completely in any one established community even though there is an almost romantic longing to do so.

FIGURE 7.2: *nómadas* cast: Allison Vicente, Amy Griffith, Anja Graham, Caitlin McKinnon, Jeremy O'Neill, Kadin Vanden Heuvel, Kaia Shukin, Kestrel Paton, Kevin Locsin, Lynnelle Sura, Montserrat Videla Samper, Nelle Lee, Seana Williams, Vienna Wong and Yian Chen.

4. An ability to recognize others in the same predicament.
5. A formal or informal indoctrination in more than one language, cultural form or institutional system.
6. An attachment to these nation-based languages, cultural forms or institutions and to the people who practice them.
7. Relocation by force or other means from any one of these institutional frameworks, systems or countries.
8. Someone who regularly and sometimes even fluidly moves between these systems, institutions or countries.
9. A desire not to be pinned down.

To give some encouragement and guidance to everyone for the task, I set up an online folder in which I deposited – throughout the 2017 summer break – images, short videos and writings that pointed to potential directions we would be pursuing once the rehearsals began. My own preparation involved visits to countries I had previously lived in or had close connections with, talking to people, making notes, collecting images and making video recordings of places and events I thought would be useful reference points.

For example, on a visit to Germany that summer I found materials on exhibit at the *Deutsches Auswandererhaus Bremerhaven* (German Emigration Centre Bremerhaven) that documented over three hundred years of emigration to the New World, as well as immigration to Germany itself since the 1800s. In this city, as well as in visits to the United Kingdom, France and Switzerland, I was quite surprised by how much the population demographic I remembered in cities such as London, Chester, Paris, Metz, München and Zürich had changed. I was also struck by the ubiquitous presence of the shipping container in every city I visited.

As a symbol of the international movement of goods, the shipping container had become transformed into any and everything from temporary housing, offices, full-time homes as well as vehicles that temporarily housed those who were desperately trying to reach distant lands. In London, the containers were restaurants in the Brixton Market area.[3] In the city of Metz in northern France I saw one that housed an impressive art exhibition.[4] And in Münster, Germany, where the railway station was being renovated, they were temporary offices. This ubiquity inspired me to convert a set of boxes that had been sitting in my garage for some years after the production of *Imprint II* into a new set design for *nómadas* (2017).[5] The design was also adapted for use in *nómadas_the installation* (2017) and *nómadas 2018_excerpts* (2018) (see Figures 7.2–7.6). Once this decision was made, I felt strongly that the installation and the live performance should function independently as well as in a combined dance, theatre, live art and performance art event. In fact, the first

FIGURE 7.3: *nómadas* cast: Allison Vicente, Amy Griffith, Anja Graham, Caitlin McKinnon, Jeremy O'Neill, Kadin Vanden Heuvel, Kaia Shukin, Kestrel Paton, Kevin Locsin, Lynnelle Sura, Montserrat Videla Samper, Nelle Lee, Seana Williams, Vienna Wong and Yian Chen.

iteration of *nómadas* had the installation introducing the live performance event and later re-emerging briefly to close it. In this way, the audience had the opportunity to interact with the boxes and the installation prior to the live performance as well as after the live event ended. In Figure 7.2, one can see the enhanced cast in the individual boxes that were assembled in the software program *Isadora* by the Chien brothers Sammy and Shanghan for a third version of the audio-visual installation. In this image, the entire feature is tripled vertically to exaggerate the effect. In this version, there were three video projectors, one for each of the screens.

The videos in the three horizontal screens and the sound score all had different lengths such that the spoken text and electronic score never coincided with the same image throughout their individual cycles. This organization meant that one could only guess who was speaking by viewing several cycles of the roughly fifteen-minute installation and making informed guesses that hopefully matched content to voices and bodies. As the reader may remember, this was a strategy that I first employed in Project Barca to good effect. There were, however, several trick images or sound sequences that could throw the viewer off. For example, a couple of the speakers were never present in the video and some of the individuals in the composite video image – those in the boxes or in the black and white images in the central part of the frame – had texts that were not in the sound score. In effect, I was playing with Barrett's theory of how stereotypes are constructed (Barrett

2017).[6] And, as I always do with my installation works, I would walk through the audiences present listening to their conversations and sometimes asking about what they thought they were looking at.

nómadas 2018_excerpts

As far as the live performances were concerned, the first iteration of *nómadas* was the six-part structure listed below, which was slightly different from the five-part framework originally submitted with the grant application. The second version *nómadas 2018_excerpts* had a completely different structure even though much of the content was the same.

1. *Prologue*: The Condition
2. *Home*: To Leave...or not
3. *Departure*: The Parting
4. *Journey*: Building, Dismantling Walls
5. *Arrival/settlement*: New Home
6. *Epilogue*: In-between

While *nómadas* had a cast of students from the School for the Contemporary Arts at SFU, *nómadas 2018_excerpts* consisted mostly of a cast of professional dancers from Vancouver. Both versions used the same set design, but the second featured a live percussion quartet with three different composers and four new compositions instead of Adam Basanta's original electro-acoustic score. It would be impossible to convey to the reader what these works looked like without seeing the performances themselves, excerpts of which can be found on my website here.[7] The *nómadas* audio-visual installation (Figures 7.1 and 7.6) had three separate iterations with two, four and six channels of sound and with two and three channels of video. This structure was indicative of how the research process developed, namely, as a continuous exploration of a large amount of source material presented in different formats. Indeed, each time I mounted the installation I would introduce a different constellation of sound and video. In all, my collaborators and I were able to interview around forty individuals, record the material they shared with us and, with their permission, use it in either or both the installation and the live performance works. These 40 individuals included the 15 performers in the first iteration of *nómadas,* and the many professional and non-professional performers as well as regular people we interviewed (Figure 7.6).

nómadas 2018_excerpts had a cast of six performers, two of them from the *nómadas* production and the additional four professional performers from the Vancouver dance community. Although the title has the term 'excerpts' attached to it, this was actually a completely new work with re-arranged material from the original presentation and additional material created for that specific staging.

The reason for the different staging had to do with the nature of the commission I received; I was asked to restage the original work with a percussion quartet that was

FIGURE 7.4: *nómadas 2018_excerpts* cast. Dancers: Marc Arboleda, Nelle Lee, Kaylee Louie, Eden Solomon, Juan Villegas, Seana Williams. Musicians: Luke Hildebrandt, Brian Nesselroad, Greg Samek and Daniel Tones.

FIGURE 7.5: *nómadas 2018_excerpts* cast. Dancers: Marc Arboleda, Nelle Lee, Kaylee Louie, Eden Solomon, Juan Villegas, Seana Williams. Musicians: Luke Hildebrandt, Brian Nesselroad, Greg Samek and Daniel Tones.

given four new compositions by three new composers to perform.[8] Since it was artistically impossible to recreate the same work under such conditions, I made a tactical decision to completely transform it to suit the new context. Figures 7.2 and 7.3 are from *nómadas* and Figures 7.4 and 7.5 are from *nómadas 2018_excerpts*. Figure 7.1 is from the third iteration of *nómadas the installation*. The two dancers who were in both productions are the two women in the bottom half of the composite image in Figure 7.2, who were senior students at the time. I used the commission as an opportunity to introduce them to the professional dance scene with the requisite financial reward and artistic visibility they so richly deserved. Three of the remaining four cast members were alumni of the SCA program who had joined the professional dance community and the fourth was an alumna from the Arts Umbrella Dance Program in the city whom I had witnessed performing in another choreographer's work.

The two sets of texts *On Home* are examples of the material collected from the live performance cast and from our Vancouver interviewees, all of whom had a 'presence' in some way in the three different productions. The first text is from a young female Mexican born Columbian/Mexican/Canadian/American who responded to my provocation about her nomadic identity, and the second is from three generations of an Asian/Canadian family who were interviewed about their cultural heritage. The youngest of that trio was also one of the performers in *nómadas 2018_excerpts*. The first text is framed as a 'poetic confession' and the second as an informal interview. The 'confession' is part of the Epilogue to *nómadas* and was also embedded in *nómadas 2018_excerpts*. It also became an integral part of the entire Contemporary Nomads project, appearing in virtually every edition of the live performance and the installation. The 'confessor' is the skilled Columbian/Mexican/Canadian/American performer/actress who, to me, epitomised the idea of a contemporary nomad. The text was written and spoken in both English and Spanish and I'm quite sure that anyone reading it would agree that it contains familiar information, especially with respect to the nine initial characteristics outlined earlier.

On Home

I

Where are you from?
I hate that question
If it means ancestry, then *yo soy de Colombia y España*
If it means where I was born, I am Mexican
If it means where I pay my taxes, my bills, where I see my
doctor, I'm from Canada

If it means where I grew up as a child, I'm from Texas
So I never really know how to answer that question
All I know is that home to me doesn't seem like a place to return to
I am envious of those who have found some place to go back to
Right now nowhere is home.
Some say home isn't a place but a feeling where you feel deeply intimate and connected with yourself
And if that's the case home is very elusive to me
Maybe home is a person
Perhaps a lover I've yet to meet
It could be my mother
Who am I kidding, they are them and I am me
No matter how badly I want them to be home, they aren't
You can't make a home out of a human being.

II
Last night I was watching the sunset at English Bay
And I'm standing there feeling the water pushed to my ankles and then pulled
And I'm looking out as far as I can
I think about the history of this Coast Salish territory and I try to imagine
All the different people who have stood here before me
Feeling the same water push and pull at their ankles
I think of Columbus, arriving to land after being on water for weeks
Of refugees arriving to shore
I look down at my feet and wonder what this land has witnessed
And in this moment I don't feel alone at all
And then, I just sort of went quiet
And in that silence [...] I don't know
Maybe last night was a type of home for me.

III
There is a type of healing that I believe will happen to me when my feet truly touch ground
A type of healing where my body claims the soil beneath it and I am able to go deep
To dig deep into the rot of my life and its surroundings with my

own two hands I'll lift my eyes and look around and take a deep
breath.

IV
Oh God, is this earth mine?
Can I even call it mine?
Is any of it ours?
I don't know what belongs to me or what I belong to
And belong, what an encasing word
I mean [...] I don't want to be owned or held or possessed by
anything or anyone
But belonging to myself seems so insubstantial
But maybe ownership is insubstantial
I don't know.

V
Hoy cuando regresábamos de Nueva York, Nena me dijo:
¨¡Ah! ¡Ahora estamos en tu pais!¨
Y me senti triste porque no siento que tengo un pais
Quiero ser solo de Colombia para tener ese patriotismo y estar
más conectada con toda mi familia
Solo quiero pensar en español y hablar solo en español porque
tal vez mi sentiria como si finalmente soy parte de una cultura
por completo.

VI
I am speaking of this from here, from the state of the in-between
I speak as the cross-cultured one, as the bilingual one, as the
privileged one
As the triple nationality, as the settler, as the student
As the daughter, as the seeker, as the immigrant.

(Montserrat Videla Samper)

The second text is part of a much longer interview with the three Asian/Canadian women mentioned earlier. Excerpts from both texts and all four of the speakers appear in all versions of the installation. At the point where the excerpt begins, the mother, the daughter and the grandmother are being asked several questions about their past, their relationship to one another and to the rest of their family as well as their feelings about a Canadian identity.

FIGURE 7.6: Participants in v.1 of *nómadas_the installation*. Top left to bottom right: Lynnelle Sura, Suzette Bayrock, Mike Henry, Kaylee Louie, Kenny León, Veronika Fernandez, Irene Chu-Louie, Marina Buston, Katrina Mugume, Qiuli Wu, Montserrat Videla Samper, Nestor Bayrock and Foon Sum Ma.

Interviewer: How do you identify with your cultural heritage?
Mother: Sorry, what's that question again?
Daughter: How do you identify with your cultural heritage?
Grandmother: (Speaks in Chinese, daughter laughs)
Mother: (Responds in Chinese)
Interviewer: Would you like me to repeat the question?
Mother: I'm just trying to explain to her, as close as I can, what the question is?
Grandmother: (Speaking in Chinese).
Daughter: Yes, but I feel like you're answering it.
Mother: No but...well a nomad is like [...] people moving all over the place.
Daughter: Yeah, I know, but [...]
Mother: So, what's the question again?
Daughter: Yes, please, please repeat the question sir.
Interviewer: How do you identify with your cultural heritage? And does the word nomad have any significance for you?
Mother: Oh [...] OK. That's why I had to explain to her what it means [...]
Daughter: But you're describing what it means to you.
Mother: No, I'm describing what she literally said in translation, which was [...] 'is it like those Mongolian people that move around a lot?' [...] But I don't know how to say the word nomad in Chinese.
Daughter: (laughter) I think this question is really hard to ask in Chinese.
Mother: Well, to answer the question of whether I am a nomad, I guess for me it would be no, since I always knew I was Chinese. I was always interested in the history of China, in the different dynasties and how they went from one to the other. And I don't have any problem with it. I know a lot of people who were born here really feel ashamed of being from China or Hong Kong. But I don't really have any problem [...] I don't feel ashamed, I'm actually very proud. China had thousands of years of history.

Grandmother: (Speaks in Chinese)

Daughter: Yeah.

Mother: I always pass this along to my kids. I remember when they were young I said [...] I asked them; are you Chinese or Canadian? And right away you guys said, well I'm Canadian.

Daughter: Uhmmm [...]

Mother: What I did was I put them up to the mirror and I said what do you see. What do you see in the mirror? What colour is your hair? What colour are your eyes? What colour is your skin. I know we don't want to be identified based on the colour of our skin, but, I always wanted to make sure that you guys were proud of your own heritage. That you will never be ashamed of it. And that's why I did that. Put you up in the mirror when I asked you that question.

Daughter: Thanks, mom, I guess I'm kind of Chinese.

Mother: Not kind of Chinese, you are Chinese.

Grandmother: (Speaks in Chinese)

Daughter: Uhmmm.

Grandmother: (Speaks in Chinese)

Daughter: I think following on what my Mom said about not being ashamed of our culture, I definitely feel that she has taught me well, as, now, in my adult life, I feel like I have really tried to investigate—to get to know my roots.

Mother: That's why you said you wanted to go back to Hong Kong to see where I was born.

Daughter: Yeah, definitely.

Mother: To see where I grew up.

Daughter: Yeah, I want to go back to Hong Kong and [...]

Mother: Find your roots

Daughter: Yeah, get to know my roots. I've taken courses, Asia/Canada courses studying the history of China and Canada together, which is what I am. I'm Chinese Canadian. I'm not one or the other, I'm actually both. So I think that is my relationship to both the cultures that I've grown up in.

Mother: Well, I just didn't teach you the traditional Chinese culture, I always tried to instil the Western side of it too. Cause I took both.

(Excerpted from an interview conducted in November 2017 with Irene Chu-Louie, Kaylee Louie and Foon Sum Ma)

The exchange is quite revealing, not least of all because these three generations of Chinese Canadians represent stages of a movement along an East/West axis. The text by the young Latin American woman, on the other hand, represents one along a North/South axis, also with Canada and Vancouver as destinations. Both texts reveal how these journeys of arrival and settlement unfold, and how complex questions about identity, belonging and nationality can become. The tone of the two texts is also quite interesting; the one unfolding as a poetic soliloquy and the other as a triadic autobiographical narrative provoked by questions from someone outside the family unit. It is clear, for example, that each member of the unit performs a unique role in the unfolding; the mother in the middle, sometimes translating and sometimes misunderstanding some of the nuances of the question, the daughter fine tuning explanations and providing clarity, while the grandmother, who never speaks in English, performs the role of silent but observant matriarch. All three take turns as the locus of communication, shifting language when it becomes necessary.

In *nómadas*, I wanted to speak to people who were not only interested in the nature and content of the project but were also prepared to voice issues they may have always wanted to but could only do so in a private and safe space with trusted family and friends. These individuals were informed that the content of the interviews was destined for a public performance. As such, they were free to choose how they answered the questions, or in some cases not answer them at all. The issue of what a contemporary nomad is was introduced at different points in the sessions, sometimes directly and at other times indirectly. As it turned out, the term 'nomad' was so overwhelming in its implications that the 'contemporary' preceding it often became subsumed by its power. Below are some of the questions that were asked as a way of opening up conversations. Not all of these were asked of each interviewee or in the same order and not all of the unplanned questions appear here:

1. What's your name?
2. How old are you?
3. What's your nationality?
4. What languages do you speak?
5. Can you tell me the story of your family?
6. How do you identify with your cultural heritage?
7. How many different countries have you lived in?
8. When people ask you where you're from, how do you respond?
9. Does the term nomad mean anything to you?
10. Do you have a partner?
11. Where are they from?
12. Do you have kids?
13. Where were they born?
14. As a parent, what choices have you made regarding the cultural upbringing of your child?

15. What can you tell me about your ancestral culture?
16. Does the term 'contemporary nomad' describe anything about your lifestyle?

What I hoped to achieve was an open conversation that would reveal how people felt about their movement from one place to another and how those movements affected their sense of belonging to a particular place, space, language, culture or country. Sometimes one or two questions would be enough, and at other times half a dozen might not suffice. The entire objective of the exercise was to understand what a contemporary nomad could be, and how people saw themselves in relation to that term. The interviews and conversations that followed, our rehearsals and performances, and the post-performance encounters with audience members provided ample opportunities to map out the cortical and cartographic landscape of someone's psychological and physical movements. What emerged was a sense of how much people were aware of that terrain, which in turn reminded me of a question Francisco Varela posed during an interview with Otto Scharmer in Paris in 2000.

> We all know we can become aware; it happens to us all the time. You suddenly become aware of this, become aware of that, whether it be external or internal. The question is, can it be cultivated as an ability? The structuring of this essential ability is, to me, a fundamental focus of study.
>
> (Varela and Scharme 2000: 3)

The two last sentences in Varela's commentary constitute much of what the PaR and a theory of practice in this book are about. Awareness is not just a focus of study, it is a dynamic practice geared towards developing embodied knowing, itself a key objective of my choreographic practice. The physical expertise, the contemplative attitude and the discipline that one acquires in dance play a fundamental role in cultivating awareness. Below is an excerpt of a letter a young student wrote in response to my call for research assistants at the inception of the Contemporary Nomads project. In many ways, this student was an ideal candidate for the project; someone who was prepared to bring an individual perspective to the work, but who was also willing to accommodate a shift to fit the larger objectives of the project.

> First of all, thank you again for extending the invitation to work on this project with you. In exploring your past work on Project Barca and talking to you about the direction in which you intend

> to take Contemporary Nomads, I have found that the questions you are interrogating are some that I spend a lot of time thinking about, both in an artistic context and within my daily life. Through this research proposal I have tried to merge my interests with the project at hand. I hope that what I propose is research that will add another dimension to your work; I am also very open to talking with you about how I could shift it to better fit your aims.
>
> (Annie Therrien Boulos)

Multiple presences: Movement through space/time holes

In this book, I've argued that consciousness is a spectrum with awareness as a practice that one uses to develop it. I also promised to locate dance, choreography and performance at the centre of a theory of practice that claimed human beings were cognitively embodied through their experiences of movement through space and time. In this way dance, choreography and performance became key practices for acquiring knowledge about bodies and their experiences in space/time. Movement, then, could be seen as a process of thought unfolding, with bodies as material agents facilitating, and often multiplying the directionality of that unfolding. In this theory of practice, bodies become agents of performance, and dance and choreography expert practices through which the capacity for embodied knowing is cultivated.

Drawing on the three main principles of a transdisciplinary methodology, (1) the logic of the included middle, (2) complexity and (3) levels of reality, I brought seemingly divergent philosophical and scientific ideas into dialogue with a set of historical and cultural events, the point being to understand how certain ideas were connected across disciplines even though practices in those disciplines were significantly different. Using the analogy of the quantum state, where the change from one energy level to another is discontinuous to illustrate my point, I gave the example of moving from a waking state to sleep or from sleep to wakefulness as a discontinuous stepping across the consciousness spectrum. In both examples, there was a change in the behaviour of the information as well as the rules that governed it in each state. I then suggested that these changes could be classified as states of 'forgetting' or 'remembering'. I also used the analogy of the single electron in an uncharged hydrogen atom whose position instantly drops to a lower orbit if light energy is emitted or immediately moves to a higher orbit if it absorbs light energy to draw attention to the mechanics of memory. Pushing this complex analogy further, I argued that consciousness and unconsciousness could be seen as 'down-shifts' or 'up-shifts' of awareness, with the terms 'asleep' and 'awake' understood as energetic changes with distinct perceptual correlates. For example, in traumatic situations when someone is injured, memories can be lost and never recovered. In other situations, memories may return at a later date. What this suggests is that a break at any point in the spectrum of awareness does not necessarily mean that consciousness is completely lost. What it does suggest however, is that there is a disconnection or fracture between the knowing subject and the larger consciousness field.

The experience I described at the beginning of this book of waking up from a dream while still asleep, and then waking up a second time, points to the fact that there are different levels to our awareness and hence to our perception and understanding of reality. I had a different experience of reality in each of those states of body, but not enough to understand the importance of the experience at the time it took place. It doesn't take a great deal to imagine the tremendous knowledge that can come from consciously cultivating the ability to cross these energetic boundaries and to remember what took place under those conditions. Knowledge of these other states could help us understand more about our everyday world. However, one could also say that we are protected from this knowledge for good reason, as we might not be able to deal with the consequences of that knowing. In any case, the point here is that the practice of self-remembering prepares one to deal with both normal and unusual experiences.

I argue that our creative practices can be conceived as disciplined actions that prepare us to cross real and/or virtual borders, and hence to access knowledge embodied in different layers of our system. But this can happen only if these practices are deliberately used with such an intention in mind. The experiences I described in Chapter 1 in the section 'Will the artist please stand up?' were not, but when re-membered and re-cognized they became such. There were other events that, collectively speaking, convinced me that these experiences were extremely valuable in constructing my theory of practice. Below are a few strangely connected instances that reveal the type of logic that appears to operate in situations like these. These experiences were also crucial to my artistic practice since they motivated, in one way or another, the travels that I undertook and the works that I made during those periods. They also inspired me to pursue a search for knowledge beyond the professional dance field while using the practices I learnt in that field within an academic context. This decision, I believe, was propitious, as I was able to make important disciplinary connections that gave me a sense of the scope of the knowledge field I was involved in.

The real and the virtual, reality and the dream

Event I

a. *Location*: A village in Trinidad.
b. *The Event*: My younger brother and I are walking to the Anglican Church a few miles away for our Confirmation practice. We are quite young, about eight and nine years old, respectively. On the way there, we decide to help ourselves to some sugar cane stalks from the fields of the privately-owned sugar company. We are quickly apprehended by security police who happen to be nearby. I break out of the grasp of one officer and flee, hoping my younger brother would take my cue and follow. He doesn't. I run home and hide inside the house, climbing over a neighbour's wall to get there. Moments later, the security police turn up with my younger brother in tow. Our grandmother doesn't know that I am inside the house until I emerge to explain what happened. The police drive us all to the house of the field supervisor to answer for our 'crimes'.
c. *The Aftermath*: Thanks to the fact that my grandmother has a job as housekeeper to one of these same field supervisors, we get off with just a reprimand. The entire experience is deeply imprinted in my memory.

Event II

a. *Location*: A beach on Guatemala's Pacific Coast.
b. *Context*: It is the Fall of 1983 and I am invited to teach and choreograph for the Ballet Folklorico de Guatemala in Guatemala City. While there, a group of friends offer to take me on a trip to the Pacific Coast for the weekend.
c. *The Event*: I'm swimming in the ocean and my two companions are on the beach a short distance away. The waves are quite large and the sea a bit rough. I'm about to leave the water, but as I turn my back one of those waves hits me from behind, throws me in the air and I fall on my upper back and neck. Time slows down and light disappears, there is only blackness. I scream, but no one hears me. I have no idea how long I'm in that state, but I recover and scramble up the beach.
d. *The Aftermath*: I reproach my two companions for not hearing me scream and coming to my rescue. They say they never heard me. I think it impossible for them not to have. I can only conclude that the scream was a virtual experience in my head and that I had momentarily lost all feeling except the sensation of time, which I felt was slowing down, or more accurately, running out. My friends and I return to the house where the other two members of the group are staying. My neck gets increasingly stiff to the point where I cannot turn my head. My friends get me to sit down and later put me to bed. I remember a lighted candle one of them put next to my head. For some reason, this light and the person who lit it becomes very significant in my memory of the entire event.

Event III

a. *Location*: The city of Vienna in Austria, near the *Haus des Meeres*.[9]

b. *Context*: I recently moved from the Limón Dance Company in New York to take a job with Tanzprojekt München, a dance organization in Munich, West Germany. It was my second domicile in the country, having spent six months four years earlier (in 1980), also in Munich with the same organization. I would eventually call my stay in that country the underworld period of my life because of the many bizarre experiences I had there.

c. *The Event*: It is 1984 and I'm invited to teach at the Body Dynamic Studio in Vienna. Walking around the city, I find myself looking at a monstrous concrete building with barely any windows that seems strangely familiar. But since I'd never been to Austria before and certainly never to Vienna, I am very disturbed by the building and my 'false' memory of it. I walk around the neighbourhood looking for clues as to why I would know it but I find none. I go to the door of the monstrosity and ask what exactly is inside. I'm told that it is an aquarium that was once a World War II bunker.

Event IV

a. *Location*: My apartment in Freiburg im Breisgau, Germany.

b. *Context*: It's approximately two years after the Guatemala incident and a year after my first visit to Vienna. I've moved to the city of Freiburg im Breisgau from Munich on contract with the Städtischen Bühnen there. I've been having a set of very disturbing dreams. In this one, I'm in the backyard of the house in Trinidad where I was born.

c. *The Dream*: In this dream, an airplane has crashed in the backyard of the house. I think my father is somehow involved in the accident. I see a large caption written in the space above the scene that reads 'Spock and Kirk were killed and thrown into the land of Oma Ikki'.[10] I wake up extremely puzzled.

d. I am so disturbed by this backyard dream that I eventually call my mother in Trinidad to find out if something tragic happened to me as a child there. She confirms that as a baby I crawled out the back door of our house and fell down a flight of stairs into the yard below. The fall left me unconscious. My mother claimed that she poured water over my face to revive me. She said that I did not cry throughout the entire experience. I remember having a sense of relief as well as a deep concern after our conversation; the former because I knew this incident was clearly connected to the dream, and the latter because of how that fall could possibly have affected me.

Event V

a. *Location*: An apartment in Vienna, Austria, soon after the previous event in Freiburg.
b. *The Dream*: A beach on a coastline somewhere. I and another man are running away, escaping from something. The other man is caught, but I jump over a wall and fall into the sea. Fleeing along the beach, I spot a kaleidoscopic spinning object flying towards me. I instinctively know that I cannot escape so I stop to embrace it. The object hits me in the chest and my time slows down. I hear my own voice speaking, 'The way to your butterfly is through the power of the world'. I also notice that the words are written in a caption above the scene as I voice them. I wake up laughing and muttering to myself, 'yeah really!'[11]

In trying to explain how these events, decades apart and with similar geographical reference points, images, bodily actions and emotional states are connected, I see the brain recording some of my deepest experiences in very specific geographic locations and then playing the contents back to me decades later as memories with a strange new architecture. That architecture becomes denser as the body accumulates a more comprehensive set of lived experiences, therefore influencing my waking consciousness that in turn presents the information according to its own logic. Put another way, the data that was archived in my body had specific physical, emotional and mental coordinates that were now accumulating new images from experiences that I was having from a later date and in different locations. The difficulty I had was remembering and recognizing the narrative that was playing out across these different space-times, especially since the latest events were all taking place within a span of months. I was therefore left to grapple with something that seemed illogical at best and suggested trauma and mental instability at worst. My cortical and cartographic maps were in multi-dimensional overlapping modes where time and space were non-linear. The image I had was of memory as points along a string, but that string was wrapped into a ball and my body was that ball. In other words, I felt like Whitehead's (1978) cosmos where many things were connected at the same level, but other things seemed to be connected at very different levels (1978).

I would also be reminded of Eric Kandel's claim that perception itself is creative (Kandel 2006), and that a major function of the brain is to organize information according to its own logical reasoning. The key terms here are 'own logical reasoning'. I would come to realize that there were many different logics, and at least one of them was at odds with what I had been taught. It was clear that I had entered a world with different rules, generated quite different experiences and revealed different forms of knowledge. The cognitive maps in my nervous system appeared to store and replay the memories of experiences I had, along with new ones that resonated with those older memories in a kind of simultaneity that was multi-dimensional. I had no memory whatsoever of what happened in my unconscious state in at least one of those cases, namely, the footballing incident I mentioned in Chapter 3 in the section titled 'Will the artist please stand up?' Yet my brain was able to create its own logical reasoning that would reveal new details to me. These maps were not fictions per se, but reality reconfigured. The rules governing that new reality would naturally be different from the one I was previously accustomed to, and like everything else, it came at a cost.

Nevertheless, learning how to recognize these new rules and the states that accompany them would be part of the benefits, which included a better understanding of the knowledge the body possesses, how that information is organized and how it could be creatively utilized. Although this knowledge had been unfolding in the different places I lived and visited and consequently in all of my choreographic works, it would take some time before I could create anything near a complete picture. This came in the form of a hypothesis, and consequently a theory of practice, both of which form the backbone of my artistic practices. The titles of some of the early works choreographed during that significant phase in Germany point to a beginning of sorts; *Vortex* (1980), *Pithecanthropus Erectus Part I* (1985), *Neptune Rising* (1987), *Ich Khepera* (1988), *A Tale from Atlantis* (1990) and *Red and Blue on a Purple Background* (1991) are titles that gesture towards that unfolding.[12]

Performing the self: Movement as an unfolding and initiating of thought

> *We are simply asking; maybe knowing [...] maybe knowledge, is as fundamental, or even more fundamental than reality.*
>
> (Zeilinger 2007)[13]

In a talk given by Anton Zeilinger at the Mind and Life XIV conference in Dharamshala, India in April 2007, the Austrian physicist attempted to explain to the Dalai Lama and a group of scientists, philosophers and Buddhist monks the specifics of the famous double-slit experiment and its importance in the development of quantum information and quantum computation.[14] His explanation was a way of introducing two exciting developments that he claimed were based on the conceptual foundations of quantum physics, namely, Quantum Information and Quantum Computation. Both, he claimed, were direct results of the experiment that proved light was both a wave and composed of particles. Zeilinger's point was that because the world was strange and because we needed quantum physics to help explain that strangeness, our knowledge of the behaviour of these elementary particles could be used to develop new technologies. Put another way, one did not have to understand precisely why these particles behaved the way that they did, as long as one could creatively utilize that behaviour. And this, in fact, is what his lab was actively working on in Vienna at the time.

I am making a parallel argument here for the behaviour of the human body/mind in extraordinary situations. What became very clear to me after working on Transnet, The Touched Project, Project Barca and Contemporary Nomads, was that an interesting continuity existed between these projects that could only be recognized by stepping out of the process at each one of those four stages. The randomness of my perceived thinking was not random at all. The implications were clear; self-observation changes thinking and thinking influences practice, resulting in a change in how one perceives and then engages with reality. In other words, regardless of whether one fully understands what one is going through during an experience, the body records every aspect of that memory, which later becomes available for re-cognizing and re-membering as knowledge. However, a lot depends on what lens one uses to examine that knowledge and how much of that knowledge, in turn, could be understood from different perspectives. My perspective was choreography as a tool for structuring and restructuring movement according to the different laws at different levels of being.

In a conversation with Senior Research Scientist Oliver Stelzer-Chilton at the TRIUMF Particle Accelerator at the University of British Columbia in Vancouver, Canada,[15] I proposed a choreographers approach to 'how knowledge might be translated across the disciplinary communities of art and physics in order to develop a shared understanding of the cosmos'.[16] Our conversation was centred around the idea of consciousness as something that exists not just in the human body but as a phenomenon in the universe at large. Although this idea is not shared by all scientists, it is certainly one that is at the forefront of current scientific thought (Chopra et al. 2017). It is also one that is at the foundation of certain religious philosophies, including Buddhism. During my exchange with Stelzer-Chilton, he pointed out three facts concerning an energy field that science proved permeated all of space/time, while identifying the fundamental particle that was associated with that field:

1. The Higgs field is an energy field that exists throughout the universe.
2. The Higgs boson is an excitation within that field that continuously interacts with other particles, like electrons for example.
3. Particles accumulate mass because of their movement through the Higgs field.

My questions to Stelzer-Chilton were: (1) Can we create a transdisciplinary analogy between physics and dance to say that the accumulation of *mass* (as information) by *particles* (bodies) moving through *the Higgs field* (space/time), is the primary mechanism for those bodies (human beings) to accumulate information? And can dance, as a movement practice in space/time, be used to regenerate and thus claim this naturally accumulated information in and through the body as personal knowledge? (Daniel 2019). My colleague agreed that the analogy and my proposal were theoretically sound. However, the point of this analogy for me as a choreographer was to reimagine the fundamental elements of my disciplinary creativity, i.e. space, time and material bodies, as mediums for perception and as carriers of information. Hence, if movement is the process through which everything in the Universe seeks to achieve its goal, i.e. how a thing begins and ends its life, mapping it on the scale of the cortical and the cartographic would be a process of accumulating knowledge about the very nature of reality.

But since any complex system receives input – or food if one wishes – from many different sources asynchronously, the life of that system could be maintained as long as its fundamental structure remained intact. If we think of movement as a thought that unfolds in space/time creating energy as it travels it is not impossible to imagine that a body can apprehend some of that energy and the information it carries. Choreographer Zab Maboungou's idea of her dancing as a way to create time becomes very interesting here.[17] Her example of African polyrhythms, i.e. putting several asynchronous and overlapping rhythms together, literally enabled the musician and dancer to gain time, and in so doing, to experience heightened states of being. In other words, they were able to 'exist' in different temporalities or dimensionalities simultaneously. One can find the remnants of such ritual practices in Indigenous cultures that have lasted to the present day.

To conclude, dance can be imagined as a practice for claiming the naturally accumulated information that is in the body and in the space through which it travels. As such, the dancer is someone skilled in directing the movements of his, her or their body through space/time, actions that can be seen as excitations within a field of consciousness. This field exists everywhere, in varying degrees of intensity. Therefore, we should be able to define choreography as a practice for investigating and claiming this naturally accumulated information in and through the body and in the spaces through which it travels as knowledge of the whole. The choreographer, therefore, is someone who facilitates the organization and reorganization of the dancer's and audience's cortical and cartographic landscape.

NOTES

1. www.migrationpolicycentre.eu/migprosp/publications/.
2. The Spanish term for nomads.
3. www.thenudge.com/activities/pop-brixton/.

4. www.constellations-metz.fr/pages/edition-2017/.
5. These designs were that of the artist/sculptor Alan Storey. www.alanstorey.com.
6. www.henrydaniel.ca/contemporary-nomads.
7. www.henrydaniel.ca/contemporary-nomads.
8. The commission was for the Cambridge Music Conference and was staged for the Migration and Multiculturalism Conference on 28–29 September 2018 at the Goldcorp Centre for the Arts in Vancouver.
9. The *Haus des Meeres* is a World War II bunker in Vienna, Austria, that was converted into a modern-day aquarium. www.haus-des-meeres.at.
10. This information is taken from my archived diaries. Spock and Kirk are characters from the famous American TV and Film series Star Trek, which I looked at a lot at the time.
11. See Appendix A for a complete list of works.
12. 9 April 2007. Mind and Life XIV – Day 1 p.m. – with the Dalai Lama. www.youtube.com/watch?v=fO-K13cfJwo.
13. This experiment – first conducted by British scientist Thomas Young in 1801 – demonstrates the properties of light as a wave at the time that it was thought to be composed of particles. To put the experiment in as simple a manner as possible for our purposes here, light behaves as a particle if it is given only one option and as a wave if it is given more than one. The term option is understood here as the number of parallel slits in a plate that receives electrons – or photons – fired toward it. Given one slit, it acts as a particle, given more than one it behaves as a wave. Several variations on that experiment, based on Albert Einstein's discovery that light also consisted of particles, would later be developed.
14. www.triumf.ca.
15. This quote came from the *Leaning Out of Windows Project* led by Randy Lee Cutler and Ingrid Koenig at the Emily Carr University of Art + Design. Our group was assigned the role of '*Finding common ground via metaphor*' and it consisted of Physicist: Luca Egoriti | Physicist: Oliver Stelzer-Chilton | Scholar: Shelly Rosenblum | Scholar/Artist: Henry Daniel | Artist: Carlyn Yandle (facilitator), www.ecuad.ca/calendar/leaning-out-of-windows-emergence.
16. Transnet video archive: Transnet 20050616 Day 1 Conference Tape 3 (Maboungou, Z).

An Epilogue

Fitting [Out-fitting] In

Who is he fooling and what is he really doing there?

They encountered each other in the parking lot, the one that was reserved for upper administration.

The dean looked at the professor, who was on his way to another parking lot much further away and started voicing what he probably thought was a compliment. Stopping abruptly, he tried to swallow the final words of the sentence.

'You look so much bet'

The professor smiled politely. Both knew exactly what the rest of the sentence was going to be, and both silently agreed not to pursue the issue. The professor had cut his dreadlocks.

After all, he thought, the dean seemed like a *mensch*, and surely didn't intend any bias.

In fact, he was the one who encouraged the professor when the latter's million-dollar grant application to set up a performance research centre was not allowed to leave the university on grounds that it was not likely to succeed at the federal level. However, the inside story was that the untenured assistant professor in the Faculty of Arts wouldn't have had much chance of success at that level anyway. Why not support a tenured full professor from chemistry, for example?

This dean was also the same one who commented at the professor's hiring interview that the job was contingent on him completing his Ph.D., even though the requirement for the position specified an MFA or equivalent experience. The professor was ABD at the time, with an MA and an extensive and enviable international career at the highest professional level in his field.

Back then he still had his dreadlocks. Now, in the parking lot more than seven years later, and with his title changed to tenured associate professor, Ph.D.; they were gone [...] shed. The dean had also retired but was recalled to head a newly established faculty [...] health sciences, I think.

Who am I and why am I here?

I remember precisely when and why I first started growing dreadlocks. It was a long time ago in the Caribbean, before I became a professional dancer and choreographer.

My last attempt came out of pure frustration. I had gotten tired of driving the three hours from Münster in Germany to Amsterdam in Holland every time I needed a haircut.

'Why not grow some dreadlocks again?'

Now, a few years on from the comment in the parking lot, with more than a little 'salt-and-pepper' on my head, and the title of tenured Full Professor next to my name, I wondered about the numerous 'slips' of the tongue I had experienced from colleagues and strangers *en route*.

'Who am I fooling, and why am I really here?'

'Do I really "look much better" without my dreadlocks?'

'Why did I shed them? And why are they still lying in the top drawer of my cupboard amidst numerous socks and underwear? How many other discarded masks still lie in the cupboards of my house?'

The term 'fragmented subjectivities' comes to mind.

Four different Deans and a number of institutional re-organisations at the faculty and departmental levels later and I'm still trying to fit into a system that will always see me as 'other'.

Tracy McMullen's 'riffs' on Curtis Mayfield's gospel-inspired *People get ready, there's a train a'comin'* (1965). She claims that there is no need to get ready for a future that is already here. McMullen also suggests that the African American tradition of improvisation offers perspectives on notions of the self, hope and the future that reveal a great deal about being in a world that 'does not erect fictitious boundaries around a self that cannot, in fact, be located' (McMullen in Heble and Wallace 2013: 266).

I once published an essay titled 'Performing the now: Mingus' Pithecanthropus Erectus' (Daniel in Hui and Whyton 2017), which looked at the life and work of musician/composer Charles Mingus.[1] Following McMullen, I argued that the post-colonial, post-slavery, post-institutional 'self' did not really exist and thus had little to prop itself up against or gather around. One could, however, begin to recreate such an individuality through an ongoing improvisational search that would open up possibilities for becoming.

I think about what I have become, or rather about what I have given up to become.

'Who am I fooling, and what am I really doing here? Do I look much better without my dreadlocks? Under whose gaze?'

Fitting [Out-fitting] In

This final chapter concerns itself with the performativity of identity from the perspective of a Black male artist and scholar working in a School for the Contemporary Arts within the Canadian university system. Having spent the greater part of my life in countries outside my own native land,[2] and in the professional world as dancer, performer, choreographer, media artist and scholar, one could say that I have acquired a fair degree of experience about the nature of various discourses on performance and the performativity of identity. Since I regularly lecture on and challenge many of these ideas in both my intellectual and artistic work – at the same time encouraging my students to do the same – the thematic of this book gave me an opportunity to comment on some of my experiences within a wider context.

Three issues compound the challenges someone like me faces in an average day. The first is that my job as a dance and performance studies scholar sits squarely in the realm of what is known as Research/Creation in Canada and, as such, is considered already on the margins of valid academic research. Second, in promoting an approach to art scholarship that intersects with a wide spectrum of disciplines, I am often confronted with the borders that many of these disciplines erect to protect their domains from people like me. Third, my own immigrant Caribbean/Black African ancestry makes me extremely sensitive to what I see as a certain 'colonisation of minds' that the dominant forms of discourse foster within academia, and the difficulty people like myself encounter in trying to offer alternative approaches. In short, I am no stranger to the prejudices against race, language and academic discipline, nor to the many other subtle – and not so subtle – discriminatory practices operating both inside and outside academia. Given that many of these biases are grounded in historically established configurations of inequality and impact what takes place in the classroom, the boardroom, in adjudication panels where research funding priorities are determined and in hiring, promotion and tenure committees where one's performance is being assessed, this chapter is a study of 'fitting in' as I am tasked to help 'outfit' a generation of students – mostly White – who, all too often, are more concerned with what they are entitled to rather than the possibilities that exist for their own development.

So, what's your background?

Most of us working in the realm of the arts are fairly acquainted with some form of this question. I call it the 'establishing a genealogy' question. We always want to know what someone else's intellectual lineage is, how they got to where they are now and who their mentors or influences were along the way. In many ways, the question is similar to another ambiguously worded one encountered by those who have a language, accent, racial origin or other characteristics that deviates from some tacitly agreed norm. This is the 'Where are you from?' or 'Where are you *really* from' question. When positioned within the context of academia, where disciplinary categories, theoretical and conceptual frames within particular knowledge fields and the 'impact value' of one's own research within a diverse socio-political and economic sphere play a large role in situating someone's work, these questions converge in a dynamic space that generates a great deal of tension, not to mention misunderstandings and downright fallacies of one sort or another. To put it another way, a wide range of personal and institutional prejudices come into play, and when the neoliberal politics of university administrators are added to the mix,[3] important things get sacrificed.

To be fair, the above-mentioned questions are often asked out of curiosity, and sometimes in a non-guarded or naïve manner to elicit information, start a conversation or simply to check out the competition. However, these situations also present a rich field of investigation for people like me, artists/scholars whose research involves detailed examinations of human beings 'performing' their way through the complex structures of privilege, entitlement and institutional power that White Supremacy offers. These *mise-en-scènes* are composed of so many different layers that it is not difficult to lose one's sense of self while playing several scripted and unscripted roles. Acknowledging that others may genuinely want to know more about one's background to better locate one in the intellectual machinery, the question is nonetheless how far such performances can be sustained before one or more of the many masks we wear begins to reveal themselves. A fascinating quality of these encounters is that no matter what one suspects about the nature of one's own exclusion from orbits of institutional power, there is rarely any overt admission of exclusivity until the proverbial slip of the tongue. When such slips occur, and they frequently do, the supporting cast can be left with debilitating feelings arising from the recognition of their role as mere placeholders fulfilling a mandated but vaguely articulated notion of institutional inclusivity. To put it even more colourfully, one can find oneself playing the role of the 'spice' that adds taste to a dish, but which must not be confused with being the meal itself, or even having a real influence on the decisions made at the table. Such realizations are always painful for the ego. Unfortunately, or perhaps fortunately, the stories I tell here are minor narratives in a larger discussion regarding notions of equity, diversity and inclusivity, or what I see as a process of 'fitting [out-fitting] in'.

First, how does one 'fit into' a paradigm, research or otherwise, that essentially ignores the validity of one's dance, choreographic and performance practices as critical modes of knowing? Second, how can such 'embodied' practices inscribe themselves within institutions of power when the actors themselves and the very methods they use to investigate that knowledge are already perceived as unworthy, or barely tolerable at the margins of serious research? Third, who constructs the ontological and epistemological bases that support this type of knowing, and/or the perceptive lenses and inscriptive practices through which such knowledges can be recognized and promoted? These are all extremely difficult questions to even begin to consider here. But unless they are faced head-on, I believe the 'colonisation' of minds that currently substitutes for real critique in certain quarters of the academy will continue. More importantly, unless there is a critical mass of 'bodies of difference' in the practice rooms and lecture halls of the academy to engage in such dialogue, we are being profoundly delusional in our use of the terms 'equity', 'diversity' and 'inclusivity'.

A colleague of mine spoke quite frankly at a scholarly gathering[4] about the fact that there are quite distinct approaches to and notions of diversity and inclusivity in the part of Canada from which I write. Acknowledgement comes first for the First Nations community; after all, the term 'First Nations' itself undeniably calls for such recognition. After this comes, the Chinese-speaking community and the substantial contributions they make to help keep the West Coast economy vibrant, an economy that relies to a great extent on a booming real estate business and a growing tech industry.[5] Third in line comes the South Asian or Indian community who form a powerful and important economic and cultural presence. And only then, if there is any goodwill left, could one perhaps begin to talk of a Black community. Having experienced this prioritization as an unwritten rule in my years of living amongst this 'diversity', I understood what my colleague meant.

These statements, to my mind, were certainly not meant as derogatory or prejudicial. However, this individual was called to task by a member of the audience, another colleague, who warned against articulating any hint of discrimination against Asians that was already tacitly promoted in the community. Theoretically, I saw her argument. However, I felt that my other colleague's point became lost amidst a kind of sensitivity – or institutionally-practiced conservatism – that always seems to mollify glaring problems that require address, at the same time drawing attention away from policies that are themselves inherently discriminatory.

Caught in such maddeningly contradictory circumstances, one is forced to take a step back and evaluate one's own position within what too easily turns into what Rinaldo Walcott calls 'competitive oppression exceptionalism' (Walcott in Broeck and Junker 2014: 96). Such attitudes serve no helpful purpose whatsoever and indeed create even more unwanted tensions within and across racial groups. But one could be forgiven for asking whether we can ever move away from such dichotomized modes of thinking. What, then, are we really trying to achieve here, and what could the role of the artist be as an intellectual within a system that not only ignores the potential of artistic perspectives, but actively forces them into frameworks that deny their very potential? Indeed, one can ask whether it is possible for new theoretical and conceptual models to emerge from an institutionalized framework that forces people like myself to 'fit in' to something that fundamentally was not designed to accommodate difference.

Admittedly, these same questions have dogged my extended residence in countries on both sides of the Atlantic throughout a professional career as dancer and choreographer. In the past, however, the issue had more to do with how I saw myself being presented through the lens of other people's choreographic ideas, and my own struggle to articulate an individual creative voice. These international performance stages were precisely the locations where bodies like mine desperately strove to 'train' a different type of gaze, one that could offset the negative effects of a colonial past. Now, as a scholar, I encounter some of the same institutional barriers, and I am again forced to ask: when will we be ready for such conversations and in what kinds of forms will these conversations come? Damned if I can, damned if I can't! If I'm cast in the role of trying to perform new identities for my own survival, then perform I must. However, in the meantime, I often feel that my greatest performances take place in my daily efforts to negotiate a space to exist within institutions that do not truly recognize the modes and structures of knowing that people of difference bring. We always seem to be trying to fit into an uncomfortably limited and limiting space. And for bodies and minds accustomed to wide open physical and mental vistas, this is quite disconcerting.

Where are you from? I mean, where are you really from?

These two questions, especially when they follow one another, always provoke a deep sense of frustration, and, consequently, a re-examination of the notion of self that any person of colour, immigrant or outsider feels within a system. These are complex questions, and responses can evoke tensions since one always wonders which 'you' is really under examination. Which part of me is out of place? And why does it appear to others that I do not belong? These are more than rhetorical questions, they speak to foundational aspects of who one 'is' and/or intends to 'become', and hence are profoundly philosophical.

As the only tenured Black faculty member at the time of this writing in a department of more than thirty full-time professors, and another half that number of part-timers, I am a minority. But race isn't the only criterion that problematizes issues of belonging or fitting in. When my mostly White and mostly female students in a studio class comment on what they see as a 'cultural' approach to the physical practices that I offer, what exactly do they mean? And what about the more 'diverse' student population in my lectures and seminars whose first language is not English? Or others who come from cultures that have a decidedly different epistemic logic than what is on offer? However, as the sum total of the material I teach is by no means *Black*, I often wonder if the comment about 'a cultural thing' means that the material is in some way flawed. A temporary director of a well-known contemporary dance academy in Rotterdam, Holland – where I had been invited as a guest artist – once called my studio practice 'Afro-Caribbean Limón'. This was referring to my adaptation/interpretation of a dance technique I studied at the Juilliard School and had performed as a member of the José Limón Dance Company of New York. It visibly amused me that this colleague chose to ignore the fact that all such so-called modern and/or contemporary dance techniques have had substantial input from Black bodies throughout their development,[6] input that is unacknowledged in many of the written histories that continue to be disseminated. Ironically, he also recognized that there was something I added to the technique simply by performing it, a point that is lost on many writers who should know better.

Another relevant point is that on a daily basis I do not encounter more than three or four Black students on my way through the halls of the department I teach in. Very rarely do I have two at the same time in any of my lecture courses, and never have I had more than three at any one time in the studio courses I teach. This is quite shocking for someone whose work attempts to create a dialogue between these diverse bodies. However, the more important issues at stake here and the questions that need to be asked should be: where are these people, and why are they not here? Do my teaching practices or those of colleagues like myself across the university not accommodate what they are looking for? Could it also be that there are not many of 'us' people of colour in the city in the first place? Or that those who are around do not think the programs offered are worthy of their time and effort? Whatever the case, the onus seems to be on me to go find and invite these diverse student populations into the institution, which in turn begs the question: is that part of the reason I was hired in the first place? And if this is indeed the case, why are my substantial and ongoing efforts to attract such students not being supported by said institution?

Growing up in a place where we were taught that Columbus 'discovered' the Americas more than five and a half centuries ago, and that he was followed by others who brought our ancestors here through an ignominious trade, the issue of how to go about dismantling deeply embedded modes of thinking about who we are and what our worth is continues to be of concern. But how does one go about decolonizing a mind, starting with one's own? This is a question the Kenyan writer Ngũgĩ wa Thiong'o himself wrestled with. Part of his solution was to go back to writing in his own Indigenous tongue, where I believe he felt his identity was more embodied in the rhythm, syntax, meter, colour and tone of the language. But even that was short-lived since wa Thiong'o was forced to leave Kenya for the United States where the dominant language is English and he was required to teach in an English-speaking university. Perhaps one of the ways to decolonize institutional spaces for those who have been deprived of our Indigenous languages is to resist the institutionalized forms of White discourse that continue to support the types of biases I mentioned earlier. The arts can play a key role in such efforts by looking more closely at the spaces between the verbal and the non-verbal. This then begs the question of whether the academy, with its current curricula, has the means to decolonize the spaces it claims it wants to. These questions will certainly not be addressed without the establishment of a certain 'critical mass' in the spaces where 'new knowledge' is being 'produced'.

Oh! You're a professor? What do you teach?

My first response to these two questions is almost always to say yes, I teach dance, theatre and performance studies. This elicits the inevitable follow-ups: 'What kind of dance?', 'You mean you can actually get a Ph.D. in dance?' and 'What is performance studies?' By this time, I am already preparing for the upcoming explanation of what studies in dance, theatre and performance studies entail. And if the questions appear genuinely curious, I try to explain how all of these interests combine to form a comprehensive approach to teaching, scholarship and research. Amidst the genuine surprise and obvious confusion, I'm usually enjoying the entertainment for what it's worth as I try to discover more about the nature of the personality standing in front of me. The scene is a truly fascinating one and the reader would be correct in thinking that this could be a unique opportunity to do a reverse anthropological, sociological and/or ethnographic case study; 'Kafka's Ape revisited,' if you wish.[7] And if, as 'Red Peter', I am consigned to a continual reportage of gratitude to the academy for supporting my *Entwicklung* (educational development) then I can be forgiven for seeing the entire experience for what it is – an extended and ongoing performance of identity that's taken more than five hundred years to unfold. Walcott and others were correct in their observations that 'The colonial history that gave rise to contemporary life in the West [still] haunts our present' (Walcott in Broeck and Junker 2014: 96), and this presence is evident in all aspects of our everyday lives.

Soon after my appointment as an Assistant Professor in a Canadian university, and perhaps already sensing what lay ahead, I created a new dance and performance work titled *Relatively-Well-Centred* (2000). This would be my first attempt in Canada to implement a choreographic model I had begun developing much earlier in the United Kingdom and other parts of mainland Europe – primarily Germany – in academic, professional and community dance institutions. This model included using in my works students I was assigned to teach in several disciplinary areas, faculty members from across the university and professional artists working in the so-called 'market' outside academia. The response to this first work was quite strange to my mind at the time; I thought either no one understood my intentions, or colleagues were too polite to comment on what they saw. I received absolutely no critical feedback outside the cast and creative team, something that baffled me since I assumed that in such an environment critical dialogue was expected and even encouraged. Even gentle probing failed to squeeze much out of my colleagues.

Relatively-Well-Centred utilized text from Franz Kafka's *Ein Bericht für eine Akademie*, or 'A Report to an Academy' (1917), Mari Evans's *I am a Black Woman* (1970) and Virginia Woolf's *Orlando* (1928). Its aim was to explore some of the key issues inherent in these writings, which was essentially a critique of knowledge through the performance of culture, gender and race. The work was also part of a larger strategy to position dance and other performance practices as valid modes of academic research. This habit of drawing inter- and trans-disciplinary references through well-known works, in this case literary writings, has always been strategic to both my studio practice and my intellectual/theoretical work. Such an approach underlines the idea that we human beings exist in bodies that have complex histories, are embedded in multiple domains, have 'selves' and memories that exist simultaneously in different spatiotemporal orbits and can be investigated by methodologies that do not obey prescriptive disciplinary categories.

Relatively-Well-Centred utilized the basic concept embedded in an ellipse, which describes a trajectory that is quite different from that of the circle. The structure of the circle is described as a set of all points on a plane that is at fixed distances from a central point or focus. The ellipse, on the other hand, suggests that there are two foci, with points on a plane that are at fixed distances from two central points or foci that eventually stretches the shape of the circle into an extended form, the ellipse. One can say that the circle is a special type of ellipse, or conversely, the ellipse is a special type of circle. One can also say that if an object is moving in an elliptical trajectory with only one visible centre or focus, there must be a second invisible focus. The idea behind the *mise-en-scène* in *Relatively-Well-Centred* is that the White performers onstage were the visible focus and the second 'invisible' centre or focus was the pre-recorded images of Black bodies on a screen behind, creating a doubly centred 'elliptical path' with the audience as observing subjects. Additionally, the music for this work consisted of African drumming patterns, voice and percussion executed by my only Black colleague in the department – Albert St. Albert Smith, a highly skilled musician and lecturer who had spent decades accompanying dance classes and had run a biennial field school to Ghana until his retirement. However, none of his music was obviously recognizable, since it was deliberately electronically manipulated into something quite 'other' by another colleague, Martin Gotfrit, a White musician/composer. The musicians who contributed to this work never appeared live on stage, nor did I, but we were all instrumental in determining the trajectory of the work. A subtle message of this approach was that few artists of colour had access to the structures of institutional power and that their work could only be visible through the work of others or be presented only through the mediation of others. This, to be sure, was just one layer of the performance and, as I mentioned, the audience was not required to know this. The other layers literally spoke for themselves, since the performers danced to pre-recorded excerpts from the texts of Kafka's 'A Report to an Academy', Woolf's *Orlando*, and Evans's *I am a Black Woman.*

Kafka's 'Report' spoke of an ape that had been captured in Africa, brought to Europe and taught to become a human being. After such an accomplishment, that ape was called before representatives of 'the academy' and asked to give an account of that accomplishment – a defence, so to speak. Woolf's *Orlando* is a feminist manifesto that traces the life and adventures of a poet who changes sex from male to female and lives over centuries, meeting the key figures of English literary history along the way. Evans's *I am a Black Woman,* on the other hand, is a poem that focuses on the struggles of African American women and the experiences that made them such strong and resilient individuals. All three of these texts, to me, were unique critiques not only of how the structures of institutional power worked but also of how they could be decentred. In fact, my argument was that the protagonists were all 'relatively well centred' because of their own efforts to become something other than what was expected of them.

This initial effort to introduce what I had hoped would stimulate critical dialogue was met by polite silence. Even as I sought feedback, no one said a word about what I saw as the most important aspect of the work, namely, how to introduce a lively debate about diversity and inclusivity through an individual artistic practice and to offer a critique of an institution that seemed to discourage what it actually advertised as part of its social and educational mandate. A decade later, and after much effort in developing new works with varying degrees of criticality, I rechoreographed and restaged a section of *Relatively-Well-Centred* as *The Report* and *Kafka's Report...revisited* in two separate versions (2010 and 2016, respectively) using just Kafka's text in the original German with a partial translation by my playwright colleague Marc Diamond.[8] *The Report* presented White bodies performing classical ballet routines *en pointe*, subsequently transformed by a contemporary vocabulary that challenged the ballet's institutionalization. The 'ape' role was reprised by the original Canadian/Filipino actor/dancer Vic Ustare (2010)[9] and later by Marc Arboleda (2016).[10] These works were well received, or

I should say received very good applause from my audiences, but still no discussion about the fundamental problems that generated the work in the first place. That was left to me to introduce in my own classes.

What's ahead?

Those with an ancestry embedded in the experience of the Atlantic Slave Trade have inherited a peculiar relationship to the descendants of those who enslaved their forefathers, as well as with the institutions created to keep slaves in check. Each has become trapped in the other's orbit, rooted in each other's gaze. Escape from this cycle demands that we strive to become something 'other than', to radically shift the focus away from a dynamic that forever perpetuates an illusion that presumes its own truth. But what could this radical shift be and from whence can it come? I firmly believe that a new and more diverse set of bodies must infiltrate current institutions in order to radically change the discourses they proliferate. These bodies must challenge what has become normative, actively promote shifts in perception, and expose the many possibilities that lie hidden between the yes/no, subject/object dichotomies of an inherited rationalist mode of thinking and being. As McMullen (2013) argues, we are dealing with a future that is already here, and something 'other than' the past must describe that future.

Argentinian-born scholar Enrique Dussel put it another way by saying that 'the Latin American intellectual has the challenge, in addition to the normal academic duties of the European or American world, of having to establish the bases for the construction of an explanation of the cultural reality from which his or her own reflections emerge' (Dussel, in Alcoff and Mendieta 2000: 269). In other words, they must envisage a somewhat different epistemology. I argue that this is a challenge that everyone who questions commonly held institutional practices must accept. And in accepting that challenge, they must also find a way to position the performing body as an intelligent and knowing entity that reveals itself to its owner and to others. That owner just needs to recognize what is already inherently within his, her or their sphere. I see my own task as contributing to this not so subtle perceptual shift, a shift that includes my response to a call to:

> interrogate the established structures and the creative individual, as well as philosophical and educational processes, towards the search for decolonization of the body and the form; and by so doing effect a decolonization of knowledge specifically in dance but generally across disciplines.[11]

Perhaps this book is merely the beginning of that task, or perhaps the end of my efforts, in the sense of laying a strong theoretical base with the requisite epistemic logic to support it. I argued in my hypothesis that we human beings were fragmented subjectivities cognitively embodied through our experiences of space, place and time. In other words, the spaces we inhabit and the practices we engage in are documented in and through cortical and cartographic maps, and an investigation of these maps through movement, dance, choreography and performance reveal a great deal about who we are and what we could become. Therefore, if dance is positioned as the movement behaviour of the human body in space/time and choreography the deliberate organization of those movements into coherent and meaningful structures, then cartographical mapping is the conception, production, dissemination, representation and study of maps of geographical territory, and cortical mapping the method through which the brain dynamically represents relationships between two different kinds of territories, i.e. the body and the environments in which we as owners of those bodies exist. Movement is indeed analogous to thought unfolding.

Finale

To conclude, Cuban-born Jamaican dramatist, novelist and cultural theorist Sylvia Wynter once argued that the principal 'fantasy' with which Columbus would challenge the existing models of geographic placement came from his 'messianic apocalyptic fervor' on the one hand, and his 'psychosocial motivation as a lowly born cartographer and occasional merchant to better his social status' in an emerging Spanish society on the other (Wynter in Hyatt and Nettleford 1994: 23).[12] Wynter had first-hand experience of what it was like to live both in and out of her home country in the aftermath of official colonialism even as its effects continued to manifest in her everyday life. This condition speaks to what Meerzon (2012) called the condition of the exiled, i.e. the individual who belongs neither here nor there but who uses the condition as both punishment and privilege. Although Meerzon was referring to Poet Laureate Derek Walcott in that instance, I think the same applies to those who find themselves in similar situations.

But what about those who no longer have the option of a native home or language to return to or to gesture from. Wynter recommends that we go back five centuries to fully understand how and why we find ourselves in this position today and decide what we can do to help solve it. Though we are the inheritors of voyages we did not ask for, never wanted to be a part of, but were nevertheless drawn into, those of us who are offspring of the enslaved need to make our 'salvation' an integral part of that solution. The position statement of dislocation and displacement that began this book must transform into one of relocation and repositioning. The self and its 'being' must emerge dynamically by performing its way through all the environmental, doctrinal, political and socio-economic frameworks that colonizing processes have erected to constrain it. And this is what I hope I have achieved for myself with this publication.

NOTES

1. Charles Mingus was born in Nogales Arizona on 22 April 1922 of mixed heritage; African American, German American, British, Chinese and Native American (Horton 2007). He died in Mexico on 5 January 1979 at the age of 56, soon after working on music for an album with the Canadian singer/songwriter Joni Mitchell.
2. I was born on the Caribbean island of Trinidad and educated at Naparima College; an all-boys secondary school founded by Canadian Presbyterian missionaries for the sons of Indian indentured servants who were brought in to replace the 'emancipated' African slaves in the mid nineteenth century.
3. See Hall et al. (2015: 16) critique of Neoliberalism's project as 'a reassertion of capital's historic imperative to profit – through financialization, globalisation and yet further commodification', and Bill Readings' critique of the University and its administrative manipulation of teaching and research objectives in his 1996 monograph, *The University in Ruins*.
4. This exchange took place at the 'Continuing Conversations' 15 October 2015 roundtable discussion at the Djavad Mowafaghian Cinema, Goldcorp Centre for the Arts, Simon Fraser University, Vancouver. The discussion was part of a three-day seminar dedicated to remembering, and continuing, the work of British public intellectual Stuart Hall. Retrieved 30 January 2016, www.henrydaniel.ca/news/.
5. Ryan Holmes (3 February 2016) – *The Financial Post*. Retrieved 30 January 2016, from: 'Without affordable housing, Vancouver risks becoming an economic ghost town' https://financialpost.com/entrepreneur/fp-startups/without-affordable-housing-vancouver-risks-becoming-an-economic-ghost-town.
6. Contemporary dance techniques such as Graham, Limón and Horton have all had major influences in their developmental process from Black dancing bodies since the early part of the twentieth century. Dance historian Brenda Dixon-Gottschild (1996, 2003) has written extensively on the Black influence on modern and contemporary dance, including George Balanchine's neo-classic ballet, by a Black movement and music aesthetic.
7. I'm referring to Franz Kafka's story about an ape who is captured somewhere in Africa and trained in Europe to become human. After a rigorous education, 'Red Peter' is asked to make a report to an academic committee about his transformation. Kafka's *Ein Bericht für eine Akademie* or 'A Report to an Academy' was first published in 1917.
8. Teacher, theatre director, playwright, novelist, opera librettist, Professor Marc Diamond died suddenly at his home in Vancouver on 17 November 2005, aged 61, www.sfu.ca/~gotfrit/Marc_Diamond.htm.

9. www.henrydaniel.ca/the-report.
10. 5 August 2016, www.henrydaniel.ca/news.
11. 'Decolonizing Bodies: Engaging Performance.' 3rd Biennial International Dance Conference. The University of the West Indies, Errol Barrow Centre for Creative Imagination, Cave Hill Campus, Barbados, West Indies.
12. Wynter, Sylvia. '1492: A New World View' in *Race, Discourse and the Origins of the Americas: A New World View*.

Appendix A

Artistic Works by the Author

Note: *All works are choreographed by the author or in collaboration with him.*

Multi-year research projects referenced

Contemporary nomads (2017–21)

Academic and artistic collaborators:

Dr Ali Abdi, Dr Handel Wright, Adam Basanta, Chimerik Media Collective – Sammy Chien and Shanghan Chien

Choreography:

Nómadas 2018 (excerpts). Premiered 28 September 2018. Goldcorp Centre for the Arts, Vancouver
www.henrydaniel.ca/contemporary-nomads
Choreography: Henry Daniel
Dancers: Marc Arboleda, Nelle Lee, Kaylee Louie, Eden Solomon, Juan Villegas, Seana Williams
Musicians-Fringe Percussion: Luke Hildebrandt, Brian Nesselroad, Greg Samek, Daniel Tones
Stone, Metal, Skin – Music by Nigel Osborne
Kwak'wala Prelude (*Of Place and Language*) – Interview with Chief Robert Joseph 2010 – Used by permission of Chief Robert Joseph
Limology – I – Swell, II – Flight, III – Limbo – Music by Peter Nelson
Displacement – Music by Owen Underhill
Afterward – Music by Owen Underhill
nómadas – Text by Montserrat Videla Samper
Production Stage Manager: Kim Plough
Lighting Designer: Sophie Yufei Tang
Videographer: Asad Yahya

Assistant to the Videographer: Fegor Obuwoma
Cameras: Asad Yahya, Matthew Koropatwa, Colin Williscroft, Rithica Devireddy, Gregory Sparling

i. *nómadas*. Premiered 22 November 2017. Goldcorp Centre for the Arts, Vancouver
audio/video installation and live performance
www.henrydaniel.ca/contemporary-nomads

I. Prologue: *The Condition*
II. Home: *To Leave…or not*
III. Departure: *The Parting*
IV. Journey: *Building, Dismantling Walls*
V. Arrival/Settlement: *New Home*
VI. Epilogue: *In-between*

Performer/Collaborators

Allison Vicente, Amy Griffith, Anja Graham, Caitlin McKinnon, Jeremy O'Neill, Kadin Vanden Heuvel, Kaia Shukin, Kestrel Paton, Kevin Locsin, Lynnelle Sura, Montserrat Videla Samper, Nelle Lee, Seana Williams, Vienna Wong, Yian Chen
Henry Daniel: Choreography and Direction
Alan Storey: Set Design
Adam Basanta: Iris Garland Guest Artist – Sound Design
Chimerik 似不像: KRT Visiting Artists – Media Design
(Sammy Chien and Shanghan Chien)
Emily Bayrock: Video/Film Installation
Asad Yahya: Video/Film Installation
Jeremy O'Neill: Additional Sound Design
Sharon Lau: Lighting Designer
Nyssa Song: Rehearsal Assistance
Tabitha Alexander: Rehearsal Assistance
Sasha Kleinplatz: Dramaturgical Assistance
Laura Albert: Dramaturgical Assistance
Parmida Saeidian: Stage Manager
Kieren Eigenfeldt: Technical Director
Emma Hoogeveen: Assistant Technical Director
Jenny Jung: Assistant Stage Manager
Laura Coons: Projection Op
Joel Lagemaat: Sound Op
Jamie Sweeney: Lighting Op
Barry Hegland: Faculty Lead
Ben Rogalsky: Faculty Technical Director

Project Barca (2011–14)

Academic and artistic collaborators:

Dr Rita Dhamoon, Dr Olena Hankivsky, Professor Owen Underhill

Choreography:

i. *Isabella's Dream*. Premiered 22 May 2014. Nelson Hall (University Club Patio), UC Davis, USA. UC Davis Department of Theatre and Dance presents *Isabella's Dream* www.henrydaniel.ca/project-barca/#isabellasdream

Created by Granada Artist-in-Residence Henry Daniel in collaboration with Mary Ann Brooks, María De Los Ángeles Ceja, Daniel Davis, Brandon Gonzalez, Tiffany Martin, Deirdre Morris, Joyful Simpson, Joelle Toney, Olivia Turnross

Costume Designers: Roxanne Femling

Sound Design: Anel Zarate, Christine Richers and True Randall

Lighting Designers: Henry Daniel and Mike Hill

Stage Manager: Andrea del Moral

Asst. Stage Manager: Crystal Han

Composer Credits

Opening music from the production *Here Be Dragons/Non Plus Ultra*, composed by Owen Underhill based on the fifteenth and sixteenth century (including Sephardic, Arabic and Renaissance music), and performed by the intercultural/international ensemble consisting of Anna Casade-munt, alto gamba; Stanislas Germain, lute; Gordon Grdina, oud; Martin Fisk, percussion; and soprano Dorothea Hayley.

Lamentación En Hebreo: Mà Aidéj? Mà Adamélaj (Anónimo) by Jordi Savall's Hespèrion XXI, La Capella Reial De Catalunya.

Yanvalou drumming rhythm. *Papa legba* by Jeff Pierre

Musicians

Christine Richers – Saxophone, True Randall – Clarinet

Special Thanks

Cheryl Cox, Vice-President of Sacramento Theatrical Lighting, Conventions and Exhibitions Buerau

Donna J. Flor Production Manager, and the staff of the Mondavi Center for the Performing Arts

Caitlin Sapunor-Davis, Production Manager of the Sacramento Ballet

Randy Roberts, Katrina Wong and the rest of the staff of the Nelson Gallery

Production Team

Media Design: Henry Daniel, Mónica Martin, Muciano Miranda Ignasi Rubio

Videographers: Adrian Cacho Kiko Delacruz

Scene Shop Student Staff: Mark Merman, Cooper Wise, Ben Emerzian, Robert Bonner, Will Eberler
Dressers: Stephanie Anderson, Teryn Gray, Wendy Ortega
Costume Stock Assistant: Anel Zarate
Costume Production Crew: Kate Ackroyd, Natalie Cedillo, Vivian Cruz, Ben Emerzian, JaevWoo, Jeong Dennis Liu, Victoria Mack, Vanessa Manzo, Amanda Mitchell, Toni Postell, Taylor Relyea, Caitlin Sales, Bonnie Devon Smoti
Stitchers: Jessica Howard, Susan Huey, Lisa Romero
Arts Administration and Production Staff
Chief Administrative Officer: Karen Nofziger
Undergraduate Program Coordinator/Advisor: Kaelin J. Souza
Graduate Program Administrator/Advisor: Victoria Dye
Production Manager: Susie Owens
Facilities Manager/Audio Supervisor: Ned Jacobson
Costume Shop Director: Roxanne Femling
Publicity Director: Kathy Morison
Scene Technician/Master Properties: Byron Rudrow
Scenic Shop Carpenter: Myke Kunkel
Master Electrician: Michael Hill
Costume Shop Forewoman: Heather Brown
Costume Shop Teaching Assistant: Hannah Kagen-Moore
Company Managers: Michaela Cirimeli, Jason Moscato
Graphic Designers Publicity Assistant: Rudy Garibay, Chinh Tu, Timothy Huynh
Photographer: Abigail Alcala

ii. *Here Be Dragons/Non-Plus Ultra (HBD/NPU)*. Premiered 10–12 January 2013. Fei and Milton Wong Experimental Theatre, Goldcorp Center for the Arts, Simon Fraser University, Vancouver, Canada
Choreographer: Henry Daniel
Assistant to the Choreographer/Dramaturg (Barcelona): Rakel Ezpeleta
Assistant to the Choreographer (Vancouver): Daisy Thompson
Choreography consultant (Danza Antigua) – Anna Romani
Vancouver Performers
Dance: Arash Khakpour, Eloi Homier, Julia Carr, Karin Kato, Kyle Toy, Luciana D'Anunciação, Thoenn Glover
Oud: Gordon Grdina
Soprano: Dorothea Hayley
Barcelona Performers
Dance: Elisenda Moya, Ireneu Tranis, Laura Calvet-Butzbach, Sara Martín, Soledad Medina, Ángel Zotes

Actress: Rakel Ezpeleta
Viola de Gamba – Anna Casademunt
Renaissance Lute – Stanislas Germain-Thérien
Opening music from the production *Here Be Dragons/Non Plus Ultra*, composed by Owen Underhill based on the fifteenth and sixteenth century (including Sephardic, Arabic and Renaissance music), and performed by the intercultural/international ensemble consisting of Anna Casademunt, alto gamba; Stanislas Germain, lute; Gordon Grdina, oud; Martin Fisk, percussion; and soprano Dorothea Hayley.
Lamentación En Hebreo: *Mà Aidéj? Mà Adamélaj* (Anónimo) by Jordi Savall's Hespèrion XXI, La Capella Reial De Catalunya.
Yanvalou drumming rhythm. *Papa legba* by Jeff Pierre
Media Design Team
Costumes – Meta Vaughan
Media Design – Arrebato [Mónica Martín, Ignasi Rubio, Luciano Miranda]
Media, Web and Technical Assistant – Amit Barua
Media & Sound Design – Remy Siu
Sound Design – Nancy Tam
Isadora system programmer – Sammy Chien
Video Directors – Rheanna Toy, Sepehr Samimi
Photographs – Ágata Fornós
Technical Team
Lighting Design – Jonathan Kim
Technical Director – James Kokol
Set, Design and build – Elia Kirby and GNW Scene Shop
Stage Manager – Yovanka Contreras
Project Barca wishes to thank The Social Sciences and Humanities Research Council of Canada for funding this project; our Vancouver co-producer SFU Woodward's Cultural Programs; Area, Espai de Creació, our Barcelona host; The School for the Contemporary Arts at SFU; The Vice President Research at SFU; the FCAT Dean's Office at SFU; and all those generous people who accommodated our friends from Barcelona in their homes.

iii. *Barca: El Otro Lado*. Premiered 6 November 2012 at Nau Ivanow, Barcelona, Spain. www.henrydaniel.ca/project-barca/#elotrolado
Dancers: Elisenda Moya. Ireneu Tranis, Joahn Volmar, Laura Calvet, Mar Perera, Sara Martín, Sole Medina
Lamentación En Hebreo: *Mà Aidéj? Mà Adamélaj* (Anónimo) by Jordi Savall's Hespèrion XXI, La Capella Reial De Catalunya
Musicians: Anna Casademunt (viola de gamba), Pepe Luna (ud i percusió), Stanislas Germain (laud i percusió), Mercè Serramalera (soprano)

Choreographic Adviser: Anna Romani
Media Design: ARREBATO (Mónica Martín, Luciano Miranda i Ignasi Rubio).
Lighting Design: Rafa Tomico (EstamosDeBolo)
Video documentation: Ignacio Calo, Jordi Llorens Solé
Production Coordinator and Dramaturgical Assistant: Rakel Ezpeleta
Direction and Choreography: Henry Daniel
Project Barca wishes to thank The Social Sciences and Humanities Research Council of Canada for funding this project and Area, Espai de Creació, as our Barcelona host. We also wish to thank Avelina Argüelles, Institut del Teatre for her institutional contacts, and Nau Ivanow for presenting us at short notice

iv. *Here Be Dragons (Stage I Creative Preview)*. Premiered 1 June 2012. Studio T, Goldcorp Centre for the Arts, SFU Woodward's, Vancouver
Dr Henry Daniel: Principal Investigator
Collaborators
Prof. Owen Underhill
Dr Rita Dhamoon
Dr Olena Hankivsky
Researchers
Daisy Thompson, Marin Beck: Assistant to the Director
Nancy Tam: Sound Design
Additional Music
Remy Siu: Additional Music Composition
Gordon Grdina: Special Guest, and Performer
Performers/Contributors
Julia Carr, Thoenn Glover, Eloi Homier, Karin Kato, Arash Khakpour, Kyle Toy, Luciana D'Anunciação, Milton Lim, Janelle Reid, Erika Mitsuhashi, Caitlin Griffin
Video Documentation: Lara Amelie Abadir, Rheanna Toy
Media: Angel Chiang
Production
Jonathan Kim: Lighting Design
Amit Barua: Production Assistant

v. *Haikai*. GONG: The Gamelan Festival. Sunday 20 May 2012, 8.00 p.m. Wong Theatre, SFU Woodward's, Vancouver
Haikai
This choreography is a small section of the larger research initiative titled Project Barca: Going West to Find East/Going East to Find West
www.sfu.ca/~hdaniel/

Dr Henry Daniel – Choreographer/Director
Daisy Thompson – Assistant to the Director
Professor Owen Underhill – Collaborator
Dr Rita Dhamoon – Collaborator
Dr Olena Hankivsky – Collaborator
Performers
Julia Carr – Performer/Contributor
Thoenn Glover – Performer/Contributor
Eloi Homier – Performer/Contributor
Karin Kato – Performer/Contributor
Arash Khakpour – Performer/Contributor
Kyle Toy – Performer/Contributor
Luciana D'Anunciação – Performer/Contributor
Milton Lim – Performer/Contributor
Janelle Reid – Performer/Contributor
Erika Mitsuhashi – Understudy/Performer
Rheanna Toy – Director, Video Documentation
Lara Amelie Abadir – Video Documentation
Nancy Tam – Sound Design
Remy Siu – Sound & Media Design
Jonathan Kim – Production/Lighting Design
Amit Barua – Production Assistant/Media Design

Films:

i. *Ambos Lados*. Barcelona, Spain, 2013
www.henrydaniel.ca/project-barca/#ambos
Ambos Lados is a video performance/paper created for the World Dance Alliance Conference and Festival 'Evolve + Involve: Dance as a Moving Question' presented at the Scotia Bank Dance Centre in Vancouver, July 2013.
The work shares images and texts created during the Research/Creation 'Project Barca: New Architectures of Memory and Identity'. The material shown was created for
Here Be Dragons – A Creative Preview. Vancouver, 2012
Encounters – A video/Audio Installation. Vancouver, 2012
Stage Production *Barca: el otro lado*. Barcelona, 2012
Stage Production *Here Be Dragons/Non Plus Ultra*. Vancouver, 2013
Lead researcher, choreographer and director – Henry Daniel
Film Director – Lara Amelie Abadir
Assistant Director – Rheanna Toy
Cinematographer, Editor – Sepehr Samimi

Content Editor, translations – Rakel Ezpeleta
Media Artists – ARREBATO (Mónica Martin, Luciano Miranda, Ignasi Rubio)
Technical Team – Jonathan Kim, Remy Siu, Amit Barua
Sound Designer – Nancy Tam, Remy Siu
Performance and Text by
Vancouver – Julia Carr, Luciana D'Anunciação, Thoenn Glover, Eloi Homier, Karin Kato, Arash Khakpour, Kyle Toy, Milton Lim, Janelle Reid
Barcelona – Sara Martín, Sole Medina, Ireneu Tranis, Laura Calvet, Rakel Ezpeleta, Ángel Zotes, Elisenda Moya
Interviews – Sole Medina, Ireneu Tranis and Sara Martín

ii. *Implicados*. Barcelona, Spain, 2012
www.henrydaniel.ca/project-barca/#implicados
Choreographer and Director – Henry Daniel
Cinematography – Ignacio Calo
Montage – Amelie Lara Abadir
Dancers: Sara Martín, Joahn Volmar
Music – Jarcha Ya Amlaja Halki/Jordi Savall and Hesperion XXI
Set Management – Iamin Salcedo Garces
The choreographer would like to thank Jordi Savall and Hesperios XXI, and La Capella Reial de Catalunya for the unofficial use of the music track in this video, which is strictly for educational and non-commercial use only
Plaça de Felipe Neri, 2 August 2002, Barcelona

iii. *Voces del Vacio*. Barcelona, Spain, 2012
www.youtube.com/watch?v=gLn_kbMZmfY&t=4s
Choreographer and Director – Henry Daniel
Cinematography – Ignacio Calo
Contributors – Paula Benavente, Julia Rubies, Sara Martín, Rosana Carranza, Joahn Volmar, Iamin Salcedo, Adrian Costa, Betty Fernandez, Elena Schisano, Idalia Redondo and Rina Murakami
A special thanks to Amelie Abadir, Sonia Klamburg, Esther Sabate, Mauleon and the city of Barcelona

Installations:

i. *Encounters*. Vancouver, Canada, 2011
www.youtube.com/watch?v=K4JSZNN78BQ
A montage of the 4-channel video/8-channel audio installation in the Audain Gallery, Vancouver, June 2012

Lead researcher, choreographer – Henry Daniel
Researchers – Daisy Karen Thompson, Nancy Tam, Lara Amelie Abadir
Dancers: Julia Carr, Luciana D'Anunciação, Thoenn Glover, Eloi Homier, Arash Khakpour, Kyle Toy, Milton Lim, Janelle Reid, Karin Kato
Direction/Montage – Lara Amelie Abadir
First Assistant Director – Rhenna Toy
Camera/Lighting – Sepehr Samimi
Gaffers/Camera Assistants – Jeremy Cox, Natasha Wehn
Media – Amit Barua, Remy Siu, Jonathan Kim
A special thanks to Nancy Tam, who created the 8-channel sound for the installation. The music used for this video, however, was created and is owned by Nils Frahm and Anne Müller. *Journey for a traveller – Let my key be C*

The Touched Project (2007–10)
www.henrydaniel.ca/performance-archive
Academic and artistic collaborators:
Dr Ivan V. Bajić, Dr Jie Liang, Dr Peter Borwein

Choreography:

i. *Imprint II*. Premiered 17–20 June 2010, SFU Woodward's, Vancouver
www.henrydaniel.ca/the-touched-project/#imprintii
Choreography – Henry Daniel
Dancers – Michelle Cheung, Cai Glover, Thoenn Glover, Samantha Jane-Gray, Jessie Kwan, Felicia Lau, Peter Starr, and Matthew Waldie
Set Designer – Alan Storey
Composer – Owen Underhill
Turning Point Ensemble – Jeremy Berkman and Owen Underhill, Co-Artistic
Musicians: Lorna McGhee, Flute; David Owen, Oboe; François Houle, Clarinet; Mike Dowler, Bass Clarinet; Jesse Read, Bassoon; Benjamin Kinsman, French Horn; Marcus Goddard, Trumpet; Jeremy Berkman, Trombone; Jane Hayes, Piano; Heidi Krutzen, Harp; Vern Griffiths, Percussion; Marc Destrubé, Violin; Mary Sokol Brown, Violin; Marcus Takizawa, Viola; Ariel Barnes, Cello; David Brown, Bass
Lighting Designer – Barry Hegland
Costumes – Jay Havens, Monia Strehlke
Telepresence – Ivan Bajic, Xionan Ma
Multi View Camera System – Jie Liang, Calvin Che
Media Design – Sammy Chien

Media Assistants – Janina Schabig, Shanghan Chien
Installation Design – Majid Bagheri
Audain Gallery Installation Sound – James O'Callaghan
Graphic Design – Nazanine Parivar
Graphi/Web Design – Nasim Jahangiri
Stage Manager – Jaime Carlson
Assistant Stage Manager – Jonathan Kim
Production Assistant – Janelle Reid
Assistant Lighting Design – Shannon Wong
Film Director, camera, editor, video production – Sonia Suvagau
Videographers: Barry Liu, Riley Maruyama
Camera – Felix Olten
Production Director – Jeremy Baxter
Photographer – Chris Randall
We would especially like to thank Chief Robert Joseph who was very generous in sharing stories and the Kwak'wala language with us
Technical support: SFU Contemporary Arts, and Stefan Smulovitz
This production was made possible by a Canada Council/NSERC New Media Grant to Henry Daniel and Special Project Unique Opportunities grant to the Turning Point Ensemble from the BC Arts Council. Henry Daniel's grant administration is conducted by New Works. We would also like to thank the IRMACS Centre at SFU for their administrative and technical support in this research

ii. *Imprint.* Premiered 23 January 2010. UBC Museum of Anthropology, Vancouver, BC
www.henrydaniel.ca/the-touched-project/#imprinti
Choreography: Henry Daniel
Dancers: Brenna McLaud, Henry Daniel, Michelle Cheung, Tara Dyberg, Thoenn Glover
Advisors and special appearances by Chief Robert Joseph and William Wasden
Composer: Owen Underhill
Turning Point Ensemble – Jeremy Berkman and Owen Underhill, Co-Artistic Directors
Musicians: Lorna McGhee, flute; David Owen, oboe; François Houle, clarinet; Marie-Julie Chagnon, bass clarinet; Jeremy Berkman, trombone; Ariel Barnes, cello; David Brown, bass; Owen Underhill, conductor
Soundscape Assistance: James Maxwell, Adrian Underhill, Martin Gotfrit, Barry Truax
Sound Designer: Adam Basanta

Telepresence Technology: Ivan Bajic, Xiaonan Ma
Multiview Camera System: Jie Liang, Xiu, Xiaoyu, Clavin Che
Media Design: Sammy Chien
Videographers: Barry Liu, Adrian Underhill, Riley Maruyama
Production Manager: Allyson McGuire
Costume/Set Design: Jay Havens
Stage Manager: Kim Plough
Assistance with the projection and lighting has been provided by Robert Gardiner and UBC Department of Theatre and Film
Curatorial support in the creation of 'Imprint': We would especially like to thank Jill Baird and Jennifer Robinson of the Museum of Anthropology at UBC for working with us and facilitating and taking part in our discussions and interviews with Chief Robert Joseph and William Wasden. Both 'Bobby' and 'Wa' were very generous in sharing songs, stories and the Kwak'wala language with us
This production was made possible by a Canada Council/NSERC New Media Grant to Henry Daniel and Special Project Unique Opportunities grant to the Turning Point Ensemble from the BC Arts Council. Henry Daniel's grant administration is conducted by New Works. We would also like to thank the IRMACS Centre at SFU for their administrative and technical support in this research, Jerry Wasserman and UBC Theatre; Projects and speakers courtesy of Barry Hegland, SFU Contemporary Arts, and Stefan Smulovitz

iii. *t2_echo*. Premiered Saturday 21 November 2009. Concourse Gallery and www.henrydaniel.ca/the-touched-project/#echo
Intersections Digital Studio, ECIAD
Choreography and Direction – Henry Daniel
Dancers – Brenna McLaud, Tara Dyberg, Chengxin Wei, Donald Taruc
Music – James O'Callaghan
Violin – Julie Sun Lee
Costumes – Monica strehlke, Kate Burrows
Media Designer – Chris Ziegler
Telepresence Technology: Ivan Bajic, Xiaonan Ma
Multiview Camera System: Jie Liang, Xiu Xiaoyu
Videographers – Barry Liu, Riley Maruyama
This production was made possible by a Canada Council/NSERC New Media Grant to Henry Daniel and Special Project Unique Opportunities grant to the Turning Point Ensemble from the BC Arts Council. Henry Daniel's grant administration is conducted by New Works.

iv. *t2*. Premiered 11 July 2009, Scotia Bank Dance Centre, Vancouver, BC
www.henrydaniel.ca/the-touched-project/#t2

Choreography – Henry Daniel
Choreography and Odissi Dance – Scheherazaad Cooper
Assistant to the Choreographer – Cara Siu
Dancers: Scheherazaad Cooper, Livona Ellis, Brenna McLaud, Olivia Shaffer, Chengxin Wei
Costumes – Kate Burrows
Composers – Adam Basanta, James O'Callaghan
Tabla – Neelamjit Dhillon
Media Artists- Sammy Chien, Shanghan Chien
Telepresence Technology: Ivan Bajic, Xiaonan Ma, Choong-Hoon Kwak
Multiview Camera System: Jie Liag, Calvin Che, Xiaoyu Xiu
Robotics – Richard Vaughan, Ash Charles, Jens Wawerla, Alex Couture Biel, Adam Lein
Videographer – Barry Liu
Technical Director and Lighting Designer – Jeff Harrison
Stage Manager – Kimberly Plough
Assistant Lighting Designer – Carmen Hung
Assistant Stage Manager – Kelsey Peacock
Curator, Interurban Gallery 0 Christopher Runne
This production was made possible by a Canada Council/NSERC New Media Grant to Henry Daniel and Special Project Unique Opportunities grant to the Turning Point Ensemble from the BC Arts Council. Henry Daniel's grant administration is conducted by New Works.

v. *Touched*. Premiered 3 April 2008, SFU Mainstage Theatre, Burnaby
www.henrydaniel.ca/the-touched-project/#touched
Henry Daniel – Concept and Choreography
Mark Coniglio – Guest Artist, Troika Ranch – Media Designer
Dawn Stoppiello – Guest Artist, Troika Ranch – Choreography
Jai Govinda – Bharatanatyam Instruction
Jamie Griffiths – Media Instruction
Scheherazaad Cooper – Guest Performer
Performers – Victoria Dawe, Kim Dixon, Lily Hsu, Jeanette Kotowich, Anna Kraulis, Anny Lin (Violinist), Rachel McIlroy, Sarah Russell, Olivia Schaeffer, Janette Tseng, Jennifer Yau, Marc Arboleda, Shang-Han Chien, Chancz Perry, Justin Reist
Adam Basanta – Composer
Sammy Chien – Graphics, Media Design
Shang-Han Chien – Graphics, Media Design
Barry Liu – Videographer, Editor
Stefan Smulovitz – Interactive Technician
Richard Vaughan – Robotics

Arthur (Ted) Kirkpatrick – Motion Capture
Nelson Talbot, Graham Talbot, Nathaniel Sol – Running Crew
Rob Groeneboer – Camera/Pool Shoot
SFU Theatre Production Team
Olive Pang – Stage Manager
Kelsey Peacock and Jessica Cvjetkovic – Assistant Stage Managers
Carmen Hung – Lighting Design
Anil Chauhan – Technical Director
Scott Owens, Grace Park – Assistant Technical Directors
This performance is supported by the Iris Garland Visiting Choreographers Fund; the School for the Contemporary Arts at Simon Fraser University, Robert Gardiner's SSHRC Research/Creation Grant at the University of British Columbia, Henry Daniel's Canada Council/NSERC New Media Grant, and Theatre at UBC. Canada Council Grant Administration is by New Works
This production was made possible by a Canada Council/NSERC New Media Grant to Henry Daniel. Henry Daniel's grant administration is conducted by New Works

Films:

i. *Beyond Boxes*. Vancouver, 2011
www.henrydaniel.ca/the-touched-project/#beyondboxes
This film was produced, directed and edited by Sonia Suvagau with cinematography by Felix Oltean, cameras by Sonia Suvagau and Felix Oltean, and an original sound score by Sebastian Hugeneck
Choreography/Director – Henry Daniel of Full Performing Bodies
Dancers – Michelle Cheung, Cai Glover, Thoenn Glover, Samantha Jane-Gray, Jessie Kwan, Felicia Lau, Peter Starr, and Matthew Waldie
Set Designer – Alan Storey
Lighting Designer – Barry Hegland
Costumes – Jay Havens, Monia Strehlke
Telepresence – Ivan Bajic, Xionan Ma
Multi View Camera System – Jie Liang, Calvin Che
Media Design – Sammy Chien
Media Assistants – Janina Schabig, Shanghan Chien
Installation Design – Majid Bagheri
Graphic Design – Nazanine Parivar
Stage Manager – Jaime Carlson
Assistant Stage Manager – Jonathan Kim
Production Assistant – Janelle Reid

Assistant Lighting Design – Shannon Wong
Production Director – Jeremy Baxter
Composer/Conducter/Co-artistic Director, TPE – Owen Underhill
Shot on location at SFU Burnaby Campus, SFU Woodward's, Audain Gallery, Fei and Milton Wong Experimental Theater, Downtown East Side (DTES), 2011

Installations:

i. *IMPRINT II – the installation.* 17–20 June 2010, SFU Woodward's, Vancouver
www.henrydaniel.ca/the-touched-project/#imprintii
Media Design – Magid Bagheri
Set Design – Alan Storey
Performers – Cai Glover, Matthew Waldie, Michelle Cheung, Peter Starr, Thoenn Glover, Samantha Jane-Gray, Felicia Lau, Jessie Kwan

ii. *t2 – the installation,* Interurban Gallery, 11–25 July 2009
Robots – Richard Vaughan
Dancers – Chengxin Wei, Brenna McLaud
Media Artists – Sammy Chien, Shanghan Chien
Telepresence Technology: Ivan Bajic, Xiaonan Ma, Choong-Hoon Kwak
Multiview Camera System: Jie Liag, Calvin Che, Xiaoyu Xiu
Robotics – Richard Vaughan, Ash Charles, Jens Wawerla, Alex Couture Biel, Adam Lein
Transnet (2003–05)

Academic and artistic collaborators:
Barbara Layne, Johannes Birringer, Brian Corrie, David Kaufman, Torsten Moller Luciana Duranti, Martine Epoque, Angela Piccini, George Lewis, Carol Brown, Norma Sue Fisher-Stitt

Choreography:
Skin. Premiered 24 February 2005, Telus Theatre, Chan Centre for the Performing Arts. *A collaborative work-in-progress conceived by Henry Daniel of Full Performing Bodies*
www.henrydaniel.ca/transnet

i. Performed 17 June 2005 at the Transnet Conference at the Fei and Milton Wong Experimental Theatre, SFU
Choreography – Henry Daniel

Text – Dionne Brand (Additional text by the performers)
Performers – Courtney Bannon, Henry Daniel, Lisa C Ravensbergen, Sommer Thome, Kyle Toy, Vic Ustare
Sound Design – Arne Eigenfeldt
Bass – David Brown
Percussion – Albert St Albert Smith
Video Programming and Design – Ken Newby, Alexandra Dulic (Computational Poetics Research Group)
Lighting Design – Robert Gardiner
Technical Director and Lighting Director – Jeff Harrison
Technical Production and Stage Management – Yovanka Contreras
Costumes, Rehearsal Assistant – Monica Strehlke
Cinematographer – Dinka Pignon
House Technicians – Ernie Wai, Vera Ha
This project was supported by a SSHRC RDI Grant, a SFU Discovery Grant, the School for the Contemporary Arts and the School of Interactive Arts and Design at Simon Fraser University.

ii. *Coloured Bodies*. Premiered 17 October 2004. The Firehall, New Forms Festival, Vancouver, BC
Choreography – Henry Daniel
Performers – Courtney Bannon, Henry Daniel
Sound Design – Arne Eigenfeldt
Bass – David Brown
Percussion – Albert St Albert Smith
Video Programming and Design – Ken Newby, Alexandra Dulic (Computational Poetics Research Group)

Short-term stand-alone works mentioned

i. *Kafka's Report...reproduced*. Premiered 16–17 September 2016. Studio D, Goldcorp Center for the Arts, Simon Fraser University, Vancouver, BC
Franz Kafka's 'A Report to an Academy' (Ein Bericht für eine Akademie), and utilizes the original German text as well as Marc Diamond's English adaptation. Kafka's report is about an ape that is captured by a hunting party somewhere in Africa and brought to Europe. After what appears to be a successful transformation to human-likeness, the ape/human is called to a defense of his accomplishments by a scientific committee. Daniel's choreography builds on Kafka's mischievous commentary on the state of knowledge by adding another layer to the story. This work is danced *en pointe*.

Choreography by Henry Daniel
Music by Martin Gotfrit
Original German text spoken by Claudia Hein
English Adaptation by Marc Diamond
Performances by Marc Arboleda, Chelsea DesLauriers, Megan Morris, Nyssa Song, and Annabelle Wong
Lighting Design and Technical Direction by Kyla Gardiner
www.vimeo.com/229339928

ii. *The Report*. 4–5 March 2011 at 'The Conference on the Conference', Studio D, Goldcorp Centre for the Arts, SFU Woodward's, Vancouver, BC
Choreography and Direction – Henry Daniel
Text – Franz Kafka
English translation by Marc Diamond
Composer/Electronics – Gene Pritsker
Violin – Peter Krysa
Actor – Vic Ustare
Dancers – Thoenn Glover, Samantha-Jane Gray, Caitlin Griffin
German speakers – Ursula Baer, Andrea Dahlmann-Resing, Christine Spreter von Kreudenstein
This performance is made possible with the assistance of a SSHRC Small Institutional Grant (SIG) from the office of the VP Research Simon Fraser University, the School for the Contemporary Arts, and Full Performing Bodies
www.henrydaniel.ca/the-report

iii. *Intelligent Dancing Machines*. Premiered 10 October 2007, IRMACS Lecture Theatre, SFU, Burnaby
iv. *Kafka's Report to the Academy – Response from Dance*. Premiered 8 February 2001. SFU's Mainstage, Burnaby, BC
v. *Out of Body*. Recorded 21 March 2002 in Vancouver's CBC Studio www.henrydaniel.ca/performance-archive
vi. *Relatively-Well-Centered*. Premiered 23 November 2000 at the SFU Mainstage, Burnaby, BC
vii. *Futurist Equation*. Premiered 18 November 1999. John Stripe Theatre, Winchester, UK www.henrydaniel.ca/performance-archive
viii. *Shango Meets Ogun*. Premiered 21 December 1998. University College Scarborough, West Yorkshire, UK www.henrydaniel.ca/performance-archive
ix. *Walk-About-Timeless*. Premiered 13 July 1995. Riverside Studios, London, UK

x. *Red and Blue on a Purple Background.* Premiered 16 February 1991. Städtischen Bühnen Münster, Germany
xi. *A Tale from Atlantis/The Negro and The Mermaid.* Premiered 25 February 1990. Städtischen Bühnen Münster, Germany
xii. *Ich Khepera.* Premiered 8 March 1988. Podium, Freiburger Theatre, Freiburg, Germany
xiii. *Neptune Rising.* Premiered 25 April 1987. Balettschule Karin Wagner, Freiburg im Brsg, Germany
xl. *Pithecanthropus Erectus Part I.* Premiered 16 April 1985. Metropol, Vienna, Austria
xli. *Vortex.* Premiered 7 May 1980. Tanzprojekt München, Theatre in der Leopoldstrasse, Munich, Germany

Appendix B

MAP A

Country born in	Countries lived and worked in	Countries taught and researched in	Countries performed in	Countries presented research in	Countries visited
Trinidad and Tobago	Trinidad and Tobago, USA, Germany, UK, Canada	Trinidad and Tobago, USA, Germany, UK, Canada, Guatemala, Mexico, Spain, France, Holland, Portugal, Austria	Trinidad and Tobago, USA, Germany, UK, Canada, Guatemala, Mexico, Spain, France, Austria, Belgium, Hungary, Yugoslavia (former)/ Croatia, Denmark, Sweden, Italy, Brazil, St. Lucia	Trinidad and Tobago, USA, Germany, UK, Canada, Spain, France, Austria, Belgium, Switzerland, Finland, China, Hong Kong Australia, Barbados, Malta	Trinidad and Tobago, USA, Germany, UK, Canada, Guatemala, Mexico, Spain, Lanzarote-Canary Islands, France, Holland, Portugal, Austria, Belgium, Switzerland, Finland, China, Hong Kong, Australia, Barbados, Malta, Hungary, Yugoslavia (former)/ Croatia, Denmark, Sweden, Italy, Brazil, St. Lucia, Jamaica, St. Croix-USVI, Greece

MAP B

Countries	Cities lived in	Cities taught and researched in	Cities performed in	Cities presented research in
Trinidad and Tobago	San Fernando, Port-of-Spain	Port-of-Spain, San Fernando	Port-of-Spain, San Fernando, Sangre Grande, Scarborough	Port-of-Spain, San Fernando
United States of America	Boston, New York	Boston, New York, Davis	Boston, New York, Albany, Purchase, Chicago, Becket, Hartford, Princeton, Saratoga, Washington DC, Baltimore, Detroit, Durham, San Francisco, Ames, San Jose, Raleigh, Santa Barbara, Chapel Hill, Stanford, Wayne, Freeport, Charleston, Phoenix, Palm Beach, Fort Lauderdale	Boston, New York, San Francisco, Davis, Chicago, Los Angeles, Miami

Countries	**Cities lived in**	**Cities taught and researched in**	**Cities performed in**	**Cities presented research in**
Germany	München, Freiburg im Breisgau, Münster	München, Freiburg im Breisgau, Münster, Stuttgart, Köln, Berlin, Nuremberg, Heidelberg, Dusseldorf	München, Freiburg im Breisgau, Hamburg, Münster, Stuttgart, Köln, Berlin, Nuremberg, Heidelberg, Dusseldorf	München, Stuttgart, Berlin
United Kingdom	London, Winchester	London, Winchester, Leeds, Bristol, Exmouth, Scarbor-ough, Nottingham, Bath	London, Winchester, Leeds, Bristol	London, Winchester, Leeds, Bristol, Exmouth, Scarborough, Coventry, Guildford
Canada	Vancouver	Vancouver	Vancouver	Vancouver, Victoria, Calgary, Lethbridge, Toronto, Montreal, Ottawa, Hamilton
Guatemala		Guatemala City	Guatemala City	

(Continued)

Countries	Cities lived in	Cities taught and researched in	Cities performed in	Cities presented research in
Mexico		Mexico City	Mexico City, Guadalajara, Guanajuato, Aguascalientes	
Spain		Barcelona, Madrid, Zaragoza, Granada, Seville, Madrid, Toledo, Córdoba, Antequera, Palos de la Frontera	Barcelona, Madrid	Barcelona
France		Paris, Bordeaux, Reims	Paris, Bordeaux, Reims, Angers, Brest, Rouen, Chalon, Montpelier, Le Havre, Vienne, Grand Quevilly, Mâcon, Lyon, Clermont-Ferrand, Dijon, Nantes, Toulouse, Marseille, Strasbourg, Tarbes, Béziers, Toulon	Paris, Avignon

(*Continued*)

Countries	Cities lived in	Cities taught and researched in	Cities performed in	Cities presented research in
Holland		Amsterdam, Rotterdam		
Austria		Vienna	Vienna	Vienna, Linz
Switzerland		Zürich, Bern		Zürich
Belgium			Antwerp	Antwerp
Finland				Helsinki
Hungary		Budapest	Budapest, Székesfehérvár	
Yugoslavia (former), Croatia			Zagreb, Osijek	
Denmark			Aarhus, Copenhagen	
Sweden			Stockholm	
Italy		Palermo	Taormina	

(*Continued*)

Countries	Cities lived in	Cities taught and researched in	Cities performed in	Cities presented research in
Brazil			São Paulo, Rio de Janeiro, Porto Alegre	
St. Lucia			Castries	
China				Ningbo
Hong Kong				Hong Kong
Australia				Melbourne
Barbados				Bridgetown
Malta				Valletta

MAP C

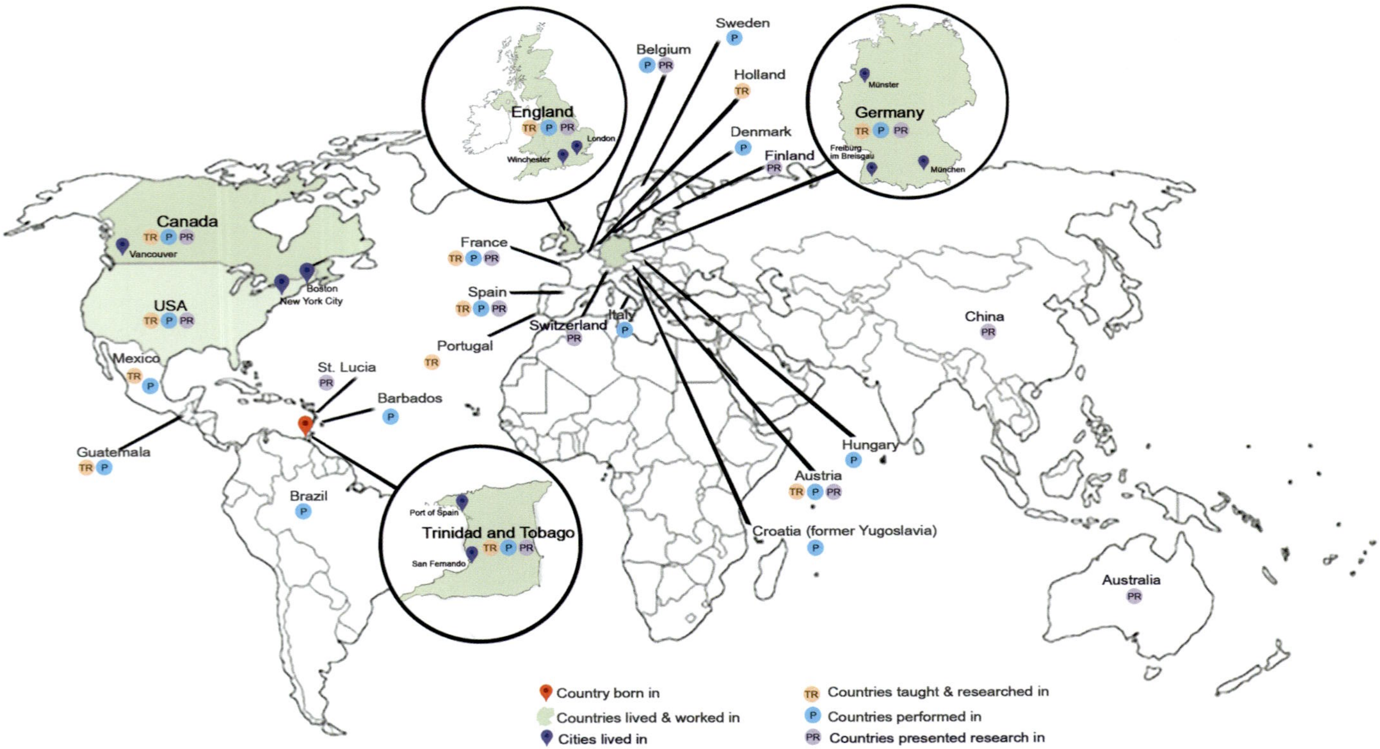

FIGURE AB.1. A choreographic mapping of countries, cities, and locations: (1) *Trinidad and Tobago*: San Fernando→ Port–of-Spain. (2) Port-of-Spain→ Boston (*United States*). (3) Boston→New York. (4) New York→Munich (*Germany*). (5) Munich→New York (*United States*). (6) New York→ Munich (*Germany*). (7) Munich→Freiburg im Breisgau. (8) Freiburg im Breisgau→Münster. (9) Münster→London (*United Kingdom*). (10) London→Winchester. (11) Winchester→Vancouver (*Canada*).

Bibliography

Achebe, Chinua. *Morning Yet on Creation Day: Essays*. Anchor Press, 1975.

Aeterni Regis, Treaty of Alcáçovas. 1481, https://clc-library-org-docs.angelfire.com/Aeterni.html. Accessed 1 Aug. 2022.

Ahmed, Sarah. *Strange Encounters: Embodied Others in Post Coloniality*. Routledge, 2000.

Ahmed, Sarah. *On Being Included: Racism and Diversity in Institutional Life*. Duke University Press, 2012.

Albright, Ann Cooper. *Choreographing Difference: The Body and Identity in Contemporary Dance*. Wesleyan University Press, 1997.

Alexander, Jeffrey C., et al. *Cultural Trauma and Collective Identity*. University of California Press, 2004.

Antliff, Mark. 'The Fourth Dimension and Futurism: A Politicized Space.' *The Art Bulletin*, vol. 82, no. 4, 2000, pp. 720–33. *JSTOR*, www.jstor.org/stable/3051419. Accessed Mar. 2022.

Apollonio, Umbro. *Futurist Manifestos*.Thames and Hudson, 1973.

Aquilina, Stefan, and Malaika Sarco Thomas editors. *Interdisciplinarity in the Performing Arts: Contemporary Perspectives*. Malta University Press, 2018.

Arbib, Michael. 'From Monkeylike Action Recognition to Human Language: An Evolutionary Framework for Neurolinguistics.' *Behavioural and Brain Science*, vol. 28, 2005, pp. 105–24.

Arbib, Michael. *How the Brain Got Language: The Mirror System Hypothesis*. Oxford University Press, 2012.

Arbib, Michael, and Derek Bickerton, editors. *The Emergence of Protolanguage Holophrasis vs Compositionality*. John Benjamins Pub. Co., 2010.

Asch, Ronald. *The Thirty Years War: The Holy Roman Empire and Europe, 1618–1648*. St. Martin's Press, 1997.

Askenasy, Jean, and Joseph Lehman. 'Consciousness, Brain, Neuroplasticity.' *Frontiers in Psychology*, vol. 4, no. 412, 2013, https://doi.org/10.3389/fpsyg.2013.00412.

Assmann, Jan. 'Communicative and Cultural Memory.' *Cultural Memory Studies: An International and Interdisciplinary Handbook*, edited by Astrid Erll and Ansgar Nünning, Springer, 2008, pp. 109–18.

Austen, John L. *How to Do Things with Words*. Clarendon Press, 1962.

Austen, John L. 'Performative Utterances.' *Austen, Philosophical Papers*. Oxford University Press, 1970, pp. 233–52.

Aveni, Anthony. 'Venus and the Maya: Interdisciplinary Studies of Maya Myth, Building Orientations, and Written Records Indicate That Astronomers of the Pre-Columbian World Developed a Sophisticated, If Distinctive, Cosmology.' *American Scientist*, vol. 67, no. 3, 1979, pp. 274–85.

Aveni, Anthony. *Skywatchers*. University of Texas Press, 2011.

Auslander, Phillip. *Theory for Performance Studies: A Student's Guide*. Routledge, 2008a.

Auslander, Phillip. *Liveness: Performance in a Mediatized Culture*. 2nd ed., Routledge, 2008b.

Ayerman, Ron. *Cultural Trauma: Slavery and the Formation of African American Identity*. Cambridge University Press, 2001.

Badmington, Neil. *Posthumanism: Readers in Cultural Criticism*. Palgrave, 2000.

Bakhtin, Mikhail. *The Dialogic Imagination*.University of Texas Press, 1981.

Bakhtin, Mikhail. *Art and Answerability: Early Philosophical Essays*, edited by Michael Holquist and Vadim Liapunov. Translated by Vadim Liapunov, University of Texas Press, 1990.

Barad, Karen. *Meeting the Universe Halfway: Quantum Physics and the Entanglement of Matter and Meaning*. Duke University Press, 2007.

Barba, Eugenio, and Nicola Savarese. *A Dictionary of Theatre Anthropology: The Secret Art of the Performer.* Routledge, 2005.

Barnes, Elizabeth. 'Ernst Haeckel's Biogenetic Law 1866.' *The Embryo Project Encyclopaedia*, 2014, https://embryo.asu.edu/pages/ernst-haeckels-biogenetic-law-1866. Accessed 21 July 2022.

Barrett, Lisa Feldman. *How Emotions Are Made: The Secret Life of the Brain*. Houghton Miflin Harcourt, 2017.

Baudrillard, Jean. *Symbolic Exchange and Death*. Translated by Iain Hamilton Grant with an introduction by Mike Gane, Sage, 1993.

Beardsworth, Sarah. *Julia Kristeva: Psychoanalysis and Modernity*. Suny Press, 2004.

Beattie, John.'Spirit Mediumship as Theatre.' *Royal Anthropological Institute News*, vol. 20, 1977, pp. 1–6.

Berghaus, Günter, editor. *New Approaches to Theatre Studies and Performance Presented at the Colston Symposium, Bristol, March 1997*. Niemeyer, 2001.

Berghaus, Günter, editor. *Critical Writings: New Edition*, edited by Filippo Tommaso Marinetti. Translated by Doug Thompson, Farrar, Straus & Giroux, 2006.

Berghaus, Günter, editor. *Futurism and the Technological Imagination*. Rodopi, 2009.

Berghaus, Günter, editor. *Handbook of International Futurism*. De Gruyter, 2019.

Bergson, Henri. *Creative Evolution*, edited by Keith Ansell Pearson, Michael Kolkman and Michael Vaughan. Translated by Arthur Mitchell. Palgrave Macmillan, 2007.

Bernstein, Jay Hillel. 'Transdisciplinarity: A Review of Its Origins, Development, and Current Issues.' *Journal of Research Practice*, vol. 11, no. 1, 2015, http://jrp.icaap.org/index.php/jrp/article/view/510/412. Accessed 21 July 2022.

Bhahba, Homi. *The Location of Culture*. Routledge, 1994.

Bhahba, Homi. *Our Neighbours, Ourselves: Contemporary Reflections on Survival*. De Gruyter, 2011.

Bleeker, Maaike, et al. *Performance and Phenomenology: Traditions and Transformations*. Routledge, 2015.

Borgdorff, Henk. 'Artistic Research as Boundary Work.' *How Does Artistic Research Change us? Proceedings of CARPA 1 – 1st Colloquium on Artistic Research in Performing Arts. Theatre Academy, Helsinki, 19–21 November 2009*. Performing Arts Research Centre, Theatre Academy, 2010.

Borgdorff, Henk. *The Conflict of the Faculties: Perspectives on Artistic Research and Academia*. Leiden University Press, 2012.

Bragato, Fernanda Frizzo, and Lewis R. Gordon, editors. *Geopolitics and Decolonization: Perspectives from the Global South*. Global Critical Caribbean Thought, 2018.

Brah, Avtar. *Cartographies of Diaspora: Contesting Identities*. Routledge, 1996.

Braidotti, Rosi. *Nomadic Subjects: Embodiment and Sexual Difference in Contemporary Feminist Theory*. Columbia University Press, 1994, 2011.

Braidotti, Rosi. *Nomadic Theory: The Portable Rosi Braidotti*. Columbia University Press, 2011.

Brand, Dionne. *A Map to the Door of No Return*. Doubleday Canada, 2001.

Brenner, Joseph. 'The Philosophical Logic of Stéphane Lupasco (1900–1988).' *Logic and Logical Philosophy*, vol. 19, 2010, pp. 243–85.

Brenner, Joseph. 'The Transdisciplinary Logic of Transdisciplinarity', 1 Sep. 2011, www.metanexus.net/transdisciplinary-logic-transdisciplinarity/. Accessed 10 Mar. 2022.

Brenner, Joseph E. 'Process in Reality: A Logical Offering.' *Logic and Logical Philosophy*, vol. 14, no. 2, 2005, pp. 165–202. https://doi.org/10.12775/LLP.2005.012.

Bunker, Jenny, et al., editors. *Thinking through Dance: The Philosophy of Dance Performance and Practices*. Dance, 2013.

Burt, Ramsay. *Alien Bodies: Representations of Modernity, 'Race', and Nation in Early Modern Dance*. Routledge, 1998.

Burton, Mark, and Jorge Mario Flores Osorio. 'Introducing Dussel: The Philosophy of Liberation and a Really Social Psychology.' *Psychology in Society*, no. 41, 2011, pp. 20–39.

Butler, Judith. *Excitable Speech: A Politics of the Performative*. Routledge, 1997.

Butler, Judith. 'On Speech, Race and Melancholia: An Interview with Judith Butler.' *Theory, Culture and Society*, vol. 16, no. 2, 1999, pp. 163–74.

Cangelosi, Angelo, and Domenico Parisi. *Simulating the Evolution of Language*. Springer, 2002.

Cannon, Walter B. *The Wisdom of the Body*. W.W. Norton. 1939, 1963.

Césaire, Aimé. *Discourse on Colonialism*. Translated by Joan Pinkham. Monthly Review Press, 1972.

Chalmers, David J. *Conscious Mind, The: In Search of a Fundamental Theory*. Oxford University Press, 1996.

Chalmers, David J. *The Character of Consciousness*. Oxford University Press, 2010.

Chalmers, David J. *Constructing the World*. Oxford University Press, 2012.

Chatwin, Bruce. *The Songlines*. Penguin Books, 1988.

Chytraeus-Auerbach, Irene, and Georg Maag. *(Hrsg.): Futurismus. Kunst, Technik, Geschwindigkeit und Innovation zu Beginn des 20*. LIT Verlag Dr. W. Hopf. Berlin, 2016.

Coates, Emily, and Sarah Demers. *Physics and Dance.*Yale University Press, 2019.

Colodny, Robert G., editor. *Paradigms and Paradoxes: The Philosophical Challenge of the Quantum Domain*. University of Pittsburgh Press, 1972.

Conquergood, Dwight, and P. Thao.'Performing as a Moral Act: Ethical Dimensions of the Ethnography of Performance.' *Literature in Performance*, vol. 5, no. 2, 1985, pp. 1–13.

Conquergood, Dwight, and P. Thao. *I Am a Shaman: A Hmong Life Story with Ethnographic Commentary*. Translated by X. Thao. University of Minnesota Press, 1989.

Copeland, Roger. *Merce Cunningham: The Modernizing of Modern Dance*. Routledge, 2004.

Corbally Stourton, Patrick. *Songlines and Dreamings: Contemporary Australian Aboriginal Painting: The First Quarter Century of Papunya Tula*. Lund Humphries, 1996.

Corbin, Henry. *Kitab al-masha'ir*, edited and translated by H. Corbin, Bibliothèque iranienne, 1964.

Costa de Beauregard, Olivier. 'Wavelike Coherence and CPT Invariance: Sesames of the Paranormal.' *Journal of Scientific Exploration*, vol. 16, no. 4, 2002, pp. 651–54.

Cox, Brian, and Jeff Forshaw. *The Quantum Universe*. Da Capo Press, 2012.

Crabtree, A. *From Mesmer to Freud: Magnetic Sleep and the Roots of Psychological Healing*. Yale University Press, 1993.

Crick, Francis. *The Astonishing Hypothesis: The Scientific Search for the Soul*. Maxwell Macmillan International, 1994.

Crider, Matthew, et al. 'A Mixing Board Interface for Graphics and Visualization Applications.' *Proceedings of Graphics Interface*, 2007, pp. 87–94.

Dallmayr, Fred. 'The Underside of Modernity: Adorno, Heidegger, and Dussel.' *Constellations: An International Journal of Critical and Democratic Theory*, vol. 11, no. 1, 2004, pp. 102–20. www.onlinelibrary.wiley.com/doi/abs/10.1111/j.1351-0487.2004.00365.x.

Daly, Ann. *Critical Gestures: Writings on Dance and Culture*. Wesleyan University Press, 2002.

Damasio, Antonio. *Descartes' Error: Emotion, Reason, and the Human Brain*. G. P. Putnam, 1994.

Damasio, Antonio. *The Feeling of What Happens: Body and Emotion in the Making of Consciousness*. Harcourt Inc., 2000.

Damasio, Antonio. *Self Comes to Mind*. Pantheon Books, 2010.

Daniel, Henry. 'Transnet, a Canadian-based Case Study on Practice-as-Research – or, Re-thinking Dance in a Knowledge-Based Society.' *Practice-as-Research: In Performance and Screen*, edited by Ludivine Allegue, Simon Jones, Baz Kershaw and Angela Piccini, Palgrave Macmillan, 2009, pp. 148–62.

Daniel, Henry. 'Organization, Control and Emergence in Choreographed Performance Systems: The Art as Research Project Touched.' *Performative Body Spaces: Corporeal Topographies in Literature, Theatre, Dance and the Visual Arts*, edited by Markus Hallensleben, Rodopi, 2010a, pp. 217–32.

Daniel, Henry. 'Writing Dance in the Age of Technology: Towards Transdisciplinary Discourse.' *Forum for Modern Language Studies*, vol. 46, no. 4, 2010b, pp. 460–73.

Daniel, Henry. *The Report*, 2011. www.henrydaniel.ca/short-term-projects/. Accessed 30 Jun. 2022.

Daniel, Henry. 'Performing Ideas… Expertly.' *Performance Matters*, vol. 2, no. 2, 2016, pp. 123–31.

Daniel, Henry. 'Performing the Now: Mingus' Pithecanthropus Erectus.' *Jazz Cosmopolitanism from East to West*, edited by Yui Hui and Tony Whyton, Zhejiang University Press, 2017, pp. 42–57.

Daniel, Henry. 'The Futurist Condition.' *Futurismus: Kunst, Technik, Geschwindigkeit und Innovation zu Beginn des 20. Jahrhunderts*, edited by Irene Chytraeus-Auerbach and Georg Maag (Hrsg.), LIT Verlag Berlin-Münster-Wien-Zürich-London, 2017.

Daniel, Henry. 'Fitting [Out-fitting] In.' *The Nuances of Blackness in the Canadian Academy*, edited by Handel Wright, Awad Ibrahim, Malinda Smith and Tamari Kitossa, University of Toronto Press, 2021, pp. 231–43.

Darwin, Charles. *The Origin of Species by Means of Natural Selection, or, the Preservation of favored Races in the Struggle for Life.* Authorized ed. 2 vols., D. Appleton, 1898.

da Vinci, Leonardo. *The Notebooks of Leonardo Da Vinci.* Arranged, rendered into English and introduced by Edward MacCurdy, J. Cape, 1977.

Dawkins, Richard. *Climbing Mount Improbable.*Viking, 1996.

de Bruin, Leon., et al., editors. *The Oxford Handbook of 4E Cognition.* Oxford University Press, 2018.

Dee Das, Joanna. *Katherine Dunham: Dance and the African Diaspora.* Oxford University Press, 2017.

DeLancey, Craig. *Passionate Engines: What Emotions Reveal About Mind and Artificial Intelligence.* Oxford University Press, 2002.

De Molina, Tirso. *El burlador de Sevilla.* Cervantes & Company, University of Wisconsin – Madison, 2003.

Deleuze, Gilles, and Félix Guattari. *What Is Philosophy?* Columbia University Press, 1994.

Dennett, Daniel Clement. *Consciousness Explained.* Little Brown and Co., 1991.

Dennett, Daniel Clement. *Kinds of Minds: Toward an Understanding of Consciousness.* Basic Books, 1996a.

Dennett, Daniel Clement. *Darwin's Dangerous Idea: Evolution and the Meanings of Life.* 1st Touchstone ed., Simon & Schuster, 1996b.

Dennett, Daniel Clement. *Intuition Pumps and Other Tools for Thinking.* 1st ed., W. W. Norton & Co., 2013.

Dennett, Daniel Clement. *Elbow Room: The Varieties of Free will Worth Wanting.* MIT Press, 2015.

Depraz, Natalie, et al. *On Becoming Aware: A Pragmatics of Experiencing*. J. Benjamins, 2003.

Derrida, Jacques. *Writing and Difference*. University of Chicago Press, 1978.

Derrida, Jacques. *Of Grammatology*. Corrected ed. Johns Hopkins University Press, 1998.

Descartes, Renée, et al. *Meditations on First Philosophy: With Selections from the Objections and Replies*. Rev. ed., Cambridge University Press, 1996a.

Descartes, Renée, et al. *Discourse on the Method; and, Meditations on First Philosophy*. Yale University Press, 1996b.

Desmond, Jane. *Meaning in Motion: New Cultural Studies of Dance*. Duke University Press, 1997.

Diamond, Jared. *Guns, Germs, and Steel: The Fates of Human Societies*. W. W. Norton and Company, 2005.

Dixon-Gottschild, Brenda. *Digging the Africanist Presence in American Performance: Dance and Other Contexts*. Greenport Press, 1996.

Dixon-Gottschild, Brenda. 'Stripping the Emperor: The Africanist Presence in American Concert Dance.' *Moving History, Dancing Cultures: A Dance History Reader*, edited by Ann Dils and Ann Cooper Albright, Wesleyan Press, 2001, pp. 332–41.

Dixon-Gottschild, Brenda. *The Black Dancing Body: A Geography from Coon to Cool*. Palgrave Macmillan, 2003.

Dowling, John E. *Creating Mind: How the Brain Works*. W. W. Norton & Co., 1998.

Drewal, Margaret Thompson. *Yoruba Ritual: Performers, Play, Agency*. Indiana University Press, 1992.

Du Bois, W. E. B. *The Souls of Black Folk*. Bantam Books, 1989.

Dussel, Enrique. *The Invention of the Americas: Eclipse of 'The Other' and the Myth of Modernity*. Translated by Michael D. Barber. Continuum, 1995.

Dussel, Enrique. *The Underside of Modernity: Apel, Ricoeur, Rorty, Taylor, and the Philosophy of Liberation*, edited and translated by Eduardo Mendieta, Humanities Press International Inc., 1996.

Dussel, Enrique. 'A New Age in the History of Philosophy: The World Dialogue between Philosophical Traditions.' *En: Prajñã Vihãra*, (Bangkok, Thailand), vol. 9, no. 1, 2008, pp. 1–22.

Dussel, Enrique. 'A New Age in the History of Philosophy: The World Dialogue between Philosophical Traditions.' Selected Papers from the XXII World Congress of Philosophy. Special Supplement. *Journal of Philosophical Research*, vol. 37, no. 9999, 2012, pp. 151–66, https://doi.org/10.5840/jpr201237Supplement32.

Dussel, Enrique. 'Agenda for a South-South Philosophical Dialogue.' *Human Architecture: Journal of the Sociology of Self-Knowledge*, vol. 11, no. 1, 2013, pp. 3–18.

Dussel, Enrique. 'Homepage.' www.enriquedussel.com. Accessed 16 Mar. 2022a.

Dussel, Enrique. 'Dussel: A Rare Lecture in English on a Non-Eurocentric Account of World History.' *YouTube*, uploaded by daniel muñoz, www.youtube.com/watch?timecontinue=516&v=5LjHdcoNthk. Accessed 10 Mar. 2022b.

Eckstein, Lars. *Re-membering the Black Atlantic: On the Poetics and Politics of Literary Memory*. BRILL, 2006.

Edelman, Gerald, and Guilio Tononi, editors. *Consciousness: How Matter Becomes Imagination*. Penguin, 2000.

Ekman, Paul. *Emotions Revealed: Recognizing Faces and Feelings to Improve Communication and Emotional Life*. Times Books, 2003.

Ekman, Paul, and Daniel Cordaro. 'What Is Meant by Calling Emotions Basic.' *Emotion Review*, vol. 3, no. 4, 2011, pp. 364–70.

Ekman, Paul, et al. 'Universals and Cultural Differences in the Judgments of Facial Expressions of Emotion.' *Journal of Personality and Social Psychology*, vol. 53, no. 4, 1987, p. 712.

Eliade, Mircea. *Yoga: Immortality and Freedom*. 2nd. ed., Princeton University Press, 1970.

Ellis, Carolyn, et al. 'Autoethnography: An Overview.' *Historical Social Research*, vol. 12, no. 1, 2011, pp. 273–90.

Evans, M. *Continuum: New and Selected Poems*. Black Classic Press, 2011.

Evans, Mari. *Continuum: New and Selected Poems*. Black Classic Press, 2007.

Eyerman, Ron. *Cultural Trauma: Slavery and the Formation of African American Identity*. Cambridge University Press, 2001.

Eze, Emmanuel Chukwudi, editor. *Myth Literature and the African World*. Cambridge University Press, 1976.

Eze, Emmanuel Chukwudi. *African Philosophy: An Anthology*. Blackwell Publishers, 1998.

Fallon, James. *The Psychopath Inside: A Neuroscientist's Personal Journey into the Dark Side of the Brain*. Current, The Penguin Group, 2013.

Fanon, Franz. *The Wretched off the Earth*. Translated by Charles Lam Markmann, Grove Press, 1967.

Fanon, Franz. 'The Fact of Blackness.' *The Visual Culture Reader*, edited by Alex Reid. 3rd ed., Routledge, 2013, pp. 463–65.

Farred, Grant. *What's my Name?: Black Vernacular Intellectuals*. University of Minnesota Press, 2003.

Ferrarelli, Fabio, et al. 'Experienced Mindfulness Meditators Exhibit Higher Parietal-Occipital EEG Gamma Activity during REM Sleep.' *PLoS One*, vol. 8, 2013, e73417.

Feynman, Richard. *The Character of Physical Law*. MIT Press, 1995.

Flint, R. W. *F. T. Marinetti: Selected Writings*, with an introduction by R. W. Flint. Translated by R. W. Flint and Arthur A. Coppotelli, Farrar, Straus and Giroux, 1972.

Fodor, Jerry A., and Jerrold J. Katz. *The Structure of Language: Readings in the Philosophy of Language*. Prentice-Hall, 1964.

Foster, Susan Leigh. *Choreographing History*. University of Indiana Press, 1995.

Foucault, Michel. 'Nietzsche, Genealogy, History.' *Language, Countermemory, Practice: Selected Essays and Interviews*, edited by Donald F Bourchard, Cornell University Press, 1977, pp. 139–64.

Foucault, Michel. *The Order of Things: An Archaeology of the Human Species*, edited by R. D. Laing, Pantheon Books, 1970.

Foucault, Michel. *Discipline and Punish: The Birth of the Prison*. 2nd Vintage Books ed., Vintage Books, 1979, 1995.

Foucault, Michel. *Foucault Live: (Interviews, 1966–84)*, edited by Sylvère Lotringer. Translated by John Johnston. Autonomedia, 1989.

Fraleigh, Sondra Horton. *Dance and the Lived Body: A Descriptive Aesthetics*. University of Pittsburgh Press, 1987.

Fraleigh, Sondra Horton. *Dancing Identity: Metaphysics in Motion*. University of Pittsburgh Press, 2004.

Freud, Sigmund, and A. A. Brill. *The Basic Writings of Sigmund Freud*. The Modern Library, 1938.

Freud, Sigmund, and A. A. Brill. *The Standard Edition of the Complete Psychological Works*. Translated from the German under the general editorship of James Strachey, in collaboration with Anna Freud, assisted by Alix Strachey and Alan Tyson, Hogarth Press [between 1900 and 1999].

Daniel, Henry, and Rakel, Ezpeleta. 'Project Barca: A Case Study on the Impact of Performance as Research, Parts I & II.' *The Impact of Performance as Research. Proceedings of CARPA 3 – Colloquium on Artistic Research in Performing Arts. Helsinki, Finland. March 4–6, 2013*. The Publication Series of the Theatre Academy Helsinki, 2014.

Gardiner, Sophie. *Just Dancing Around*. Directed by William Forsythe. Euphoria Films, 1996.

George, David. 'Performance Epistemology.' *Performance Research*, vol. 1, no. 1, 1996, pp. 16–25.

Gilroy, Paul. *The Black Atlantic: Modernity and Double Consciousness*. Verso, 1993.

Gilroy, Paul. *Small Acts: Thoughts on the Politics of Black Cultures*. Serpent's Tail, 1994.

Gilroy, Paul. *Against Race: Imagining Political Culture Beyond the Color Line*. Belknap Press of Harvard University Press, 2000.

Glissant, Édouard. *The Indies*. Issue 1 of Collection Janus Translated by Dominique O'Neill, Éditions du GREF. University of Michigan Press, 1956, 1992.

Glissant, Édouard. *Poetics of Relation*. Translated by Betsy Wing, The University of Michigan Press, 1997.

Glissant, Édouard. *The Indies: A Translation and Critical Introduction*. Ellen Richmond, Amherst College, 2012.

Goffman, Erving. *The Presentation of Self in Everyday Life*. Penguin Books, 1959, 1990.

Goldman, Derek. 'From Spectating to Witnessing: Performance in the Here and Now.' *Arts and International Affairs*. 2017, www.theartsjournal.net/2017/07/19/from-spectating-to-witnessing-performance-in-the-here-and-now/. Accessed 16 Mar. 2022.

Gómez-Peña, Guillermo, et al. *Codex Espangliensis: From Columbus to the Border Patrol*. City Lights Books, 2000.

Gordon, Lewis R. *An Introduction to Africana Philosophy*. Cambridge University Press, 2008.

Gordon, Lewis R. 'Disciplinary Decadence and the Decolonisation of Knowledge.' *Africa Development/Afrique Et Développement*, vol. 39, no. 1, 2014, pp. 81–92, www.jstor.org/stable/2448467. Accessed 16 Mar. 2022.

Gray, John, et al. *Advanced Robotics & Intelligent Machines*. Institution of Electrical Engineers, 1996.

Graziano, Michael S. A. *Consciousness and the Social Brain*. Oxford University Press, 2013.

Graziano, Michael S. A. 'Ethological Action Maps: A Paradigm Shift for the Motor Cortex.' *Trends in Cognitive Science*, vol. 20, no. 2, Feb. 2016, pp. 121–32.

Greenblatt, Stephen. *Renaissance Self-fashioning: From More to Shakespeare*. University of Chicago Press, 2005.

Grosfoguel, Ramon. 'The Epistemic Decolonial Turn.' *Cultural Studies*, vol. 21, no. 2–3, 2007, pp. 211–23.

Grosfoguel, Ramon. 'Decolonizing Western Uni-versalisms: Decolonial Pluri-versalism from Aimé Césaire to the Zapatistas.' *TRANSMODERNITY: Journal of Peripheral Cultural Production of the Luso-Hispanic World*, vol. 1, no. 3, 2012. http://dx.doi.org/10.5070/T413012884.

Grosz, Elizabeth. *Volatile Bodies: Toward a Corporeal Feminism*. Indiana University Press, 1994.

Grossman, Lawrence. *Cultural Studies in the Future Tense*. Duke University Press, 2010.

Guattari, Felix. *Chaosmosis: An Ethico-aesthetic Paradigm*. Translated by Paul Bains and Julian Pefanis, Indiana University Press, 1995.

Gurdjieff, George I. *Beelzebub's Tales to his Grandson*. Routledge and Kegan Paul, 1950.

Gurdjieff, George I. *Meetings with Remarkable Men*. Translated by A. R. Orage, revised and reworked from the Russian manuscript. Routledge & Kegan Paul, 1963.

Gurdjieff, George I. *Views from the Real World: Early Talks in Moscow, Essentuki, Tiflis, Berlin, London, Paris, New York, and Chicago as Recollected by his Pupils*. With a Foreword by Jeanne de Salzmann. Dutton, 1973.

Gurdjieff, George I. *In Search of the Miraculous: Fragments of an Unknown Teaching*. Routledge & Kegan Paul, 1983.

Gyatso, Tenzin. His Holiness, The Dalai Lama. *The Universe in a Single Atom: The Convergence of Science and Spirituality*. Morgan Road Books, an Imprint of Doubleday, 2005.

Hacker, P. M. S. *An Intellectual Entertainment: A Dialogue on Mind and Body*. The Royal Institute of Philosophy, 2014.

Haeckel, Ernst. *Anthropogenie: oder, Entwickelungsgeschichte des Menschen. Keimes – und Stammesgeschichte (Anthropogeny, or the Evolutionary History of Humans)*. 1 vol. Engelmann, 1877.

Hall, Stanley G. *Adolescence: Its Psychology and Its Relation to Physiology, Anthropology, Sociology, Sex, Crime, Religion and Education*. Prentice-Hall, 1904.

Hall, Stuart. 'Cultural Identity and Diaspora.' *Identity: Community, Culture, Difference*, edited by Jonathan Rutherford, Lawrence & Wishart, 1990, 1998, pp. 222–37.

Hall, Stuart, et al. 'After Neoliberalism: Analysing the Present.' *After Neo-liberalism?: The Kilburn Manifesto*, edited by Stuart Hall, Doreen Massey and Michael Rustin. Maryland: Lawrence & Wishart, 2015, pp. 9–23.

Hall, Stuart, author, and B. Schwartz, editor. *Familiar Stranger: A Life Between Two Islands*. Duke University Press, 2017.

Harris, Jay. *How the Brain Talks to Itself: A Clinical Primer of Psychotherapeutic Neuroscience*. Haworth, 1998.

Hawkin, David J., editor. *The Twenty-First Century Confronts Its Gods: Globalization, Technology, and War*. State University of New York, 2004.

Hayles, N. Katherine. *How We Became Posthuman: Virtual Bodies in Cybernetics, Literature, and Informatics*. University of Chicago Press, 1999.

Hazard, W. Harry, editor. *A History of the Crusades. Volume III: The Fourteenth and Fifteenth Centuries*. University of Wisconsin Press, 1975.

Heble, Ajay, and Rob Wallace, editors. *People Get Ready: The Future of Jazz Is Now!* Duke University Press, 2013.

Heidegger, Martin. *Being and Time*. Blackwell, 1962.

Heidegger, Martin. *The Concept of Time*. English-German ed., B. Blackwell, 1992.

Heidegger, Martin, and Werner Brock. *Existence and Being*. 2nd ed., Vision, 1956.

Henry, Frances, et al. *The Equity Myth: Racialization and Indigeneity in Canadian Universities*. UBC Press, 2017.

Hermes, and Walter Scott. *Hermetica: The Ancient Greek and Latin Writings Which Contain Religious or Philosophic Teachings Ascribed to Hermes Trismegistus*. 4 vols, Shambhala, 1985.

Hindley, Meredith, *Destination Casablanca: Exile, Espionage, and the Battle for North Africa in World War II*. Public Affairs, 2017.

hooks, bell. *Talking Back: Thinking Feminist, Thinking Black*. South End Press, 1989.

hooks, bell. *Black Looks: Race and Representation*. South End Press, 1992.

Horton, Ernest Aaron. *Charles Mingus and the Paradoxical Aspects of Race as Reflected in His Life and Music*. Unpublished Ph.D. thesis, University of Pittsburgh, 2007.

Hölzel, Britta K., et al. 'Mindfulness Practice Leads to Increases in Regional Brain Gray Matter Density.' *Psychiatry Research*, vol. 191, no. 1, 2011, pp. 36–43.

Huebner, Bryce, editor. *The Philosophy of Daniel Dennett*. Oxford University Press, 2018.

Hunter, Lynette, et al., editors. *Sentient Performativities of Embodiment: Thinking Alongside the Human*. Lexington Books, Rowman and Littlefield, 2016.

Husserl, Edmund. *Cartesian Meditations: An Introduction to Phenomenology*. M. Nijhoff, 1960.

Husserl, Edmund. *Phenomenology of Internal Time-Consciousness*. Indiana University Press, 1964.

Husserl, Edmund. *Ideas: General Introduction to Pure Phenomenology*. Allen & Unwin, 1969.

Husserl, Edmund. *The Idea of Phenomenology*. Kluwer Academic, 1999.

Husserl, Edmund, et al. *Husserl at the Limits of Phenomenology: Including Texts by Edmund Husserl*. Northwestern University Press, 2002.

Hume, Lynne. *Ancestral Power: The Dreaming, Consciousness and Aboriginal Australians*. Melbourne University Press, 2002.

Hutchby, Ian, and Robin Wooffitt. *Conversation Analysis: Principles, Practices and Applications*. Polity Press, 1998.

Ingold, Tim. *Perception of the Environment: Essays on Livelihood, Dwelling & Skill*. Routledge, 2000.

Irigaray, Luce. *This Sex Which Is Not One*. Cornell University Press, 1985.

Jacob, Francois. *The Statue Within: An Autobiography*. Translated by Franklin Philip, Basic Books, 1988.

Jacob, Francois. *Of Flies, Mice, and Men*. Harvard University Press, 1998.

Jacob, Pierre. *What Minds Can Do: Intentionality in a Non-Intentional World*. Cambridge University Press, 1997.

James, Cyril Lionel Robert. *The Black Jacobins*. Secker & Warburg, 1938.

James, Cyril Lionel Robert. *State Capitalism and World Revolution*, in collaboration with Raya Dunayevskaya & Grace Lee; with a new introduction by Paul Buhle. Charles H. Kerr Publishing Company, 1986.

Jáuregui, José Antonio. *The Emotional Computer*. Blackwell Publishers, 1995.

Jones, Bill T. *Story/Time, The Life of an Idea*. Princeton University Press, 2014.

Jones, Steve. *The Language of the Genes: Biology, History and the Evolutionary Future*. Rev. ed., Flamingo, 2000.

Jung, Carl G. *The Archetypes and the Collective Unconscious*. 2nd ed., Princeton University Press, 1969.

Jung, Carl G., et al. *Man and His Symbols*. Aldus, 1964.

Kafka, Franz. *Ein Bericht für eine Akademie*, Der Jude, 1917.

Kafka, Franz. *Erzählungen*. S. Fischer, 1967.

Kahn, Charles H. *Pythagoras and the Pythagoreans: A Brief History*. Hackett Pub., 2001.

Kalin, Ibrahim. *Knowledge in Later Islamic Philosophy: Mullā Sadrā on Existence, Intellect, and Intuition*. Oxford University Press, 2010.

Kandel, Eric. *In Search of Memory: The Emergence of a New Science of Mind*. W. W. Norton & Company, 2006.

Kant, Immanuel. *The Conflict of the Faculties (Der Streit der Fakultäten)*. University of Nebraska Press, 1798, 1992.

Katrak, Ketu. *Wole Soyinka and Modern Tragedy: A Study of Dramatic Theory and Practice*. Greenwood Press, 1986.

Keegan, W. F. 'Sailing into History' and other articles, in *VISTA Magazine*. Caribbean Archaeology. Florida Museum of Natural History, 1991, www.flmnh.ufl.edu/caribarch/columbus.htm. Accessed 16 Mar. 2022.

Kelly, Kevin. 'What Is the Quantified Self.' *Quantified Self*, www.quantifiedself.com/. Accessed Jun. 2022.

Kindt, Merel. 'The Surprising Subtleties of Changing Fear Memory: A Challenge for Translational Science.' *Philosophical Transactions of the Royal Society, Series B, Biological sciences*, vol. 373, no. 1742, 2018. https://doi.org/10.1098/rstb.2017.0033.

Klein, Julie Thompson, et al., editors. *Transdisciplinarity: Joint Problem Solving Among Science Technology and Society*. Birkhäuser Verlag Basel, 2001.

Kraus, Hildegard. *Regie im Theater: Johann Kresnik*. Fischer Taschenbuch Verlag, 1990.

Kraut, Anthea. *Choreographing Copyright; Race, Gender, and Intellectual Property Rights in American Dance*, Oxford University Press, 2016.

Kristeva, Julia. *Revolution in Poetic Language*. Columbia University Press, 1984.

Kristeva, Julia. *Language – The Unknown: An Initiation into Linguistics*. Columbia University Press, 1989.

Kugler, Paul. *The Alchemy of Discourse: An Archetypal Approach to Language*. Bucknell University Press, 1982.

Kuhn, Thomas S. *The Structure of Scientific Revolutions*. 3rd ed., University of Chicago Press, 1996.

Kurzweil, Ray. *The Age of Spiritual Machines: When Computers Exceed Human Intelligence*. Viking, 1999.

Langton, Christopher G., editor. *Artificial Life: An Overview*. MIT Press, 1995.

Latour, Bruno. *An Enquiry into Modes of Existence: An Anthropology of the Moderns*. Translated by Catherine Porter, Harvard University Press, 2013.

Latour, Bruno. *Down to Earth: Politics in the New Climatic Regime*. Translated by Catherine Porter, Polity Press, 2018.

Laureys, Steven, and Giulio Tononi, editors. *The Neurology of Consciousness: Cognitive Neuroscience and Neuropathology*. Academic, 2009.

Lawlor, Robert. *Sacred Geometry: Philosophy and Practice*. Thames and Hudson, 1982.

Layzer, David. *Cosmogenesis: The Growth of Order in the Universe*. Oxford University Press, 1990.

Leder, Drew. *The Absent Body*.University of Chicago Press, 1990.

Lenarcic, Jadran, and Federico Thomas. *Advances in Robot Kinematics: Theory and Applications*. Kluwer Academic, 2002.

Levinas, Emmanuel. *Totality and Infinity: An Essay on Exteriority*. Translated by Alphonso Lingis, Duquerne University Press, 1969.

Lewin, Roger. *Complexity: Life at the Edge of Chaos*. 2nd ed., University of Chicago Press, 1999.

Lyotard, Jean François. *The Postmodern Condition: A Report on Knowledge*. University of Minnesota Press, 1984.

Mackay, Donald G., et al. 'Relations Between Emotion, Memory, and Attention: Evidence from Taboo Stroop, Lexical Decision, and Immediate Memory Tasks.' *Memory & Cognition*, vol. 32, no. 3, 2004, pp. 474–88.

MacCurdy, Edward, and Leonardo da Vinci. *The Notebooks of Leonardo Da Vinci*. Jonathan Cape, 1977.

Madison, Soyini D. 'Co-Performative Witnessing.' *Cultural Studies*, vol. 21, no. 6, 2007, pp. 826–31.

Magnani, Lorenzo, et al., editors. *Model-Based Reasoning in Science and Technology*. Springer-Verlag, 2010.

Maldonado Torres, Nelson. *Against War: Views from the Underside of Modernity*. Duke University Press, 2008.

Marinetti, Filippo Tommaso, and R. W. Flint. *Let's Murder the Moonshine: Selected Writings*. 1st ed., Sun & Moon Press, 1991.

Marks, Laura. *Enfoldment and Infinity: An Islamic Genealogy of New Media Art*. MIT Press, 2010.

Marks, Laura U. *The Skin of the Film: Intercultural Cinema, Embodiment, and the Senses*. Duke University Press, 2000.

Martin, John Joseph. *The Modern Dance*. Dance Horizons, 1965.

Martin, John Joseph. *America Dancing: The Background and Personalities of the Modern Dance*. Dance Horizons,1968.

Martin, John Joseph. *The Dance in Theory*. Princeton Book Co., 1989.

Marvel, Leon. *The Physics of Transfigured Light: The Imaginal Realm and the Hermetic Foundations of Science*. Inner Traditions, 2016.

Mascia-Lees, F. E., editor. *A Companion to the Anthropology of the Body and Embodiment*. Wiley-Blackwell, 2011.

Maturana, Humberto R., and Francisco J. Varela. *The Tree of Knowledge: The Biological Roots of Human Understanding*. Random House, 1992.

Mawere, Munyaradzi, and Tapuwa R. Mubaya. *African Philosophy and Thought Systems: A Search for a Culture and Philosophy of Belonging*. Langaa Research & Publishing CIG, 2016.

Mbembe, Achille. 'Decolonizing Knowledge and the Question of the Archive.' Lecture given at the University of the Witwatersrand, Johannesburg, 2015, https://wiser.wits.ac.za/system/files/Achille%20Mbembe%20-%20Decolonizing%20Knowledge%20and%20the%20Question%20of%20the%20Archive.pdf. Accessed 10 Aug. 2022.

Mbembe, Achille. *Critique of Black Reason*. Translated by Laurent Dubois, Duke University Press, 2017.

McCarthy, Cameron, et al. editors. *Race, Identity, and Representation in Education*. 2nd ed., Routledge, 2005.

McFee, Graham. *Understanding Dance*. Routledge, 1992.

McFee, Graham. *The Philosophical Aesthetics of Dance: Identity, Performance and Understanding*. Dance Books Ltd, 2011.

McMullen, Tracy. 'People, Don't Get Ready: Improvisation, Democracy, and Hope.'*People Get Ready*, edited by Ajay Heble, Rob Wallace and Rob Wallace, Duke University Press, 2013, pp. 265–80.

McNeely, Ian F. 'Current Trends in Knowledge Production: An Historical–Institutional Analysis.' *Prometheus: Critical Studies in Innovation*, vol. 27, no. 4, 2009, pp. 335–55. Special issue: *Beyond the Information Revolution*? https://doi.org/10.1080/08109020903414085.

McNeely, Ian F. 'The University in Ruins? A Report on Knowledge.' Paper delivered at Le Centre canadien d'études allemandes et européennes, Université de Montréal, Montreal, Canada, 13 March 2009. https://scholarsbank.uoregon.edu/xmlui/bitstream/handle/1794/9223/univin-ruins-mcneely.pdf?sequence=1&isAllowed=y Accessed 10 Mar. 2022.

McNeil, Daniel. *Sex and Race in the Black Atlantic: Mulatto Devils and Multiracial Messiahs*. Routledge, 2010.

Meerzon, Yana. *Performing Exile, Performing Self: Drama, Theatre, Film*. Palgrave Macmillan, 2012.

Melrose, Susan. 'Entertaining Other Options. Restaging "Theory" in the Age of Practice as Research.' Inaugural Lecture, 15 January 2002. https://eprints.mdx.ac.uk/23053/. Accessed 6 Aug. 2022.

Menary, Richard. 'Introduction to the Special Issue on 4E Cognition.' *Phenomenology and the Cognitive Sciences*, vol. 9, 2010, pp. 459–63.

Merleau-Ponty, Maurice. *Phenomenology of Perception*. Humanities Press, 1962.

Merleau-Ponty, Maurice, and Claude Lefort. *The Visible and the Invisible: Followed by Working Notes*. Northwestern University Press, 1968.

Merleau-Ponty, Maurice, et al. *The Incarnate Subject: Malebranche, Biran, and Bergson on the Union of Body and Soul*. Humanity Books, 2001.

Mesle, Robert C. *Process-Relational Philosophy: An Introduction to Alfred North Whitehead*. Templeton Foundation Press, 2008.

Messiaen, Olivier. *The Technique of My Musical Language*. A. Leduc, 1956.

Metanexus Institute – John van Breda: 'Towards a Transdisciplinary Hermeneutics', *Vimeo*, www.vimeo.com/11235383. Accessed 2 Aug. 2022.

Mingus, Charles. *Beneath the Underdog*, edited by Nel King, Alfred Knopf, 1971.

Minian, Ana Raquel. *Undocumented Lives: The Untold Story of Mexican Migration*. Harvard University Press, 2018.

Mirzoeff, Nicholas. *Diaspora and Visual Culture: Representing Africans and Jews*. Routledge, 2000.

Mitchell, J. Kevin. *Innate: How the Wiring of Our Brains Shapes Who We Are*. Princeton University Press, 2018.

Mitkov, Ruslan. *The Oxford Handbook of Computational*. Oxford University Press, 2003.

Mohanty, Jitendranath. *Phenomenology: Between Essentialism and Transcendental Philosophy*. Northwestern University Press, 1997.

Mohr, Richard D., and Barbara M. Sattler, editors. *One Book, the Whole Universe Plato's Timaeus Today*. Parmenides Pub, 2010.

Morison, Samuel Eliot. *Admiral of the Ocean Sea: A Life of Christopher Columbus*. Little, Brown and Company, 1942.

Morison, Samuel Eliot. *The European Discovery of America: The Northern Voyages, A.D. 500–1600*. Oxford University Press, 1971.

Morison, Samuel Eliot. *The European Discovery of America: The Southern Voyages, 1492–1616*. Oxford University Press, 1974.

Morris, James Winston. *The Wisdom of the Throne: An Introduction to the Philosophy of Mullā Sadrā*. Princeton University Press, 1981.

Morrison, Toni. *Playing in the Dark: Whiteness and the Literary Imagination*. Harvard University Press, 1992.

Moten, Fred. *In the Break: The Aesthetics of the Black Radical Tradition*. University of Minnesota Press, 2003.

Mureşan, Mirela. 'Practicing Transdisciplinary Methodology within the Frame of a Traditional Educational System.' *Transdisciplinary Journal of Engineering & Science*, vol. 4, 2013, pp. 137–47.

Needleman, Jacob, and George Baker (English version editors). Associate Editor Mary Stein. *Gurdjieff: Essays and Reflections on the Man and His Teaching*. Continuum, 2004.

Newen, Albert, et al., editors. *The Oxford Handbook of 4E Cognition*. Oxford University Press, 2018.

Nettleford, Rex M. 'Unsettling the Coloniality of Being/Power/Truth/Freedom: Towards the Human, After Man, Its Overrepresentation-An Argument.' *CR: The New Centennial Review, Michigan State University Press*, vol. 3, no. 3, 2003, pp. 257–337.

Nicolescu, Basarab. *Manifesto of Transdisiplinarity*. Translated from the French by Karen-Claire Voss, SUNY Press, 2002.

Nicolescu, Basarab. 'Transdisciplinarity – Past, Present and Future.' *Moving Worldviews – Reshaping Sciences, Policies and Practices for Endogenous Sustainable Development*, edited by Bertus Haverkort and Coen Reijntjes, COMPAS Editions, 2006, pp. 142–66.

Nicolescu, Basarab, and A. Ertas. *Transdisciplinary Education, Philosophy, & Applications*. The Atlas Publishing (The Academy of Transdisciplinary Learning & Advanced Studies), 2014.

Nicolis, Gregoire, and Ilya Prigogine. *Self-organization in Nonequilibrium Systems: From Dissipative Structures to Order through Fluctuations*. Wiley, 1977.

Noë, Alva. *Strange Tools: Art and Human Nature I*. New York: Hill and Wang, a division of Farrar, Straus and Giroux, 2012.

Noë, Alva, editor. *Varieties of Presence*. Harvard University Press, 2015.

Nolan, Yvette, and Richard Knowles, editors. *Performing Indigeneity*. Playwrights Canada Press, 2016.

Nowotny, Helga. *Cultures of Technology and the Quest for Innovation*. Berghahn Books, 2006.

Okagbue, Osita. *Culture and Identity in African and Caribbean Theatre*. Adonis and Abbey Publishers Ltd., 2009.

Olivares, Francisco A., et al. 'Neurophenomenology Revisited: Second-person Methods for the Study of Human Consciousness.' *Frontiers in Psychology*, vol. 6, 2015, pp. 1–12. www.frontiersin.org/article/10.3389/fpsyg.2015.00673. Accessed 10 Mar. 2022.

Olivella, Manuel Zapata. *Changó, the Biggest Badass*. Translated by Jonathan Tittler; introduction by William Luis, Texas Tech University Press, 2010.

Ong, Walter J. *Orality and Literacy: The Technologizing of the Word*. Routledge, 2002.

Ouspensky, Pyotr D. *In Search of the Miraculous: Fragments of an Unknown Teaching*. Routledge & Kegan Paul, 1983.

Parvizi, Javad, and Antonio Damasio. 'Consciousness and the Brainstem.' *Cognition*, vol. 79, no. 1–2, 2001, pp. 135–60. www.sciencedirect.com/science/article/pii/S001002770000127X. Accessed 2 Aug. 2022.

Pavis, Patrice. *Analyzing Performance: Theater, Dance, and Film*. Translated by A. David Williams, University of Michigan Press, 2003.

Penrose, Roger. *The Emperor's New Mind Concerning Computers, Minds, and the Laws of Physics*. Oxford University Press, 1989.

Penrose, Roger. *Shadows of the Mind: A Search for the Missing Science of Consciousness*. Oxford University Press, 1994.

Penrose, Roger., et al. *How Consciousness Became the Universe: Quantum Physics, Cosmology, Neuroscience, Parallel Universes*. 2nd ed., Science Publishers, 2017.

Pepperell, Robert. *The Posthuman Condition: Consciousness Beyond the Brain*. Intellect, 2003.

Phillips, Anthony C. *Introduction to Quantum Mechanics*. Manchester Physics Series, Wiley, 2003.

Pinker, Steven. *How the Mind Works*. Alan Lane, 1998.

Plato. *The Republic*, edited by G. R. F. Ferrari. Translated by Tom Griffith, Cambridge University Press, 2000.

Polanyi, Michael. *Personal Knowledge: Towards a Post-Critical Philosophy*. Routledge, 1998.

Poli, Roberto. 'The Basic Problem of Levels of Reality.' *Axiomathes*, vol. 12, no. 3–4, 2001, pp. 261–83.

Poli, Roberto. 'Levels of Reality and the Psychological Stratum.' *Revue international de philosophie*, vol. 236, no. 2, 2006, pp. 163–80.

Poli, Roberto. 'Two Theories of Levels of Reality: In Dialogue with Basarab Nicolescu.' *Transdisciplinarity in Science and Religion*. Curtea Veche Publ., vol. 6, 2009, pp. 135–50.

Pollack, Robert. *The Missing Moment: How the Unconscious Shapes Modern Science*. Houghton Mifflin Harcourt, 1999.

Popper, Karl. *The Logic of Scientific Discovery*. Routledge, 1959.

Popper, Karl. *Objective Knowledge: An Evolutionary Approach*. Rev. ed., Clarendon Press, 1983.

Priestly, Brian. *Mingus: A Critical Biography*. Quartet Books, 1982.

Prigogine, Ilya, and Isabelle Stengers. *Order Out of Chaos: Man's New Dialogue with Nature*. Bantam Books, 1984.

Prinsloo, Estelle. 'The Role of the Humanities in Decolonising the Academy.' *Arts & Humanities in Higher Education*, vol. 15, no. 1, 2016, pp. 164–68. www.historicalstudies.uct.ac.za/sites/default/files/image_tool/images/149/The%20role%20of%20the%20Humanities%20in%20decolonising%20the%20academy%20-%20Estelle%20H%20Prinsloo.pdf. Accessed 10 Aug. 2022.

Pugh, Megan. *America Dancing: From the Cakewalk to the Moonwalk*. Yale University Press, 2015.

Rabaka, Reiland. *The Negritude Movement: W. E. B. Du Bois, Leon Damas, Aimé Césaire, Leopold Senghor, Frantz Fanon, and the Evolution of an Insurgent Idea*. Lexington Books, 2015.

Readings, Bill. *The University in Ruins*. Harvard University Press, 1996.

Reid-Pharr, Robert F. *Archives of Flesh: African America, Spain, and Post-humanist Critique.* New York University Press, 2016.

Rizvi, Sajjad H. *Mullā Sadrā and Metaphysics: Modulation of Being*. Routledge, 2009.

Rolls, Edmund T. *Emotion and Decision Making Explained*. Oxford University Press, 2014.

Rothberg, Michael. *Multidirectional Memory: Remembering the Holocaust in the Age of Decolonization*. Stanford University Press, 2009.

Rutherford, Ian, editor. *Greco-Egyptian Interactions: Literature, Translation and Culture 500 BCE–300 CE*. Oxford University Press, 2016.

Sacks, Oliver. *An Anthropologist on Mars*. Vintage Books, 1955.

Sacks, Oliver. *Awakenings*. Doubleday, 1974.

Sacks, Oliver. *The Mind's Eye*. Alfred A. Knopf, 2010.

al-Ṣafā, Ikhwān. *Epistles of the Brethren of Purity: On the Natural Sciences: An Arabic Critical Edition and English Translation of Epistles 15–21*, edited and translated by Carmela Baffioni; foreword by Nader El-Bizri, Oxford University Press in association with the Institute of Ismaili Studies, 2013.

Said, Edward. *The Edward Said Reader*, edited by Moustafa Bayoumi and Andrew Rubin, Vintage Books, 2000.

Said, Edward. *Power, Politics, and Culture: Interviews with Edward W. Said*, edited and with an introduction by Gauri Viswanathan, Pantheon Books, 2001.

Said, Edward. *Orientalism*. Penguin, 2003.

Salter, Chris. *Entangled: Technology and the Transformation of Performance*. Foreword by Peter Sellars, MIT Press, 2010.

Santoro, Gene. *Myself When I am Real: The Life and Music of Charles Mingus*. Oxford University Press, 2001.

Saussure, Ferdinand de, et al., *Course in General Linguistics*. 3rd ed., Duckworth, 1983.

Saussure, Ferdinand de, et al., *Course in General Linguistics/Ferdinand de Saussure*. Translated and annotated by Roy Harris; with a new introduction by Roy Harris, Bloomsbury Academic, 2013.

Schechner, Richard. *Between Theater and Anthropology*. University of Pennsylvania Press, 1985.

Schechner, Richard, and S. Lucie. *Performance Studies: An Introduction*. 4th ed, Routledge, 2020.

Schwab, Karl. *The Fourth Industrial Revolution*. New York: Crown Publishing, 2017.

Schieve, William C., and Peter M. Allen, editors. *Self-organization and Dissipative Structures: Applications in the Physical and Social Sciences*. University of Texas Press, 1982.

Scholz, Roland W., et al. editors. *Joint Problem-Solving among Science, Technology and Society*. Haffmans Sachbuch Verlag AG, 2001.

Searle, John. *Speech Acts: An Essay in the Philosophy of Language*. Cambridge University Press, 1969.

Searle, John. *Minds, Brains, and Science*. Harvard University Press, 1984.

Searle, John. *The Rediscovery of the Mind*. MIT Press, 1992.

Sedgwick, Eve Kosovsky. *Touching Feeling: Affect, Pedagogy, Performativity*. Duke University Press, 2003.

Serequeberhan, Tsenay. *Existence and Heritage: Hermeneutic Explorations in African and Continental Philosophy*. SUNY Press, 2015.

Shadmehr, Reza, and Sandro Mussa-Ivaldi. *Biological Learning and Control: How the Brain Builds Representations, Predicts Events, and Makes Decisions*. MIT Press, 2012.

Shakespeare, William. *As You Like It*, Act II, Scene VII, Line 138. Edward Blount and William and Isaac Jaggard, 1623.

Shakespeare, William. *As You Like It*, edited by Samuel C. Burchell, Yale University Press, 1965.

Shear, Jonathan. *Explaining Consciousness: The 'Hard Problem.'* MIT Press, 1997.

Sheets-Johnstone, Maxine. *The Phenomenology of Dance*. Dance Books for Libraries, 1980.

Sheets-Johnstone, Maxine. *The Primacy of Movement*. John Benjamins Pub. Co., 1999.

Shermer, Michael. *Why People Believe Weird Things: Pseudoscience, Superstition, and Other Confusions of Our Time*. W. H. Freeman & Co., 1997.

Simpson, Audra. *Mohawk Interruptus: Political Life Across the Borders of Settler States*. Duke University Press, 2014.

Smith, Anna. *Julia Kristeva: Readings of Exile and Estrangement*. Macmillan, 1996.

Smith, Anna. *Julia Kristeva: Speaking the Unspeakable*. Pluto Press, 1998.

Smith, John, and Chris Jenks. *Qualitative Complexity: Ecology, Cognitive Processes and the Re-emergence of Structures in Post-Humanist Social Theory*. Routledge, 2006.

Snyder, Allan W., and Mandy Thomas. 'Autistic Artists give Clues to Cognition.' *Perception*, vol. 26, 1997, pp. 93–96, www.centreforthemind.com/publications/Autistic_artists.cfm. Accessed 10 Aug. 2022.

Soja, Edward William. *Postmodern Geographies: The Reassertion of Space in Critical Social Theory*. Verso Press, 1989.

Soja, Edward William. *Thirdspace: Journeys to Los Angeles and Other Real-and-Imagined Places*. Basil Blackwell, 1996.

Sokal, Alan D., and Jean Bricmont. *Fashionable Nonsense: Postmodern Intellectuals' Abuse of Science*. Picador, 1998.

Soyinka, Wole. 'The Fourth Stage: Through the Mysteries of Ogun to the Origin of Yoruba Tragedy.' *African Philosophy: An Anthology*, edited by Emmanuel Chukwudi Eze, Blackwell Publishers, 1998, pp. 438–46.

Soussloff, Catherine, and Mark Franko. 'Visual and Performance Studies, A New History of Interdisciplinarity.' *Social Text 73*, vol. 20, no. 4, Winter 2002, pp. 29–45.

Spatz, Ben. *What a Body Can Do: Technique as Knowledge, Practice as Research*. Routledge, Taylor & Francis Group, 2015.

Spier, Steven. 'Dancing and Drawing, Choreography and Architecture.' *Journal of Architecture*, vol. 10, no. 4, 2005, p. 352.

Spinoza, Benedictus de. *A Spinoza Reader: The Ethics and Other Works*. Translated by Edwin M. Curley, Princeton University Press, 1994.

Spinoza, Benedictus de. *The Essence of Spinoza's Ethics*, edited, with an introduction by Hunter Lewis; revised and updated version of an original translation from the Latin by R. H. M Elwes. Axios Press, 2012.

Spivak, Gyatri. *A Critique of Postcolonial Reason: Toward a History of the Vanishing Present.* Harvard University Press, 1999.

Strachan, Anna Lee (Director/Producer), and Michael Bicks (Writer/Producer). *Memory Hackers.* A Nova Film Production, WGBH Educational Foundation, 2016.

Sweeney, Fionnghuala, and Kate Marsh, editors. *Afromodernisms: Paris, Harlem and the Avant-Garde.* Edinburgh University Press, 2013.

Thompson, Evan. *Mind in Life: Biology, Phenomenology, and the Sciences of Mind.* Harvard University Press, 2007.

Thompson, Jeff. 'Embodied Cognition: What It Is & Why It's Important.' *Beyond Words*, www.psychologytoday.com/ca/blog/beyond-words/201202/embodied-cognition-what-it-is-why-its-important. Accessed 2 Aug. 2022.

Tisdall, Caroline, and Angelo Bozzola. *Futurism.* Oxford University Press, 1978.

Todd, Mabel E.*The Thinking Body: A Study of the Balancing Forces of Dynamic Man.* Foreword by E. G. Brackett, Dance Horizons, 1968, 2008.

Todd, Zoe. 'Indigenizing Canadian Academia and the Insidious Problem of White Possessiveness.' https://zoestodd.com/2018/05/04/indigenizing-academia-and-the-insidious-problem-of-white-possessiveness/. Accessed 10 Aug. 2022.

Todes, Samuel. *Body and World.* MIT Press, 2001.

Tononi, Guilio. *Phi: A Voyage from the Brain to the Soul.* Random House LLC, 2012a.

Tononi, Guilio. 'The Integrated Information Theory of Consciousness: An Updated Account.' *Archives italiennes de biologie*, vol. 150, no. 2–3, 2012b, pp. 56–90.

Tononi, Guilio, and Christ of Koch. 'Consciousness: Here, There and Everywhere?' *Philosophical Transactions of the Royal Society B*, vol. 370, no. 20140167, 2015, https://royalsocietypublishing.org/doi/10.1098/rstb.2014.0167. Accessed 10 Aug. 2022.

Trumble, Michele. 'Comfort and Conflict: Story/Time: The Life of An Idea.' *Dance Chronicle Journal*, vol. 39, no. 1, 2016, pp. 102–04.

Truth and Reconciliation Commission of Canada. *Honouring the Truth, Reconciling for the Future: Summary of the Final Report of the Truth and Reconciliation Commission of Canada, Vol. 1.* James Lorimer & Co. Ltd., 2015.

Tucker, Jim B. *Life Before Life: Children's Memories of Previous Lives.* St Martin's Press, 2008.

Turing, Alan. 'Computing Machinery and Intelligence.' *MIND The Journal of the Mind Association LIX*, vol. 236, 1950, pp. 433–60.

Turner, David H. *Tradition and Transformation: A Study of the Groote Eylandt Area Aborigines of Northern Australia.* Australian Institute for Aboriginal Studies, 1974.

Turner, David H. *Australian Aboriginal Social Organization.* Humanities Press, 1980.

Turner, Victor Witter. *The Forest of Symbols: Aspects of Ndembu Ritual.* Cornell University Press, 1967.

Turner, Victor Witter. *From Ritual to Theatre: The Human Seriousness of Play*. Performing Arts Journal Publications, 1982.

Turner, Victor Witter. *The Anthropology of Performance*. PAJ Publications, 1986.

Ukpokolo, Isaac E., editor. *Themes, Issues and Problems in African Philosophy*. Springer International Publishing: Imprint: Palgrave Macmillan, 2017.

Van der Kolk, Bessel A., et al. 'Exploring the Nature of Traumatic Memory: Combining Clinical Knowledge with Laboratory Methods.' *Journal of Aggression, Maltreatment & Trauma*, vol. 4, 2001, www.tandfonline.com/doi/pdf/10.1300/J146v04n02_02?needAccess=true. Accessed 10 Aug. 2022.

Van Gennep, Arnold. *The Rites of Passage*. Translated by Monika B. Vizedom and Gabrielle L. Caffe; introduction by Solon T. Kimball, University of Chicago Press, 1960.

Varela, Francisco J. 'The Re-enchantment of the Concrete.' *Incorporations*, edited by Jonathan Crary and Sanford Kwinter, Zone. Distributed by the MIT Press, 1992, pp. 320–40.

Varela, Francisco J. *Principles of Biological Autonomy*. North Holland, 1979.

Varela, Francisco J., and Humberto R. Maturana. *The Tree of Knowledge: The Biological Roots of Human Understanding*. Translated by Robert Paolucci, Shambhala, 1992.

Varela, Francisco J., and Jonathan Shear. 'First-Person Methodologies: What, Why, How?' *Journal of Consciousness Studies*. *Journal of Consciousness Studies*, vol. 6, no. 2–3, 1999, pp. 1–14.

Varela, Francisco, and Clause Otto Scharmer. *Three Gestures of Becoming Aware*. Paris, 2000, https://pdfslide.net/documents/three-gestures-of-becoming-aware-varela-2000.html?page=1 Accessed 2 Aug. 2022.

Varela, Francisco J., et al. *The Embodied Mind: Cognitive Science and Human Experience*. MIT Press, 1993.

Vass-Rhee, Freya. 'Integrating Dance and Cognitive Science: Toward Emancipatory Research.' *Continuing Dance Culture Dialogues, 38th Annual Conference of the Congress on Research in Dance, 2–5 Nov. 2006, Tempe, Arizona*.

Vaughan, Richard T. 'Massively Multi-robot Simulations in Stage.' *Swarm Intelligence*, vol. 2, no. 2–4, 2008, pp. 189–208.

Velmans, Max. *Understanding Consciousness*. Routledge, 2000.

Von Neumann, John. *The Computer and the Brain*. Yale University Press, 1958.

Von Neumann, John, et al. *The Computer and the Brain*. 2nd ed., Yale University Press, 2000.

Xin-wei, Sha, with an afterword by Arkady Plotnitsky. *Poiesis and Enchantment in Topological Matter*. MIT Press, 2013.

wa Thiong'o, Ngũgĩ. *Decolonising the Mind: The Politics of Language in African Literature*. James Currey, Heinemann Kenya, Heinemann, Zimbabwe Publishing House, 1986.

Walens, Stanley. *Feasting with Cannibals: An Essay on Kwakiutl Cosmology*. Princeton University Press, 1981.

Walcott, Derek. *The Arkansas Testament*. Farrar, Straus and Giroux, 1987.

Walcott, Derek. *Omeros*. Farrar, Straus, and Giroux, 1992.

Walcott, Derek. *The Odyssey: A Stage Version*. Farrar Straus Giroux, 1993.

Walcott, Derek. *The Joker of Seville*. Alexander Street Press, 2003.

Walcott, Rinaldo. *Black Like Who?: Writing Black Canada*. 2nd rev. ed., Insomniac Press, 2003.

Walcott, Rinaldo. 'The Problem of the Human: Black Ontologies and 'the Coloniality of Our Being.' *Postcoloniality – Declononiality – Black Critique: Joints and Fissures*, edited by S. Broeck and C. Junker, Campus Verlag, 2014, pp. 93–105.

Walcott, Rinaldo. *Queer Returns: Essays on Multiculturalism, Diaspora, and Black Studies*. Insomniac Press, 2016.

Waldrop, M. Mitchell. *Complexity: The Emerging Science at the Edge of Order and Chaos*. Simon & Schuster, 1992.

Walker Performing Arts Centre. 'Bill T. Jones in Conversation with Philip Bither.' *YouTube*, 6 Sept. 2011, www.walkerart.org/channel/2011/bill-t-jones-in-conversation-with-philip-bith. Accessed 2 Aug. 2022.

Warden, Claire. *Modernist and Avant-Garde Performance: An Introduction*. Edinburgh University Press, 2015.

Wegerif, Rupert. 'Dialogic or Dialectic? The Significance of Ontological Assumptions in Research on Educational Dialogue.' *British Educational Research Journal*, vol. 34, no. 3, 2008, pp. 347–61.

Welton, Donn. *Body and Flesh: A Philosophical Reader*. Blackwell Publishers, 1998.

Welton, Donn. *The Body: Classic and Contemporary Readings*. Blackwell Publishers, 1999.

Wenger, Susanne, and Gert Chesi. *A Life with the Gods in Their Yoruba Homeland*. Perlinger Verlag, 1983.

White, Frank. *The Overview Effect: Space Exploration and Human Evolution*. Houghton Mifflin, 1987.

White, Hayden. *The Content of the Form: Narrative Discourse & Historical Representation*. Johns Hopkins University Press, 1987.

Whitehead, Alfred North. *Process and Reality: An Essay in Cosmology*, edited by David Ray Griffin and Donald W. Sherbourne, Free Press, 1978.

Wiener, Norbert. *Cybernetics: Or Control and Communication in the Animal and the Machine*. The Technology Press, John Wiley & Sons, Inc., 1948.

Williams, Eric. *Capitalism and Slavery*. New York: Russell & Russell, 1961.

Wiredu, Kwasi, editor. *A Companion to African Philosophy*. Blackwell Publishing Ltd., 2006.

Woolf, Virginia. *Orlando: A Biography*. L. and V. Woolf at the Hogarth Press, 1928.

Wynter, Sylvia. '1492, A New World View.' *Race, Discourse, and the Origins of the Americas: A New World View*, edited by Vera Lawrence Hyatt and Rex Nettleford. Smithsonian Institution Press, 1994, pp. 5–57.

Yasua, Yasuo. *The Body: Toward an Eastern Mind-Body Theory*, edited by T. Kasulis. Translated by Nagamoto Shigenori and T. P. Kasulis, State University of New York Press, 1987.

Zohar, Danah, and I. N. Marshall. *The Quantum Self: Human Nature and Consciousness Defined by the New Physics*. 1st ed., Morrow, 1990.

Zohar, Danah, and I. N. Marshall. *The Quantum Society: Mind, Physics and a New Social Vision*. Bloomsbury Publishing, 1993.

Zohar, Danah, and I. N. Marshall. *Spiritual Capital: Wealth We Can Live*. Berrett-Koehler Publishers, 2004.

Index